Jurists: Profiles in Legal Theory

General Editor:
William Twining

Max Weber

Anthony T. Kronman

STANFORD UNIVERSITY PRESS
Stanford, California   1983

Stanford University Press
Stanford, California
© Anthony Kronman 1983
Originating publisher: Edward Arnold (Publishers) Ltd, London, 1983
Stanford edition printed in the U.S.A.
ISBN 0-8047-1140-2
LC 82-80923

Contents

Preface

I first encountered the work of Max Weber more than ten years ago while a graduate student in the philosophy programme at Yale, and am indebted to my friend and teacher Kenley Dove for having impressed upon me the philosophical importance of Weber's work. Bruce Ackerman, Joshua Cohen, Robert Cover, Mirjan Damaska, Owen Fiss, Reinier Kraakman, Arthur Leff, Adina Schwartz and William Twining all made helpful comments on earlier drafts and I have benefited from their suggestions. Arthur Leff died before this book was completed, leaving me with an undischargeable debt of gratitude for his generosity and wise criticism. Diane Hart helped me prepare the manuscript and I am thankful for her patient and professional assistance. I am also grateful to the Yale Law School for two summer research grants and to Harry Wellington, Dean of the Law School, for his encouragement and support.

To my wife, Nancy, I owe the wholeness that gives everything its relish and delight.

List of works by Max Weber

German texts.

1. *Zur Geschichte der Handelsgesellschaften im Mittelalter* (Stuttgart, 1889).
2. *Die römische Agrargeschichte in ihrer Bedeutung für das Staats- und Privatrecht* (Stuttgart, 1891).
3. *Die Verhältnisse der Landarbeiter im ostelbischen Deutschland* (Berlin, 1892).
4. *Gesammelte Aufsätze zur Religionssoziologie* (Tübingen, 1924).
5. *Gesammelte Aufsätze zur Soziologie und Sozialpolitik* (Tübingen, 1924).
6. *Gesammelte Aufsätze zur Sozial- und Wirtschaftgeschichte* (Tübingen, 1924)
7. *Gesammelte Aufsätze zur Wissenschaftslehre* 2nd edn (Tübingen, 1951).
8. *Wirtschaft und Gesellschaft. Grundriss der verstehenden Soziologie* 4th edn (Tübingen, 1956).
9. *Gesammelte Politische Schriften* 2nd ed (Tübingen, 1958).
10. *Wirtschaftgeschichte. Abriss der universalen Sozial- und Wirtschaftgeschichte* 2nd edn (Berlin, 1958).

English translations.

1. *The Methodology of the Social Sciences* (trans. E. Shils and H. Finch, Glencoe, Ill., 1949).   MSS
2. *Roscher and Knies: The Logical Problems of Historical Economics* (trans. G. Oakes, New York, 1975).   RK
3. *Critique of Stammler* (trans. G. Oakes, New York, 1977).   CS
4. *From Max Weber: Essays in Sociology* (trans. H. Gerth and C. Wright Mills, New York, 1946).   FMW
5. *The Protestant Ethic and the Spirit of Capitalism* (trans. T. Parsons, New York, 1958).   PE
6. *The Religion of China: Confucianism and Taoism* (trans. H. Gerth, Glencoe, Ill., 1952).   —
7. *Ancient Judaism* (trans. H. Gerth and D. Martindale, Glencoe, Ill., 1958).   AJ
8. *The Religion of India: The Sociology of Hinduism and Buddhism* (trans. H. Gerth and D. Martindale, Glencoe, Ill., 1958).   RI

9. *Economy and Society: An Outline of Interpretive Sociology* (ed. G. Roth and C. Wittich, New York, 1968).   *ES*
10. *Max Weber on Law in Economy and Society* (trans. M. Rheinstein and E. Shils, Cambridge, Mass., 1954).   *LES*
11. *General Economic History* (trans. F. Knight, New York, 1961).   —
12. *The Rational and Social Foundations of Music* (trans. D. Martindale, J. Riedel, and G. Neuwirth, Carbondale, Ill., 1958).   —
13. *Max Weber on Universities* (trans. E. Shils, Chicago, 1973).   —
14. *The Agrarian Sociology of Ancient Civilizations* (trans. R. I. Frank, London, 1976).   —
15. 'The Social Causes of the Decay of Ancient Civilization' (1950) *Journal of General Education* pp. 75–88 (trans. C. Mackauer).   —
16. 'Socialism,' in *Max Weber: The Interpretation of Social Reality* (trans. J.E.T. Eldridge, London, 1971) pp. 191–219.   —

All references in the text are to English translations of Weber's writings. Abbreviations are used for certain frequently cited works. For convenience, references to the *Rechtssoziologie* give the appropriate passage both in *Economy and Society* and in the separate edition of the *Rechtssoziologie* published under the title *Max Weber on Law in Economy and Society.*

In late antiquity, amid a levelled world that had lost its faith, the individual looked to Stoic philosophy for support. For philosophy Socrates showed the way, because as a real man he had been, done and suffered what philosophy for centuries thereafter sought to understand. In the world into which we are entering, in a time of mass accumulation and mass domination, of universal utilitarianism, crushing misery and banal happiness, it will again be the task of the individual to seek his philosophical truth. No objectivity will teach him. Perhaps the open secret of a man such as Max Weber will speak to him and kindle him. If this happens, we may say: Those who understand failure and death can approach him. He will remain incomprehensible to those who, entranced by the beauties of the world which Max Weber also enjoyed in moments of serenity, forget death.

Karl Jaspers

1

Introduction

Max Weber was trained as a lawyer and legal historian and his lifelong interest in the law is reflected in nearly everything he wrote, from his two student dissertations (one on Roman agrarian history, the other on risk-sharing techniques in medieval commerce) to his celebrated lecture, 'Politics as a Vocation', which he delivered in the winter of 1918, a year and a half before his death.[1] Each of Weber's principal works touches on legal issues. If one were to catalogue all of the passages in his writings that are addressed to some aspect of the legal order, the list would be a long one indeed; *Economy and Society* alone contains dozens of such passages, scattered throughout the text.

In most cases, however, Weber's treatment of legal issues is ancillary to some other concern, for example, his interest in the nature of political authority or economic action. At only one point in his writings is his attention focused primarily on the legal order itself – in the lengthy essay entitled 'Sociology of Law' (*Rechtssoziologie*) which constitutes the seventh chapter in the German edition of *Economy and Society* (the eighth in the English translation).[2] Anyone interested in Weber's theory of law must begin with this essay and work out from it by attempting to organize his other, less systematic observations concerning legal phenomena on the basis of the more explicit and sustained treatment they receive here. In this respect, Weber's *Rechtssoziologie* provides the key to understanding, and assessing, his achievement as a jurist.

However, despite its reputation as a classic and the enormous influence that it has had in both the German and English-speaking worlds, the *Rechtssoziologie* is likely to seem nearly unintelligible to someone – even an experienced lawyer or law teacher – reading it for the first time. In part, this is attributable to the fact that it is written in a dense prose style and encumbered by a heavy use of technical terms, some drawn from existing legal vocabularies and others invented by Weber himself. The *Rechtssoziologie* also deals with a forbiddingly wide range of doctrines and institutions: to appreciate the details of Weber's argument, one must know something about Roman Law, Canon Law, Germanic customary law, modern commercial law, the English common law, and a half-dozen religious legal systems – to know more, in short, than anyone but the most erudite comparative legal historian is likely to know.*

In addition to the density of its prose and the breadth of its coverage, there is a third reason why the *Rechtssoziologie* is such a difficult text. Although it contains many individual passages whose significance can be appreciated even on a first reading, the overall impression one receives is of a vast hodge-podge of ideas and observations ranging in generality from very specific historical analyses to the most abstract conceptual schemata, all thrown together in a random fashion so that the reader moves from one topic and level of generality to another without ever quite seeing the connection between them. Unlike some of Weber's other writings – his essay on *The Protestant Ethic and the Spirit of Capitalism*, for example – the *Rechtssoziologie* lacks polish and organizational unity; it is a great, rough-hewn mass of thoughts which, although often suggestive, do not together form a recognizable whole – which do not, in other words, constitute a *work*.³ The entire Weberian *corpus* resembles a stone quarry filled with monumental statues in varying degrees of completion, some only beginning to emerge from the rock, others finished to perfection. The *Rechtssoziologie* is one of the least finished works in the quarry, and the temptation is strong to treat it as a rich but disorderly storehouse whose contents may be plundered at will without fear of damaging its organizational structure.

In this book, I offer an interpretation of the *Rechtssoziologie* which is intended to show that it does have an overarching conceptual unity and is closely connected, as well, to the other branches of Weber's general social theory – in particular, those dealing with authority, religion and economic action. My interpretation is a philosophical one; it elaborates and empha-sizes the common philosophical assumptions underlying Weber's treatment of many different topics in the *Rechtssoziologie* – the nature of oracular adjudication, the varieties of legal systematization, the modes of juristic thought and forms of contractual association, and the difference between formal and substantive legal rationality. All reveal an implicit commitment, on Weber's part, to a few simple philosophical ideas; it is these that provide the unifying link between what is otherwise likely to seem a jumble of some-times brilliant but esssentially unconnected insights.

The effort to construct an interpretation along these lines might seem misguided: the *Rechtssoziologie* is not usually thought of as a work in philo-sophy and Weber himself denied that he was a professional philosopher.** But although it is not centrally and explicitly concerned with the exposition of philosophical ideas, the *Rechtssoziologie* contains many philosophically suggestive passages. To take only one example, in his discussion of the forms

---

*'Weber's sociology of law is better evidence of his encyclopedic learning than any of his other sociological studies.' J. Freund, *The Sociology of Max Weber* (trans. M. Ilford, New York, 1968) p. 245.

**RK, p. 209 n. 1. It is somewhat ironical that Weber makes this disclaimer at the beginning of his most explicitly philosophical essay.

of contractual association, Weber draws a distinction between two types of contracts – 'status' contracts and 'purposive' contracts.[4] The terms in which this distinction is drawn are strikingly philosophical – so much so that the passage in question could easily be confused for one from, say, Hegel's *Philosophy of Right*.[5] But here, as elsewhere, Weber does not elaborate the philosophical ideas that underlie his discussion of the problem at hand and the philosophical dimension of the essay therefore remains undeveloped. Weber is, in short, something of a philosophical coquette: he teases the reader by using philosophical ideas in a suggestive way but never examines their consequences and presuppositions in a systematic fashion.

Nowhere is this more evident than in his use of the concept of legal rationality, the single most important concept in the *Rechtssoziologie*. Much of the essay is organized around the idea of legal rationality and despite its ambiguity – I shall argue that it has at least four different meanings – this is a concept that clearly invites philosophical reflection.[6] Indeed, it is difficult to think of an idea that does so more compellingly. Anyone who reads the *Rechtssoziologie* is bound to wonder what Weber means when he says that a particular legal institution or mode of thought is peculiarly rational, and this question raises philosophical difficulties because it touches on the nature of reason itself. But Weber never pursues these philosophical issues; here, too, one is left with the impression that the *Rechtssoziologie* has an implicit but undeveloped philosophical dimension, that it is a work of philosophical significance even though it is not a work *in* philosophy.

This book accepts the invitation to philosophical reflection implicit in Weber's *Rechtssoziologie* and attempts to demonstrate that the unstated philosophical assumptions that underlie its central concepts give the work as a whole a significant degree of intellectual coherence. I shall also attempt to show that these same philosophical ideas provide a connecting link between the *Rechtssoziologie* and other aspects of Weber's general theory of society. One might expect there to be some such connection between the *Rechtssoziologie* and his theory of authority since the latter deals with closely related phenomena; an equally important, if less obvious, connection also exists, however, between the *Rechtssoziologie*, on the one hand, and Weber's sociology of religion and theory of economic action on the other. Because much of my book deals with the philosophical connections between these different aspects of Weber's work, the interpretation it offers is, in an important sense, an interpretation of the whole of his sociology, one that is focused on the *Rechtssoziologie* and that takes that essay as its central point of reference, but which seeks to place Weber's theory of law in the context of his other writings.* The *Rechtssoziologie* is part of a larger system

*Talcott Parsons, Weber's principal expositor in the United States, has called the *Rechtssoziologie* the 'core' of Weber's substantive sociology, and 'an essential key to the understanding of his analysis of political and economic phenomena'. T. Parsons, 'Value-Freedom and Objectivity', in *Max Weber and Sociology Today* (O. Stammer, ed., New York, 1971), pp. 40–2.

of ideas and can only be understood as such.

The philosophical ideas which are implicit in the *Rechtssoziologie* have their foundation, and are given their most explicit expression, in Weber's methodological writings. These writings deal in a general and abstract way with the nature of the social sciences and are primarily concerned with the special epistemological presuppositions that underlie all sociological inquiry; since they address problems of a more philosophical sort and treat them in a more deliberately philosophical fashion, they are the natural place to look for a clear statement of the philosophical ideas that underlie Weber's theory of human society, including his theory of law.

The philosophical underpinnings of Weber's theory of law are to be found in his theory of value, which in turn provides the basis for his account of the distinctive characteristics of sociological knowledge. By 'theory of value', I mean a theory that purports to describe the manner in which norms are established and the kind of reality they possess. Chapter 2 examines Weber's methodological views in some detail in order to show that his conception of sociological knowledge – of sociology as a discipline – rests upon a particular theory of value, one I call 'positivistic' for reasons that will be explained. Chapter 2 also attempts to show that his positivistic theory of value is associated with a special view of what it means to be a person. Weber's theory of value and the distinctive conception of personhood associated with it inform various centrally important aspects of the *Rechtssoziologie* and link his treatment of legal phenomena to his analysis of many other problems as well. Chapter 2 provides the foundation for this claim and succeeding chapters attempt to confirm it.

I should stress one other related theme that runs through the book as a whole. Weber was fascinated with the meaning of modern European civilization and devoted a lifetime to explaining the historical genesis and intellectual significance of the various institutions which are marked by the special form of rationalism he considered uniquely characteristic of the modern West. The *Rechtssoziologie* is no exception; here, too, Weber's interest is centred on the *modern* legal order, on 'the ways and consequences of the "rationalization" of the law, that is, the development of those juristic qualities which are characteristic of it today.'[7] In part, the *Rechtssoziologie* is concerned with a problem of historical causation: how did these distinctively modern 'juristic qualities' evolve and what prevented their development elsewhere? It is also concerned, however, with what I shall call a problem of exegetical interpretation. Exegesis seeks to establish the relationships of meaning – as distinct from the causal connections – that link different events, practices, institutions and forms of thought. As an exegetical essay, the *Rechtssoziologie* is concerned with the meaning of the modern legal order as well as its historical origins: to what extent do its most prominent elements reflect common ideas or attitudes and represent related aspects of a meaningfully integrated whole?

The distinction between causal and exegetical explanation is developed at greater length in Chapter 2. While much can be said about the

Rechtssoziologie from both perspectives, this book concentrates on Weber's achievement as an exegetical interpreter of the modern legal order and, more generally, of modernity as a whole. The *Rechtssoziologie's* exegetical contribution has been insufficiently appreciated and Weber's causal hypotheses given more weight than their inconclusiveness justifies; I have tried, here, to correct this imbalance.

Weber's examination of the meaning of modern law is closely tied to his own philosophical beliefs. As I shall attempt to show, each of the institutions and analytic techniques that he associates with the modern legal order rests, implicitly, upon an acceptance of the same theory of value and conception of personhood that he himself embraces in his methodological writings; indeed, it is their common dependence on these two related ideas that distinguishes the most characteristic components of the modern legal order from their pre-modern counterparts. These same philosophical ideas also underlie the political and economic institutions, as well as the religious beliefs, that Weber associated with modern European civilization (formally rational bureaucratic administration, capitalist production, and the Judeo-Christian belief in a transcendent, personal lord of creation). To this extent, Weber's positivistic theory of value provides the foundation not only for his conception of modern law but for his understanding of modernity in general.

Although Weber was fascinated with the problem of modernity, he was by no means an enthusiastic supporter of its most characteristic institutions. In fact, Weber was highly critical of certain features of contemporary social life – in particular, the growing predominance of bureaucratic organizations administered in a spirit of formal legality and the dehumanizing regimentation typical (so he believed) of the rationally managed capitalist factory. Weber's writings contain the suggestive beginnings of two different critiques of modern society, each starting from different premises and leading to radically different diagnoses. One is consistent with his own theory of value and with the ethical beliefs on which the most important institutions of modern European civilization are themselves based. The other is inconsistent with Weber's positivistic theory of value and the conception of personhood associated with it. In the final chapter of the book, I describe these two critiques, examine their philosophical presuppositions, and attempt to show how the irreconcilable tension between them creates an ambiguity in Weber's attitude toward the modern world. This raises philosophical issues of the first importance, issues of which Weber may or may not have been aware but in any case chose not to pursue. In this respect, his work again invites a philosophical inquiry that goes beyond the limits of what he himself actually wrote. It may have been this that led Karl Jaspers, many years ago, to describe Max Weber as the true philosopher of our age – a remarkable claim given that Weber was not himself a professional philosopher and did not ascribe any special philosophical significance to his own work.[8] My hope is that this book makes Jasper's claim more plausible.

2

Methodological foundations

What kind of discipline did Weber conceive the sociology of law to be? It is with this methodological question that the present chapter is concerned. Of course, to ask what kind of discipline the sociology of law is, is not to raise a question *in* the sociology of law itself; like any methodological inquiry, this one necessarily has its standpoint outside the discipline it investigates since it seeks to clarify issues that concern the status of the discipline as a whole. The questions such an inquiry raises are in reality epistemological ones and belong to the branch of philosophy that is concerned with the conditions, forms and limits of human knowledge.

Despite their abstract character, the methodological concepts discussed in this chapter provide the necessary background for understanding Weber's more concrete treatment of legal ideas and institutions in the *Rechtssoziologie*. In this respect, particular emphasis must be placed upon his theory of value and the conception of personhood associated with it. Weber's views regarding the foundations of the sociology of law – its special conditions and defining characteristics – are based upon a *positivistic* theory of value and presuppose a *will-centred* conception of the person (in a sense to be explained later in the chapter). This same theory of value provides the key to many important themes in the *Rechtssoziologie* and uniquely illuminates the connection between this and other aspects of his general theory of society including, most importantly, his theory of authority.

In this chapter, I shall attempt to provide a foundation for this claim by clarifying the philosophical premises on which Weber's conception of the sociology of law is based. To do so, it will be necessary to make use of the full range of his methodological writings since Weber's views regarding the sociology of law must, to a large degree, be deduced from his general conception of the nature of all sociological explanation. Throughout, however, my focus will be on the sociology of law as a discipline with distinguishing characteristics of its own.

What, then, is the sociology of law as Weber conceives it? It will simplify matters if we resolve this single question into two different, but related ones. First, what is the subject-matter of the sociology of law? What sorts of things does a sociologist of law study or investigate? Second, how does a sociologist of law approach his subject-matter? What method or technique does he employ in his inquiry? If we know what a sociologist of law studies and how he studies it, we should be able to give an account of his discipline which reveals the ways in which it is like, and unlike, other forms of scientific inquiry.

Without knowing anything about Weber or the sociology of law, it is possible to answer the first question in at least a provisional way. Obviously, the sociologist of law studies *the law*, the legal order, and we all have a rough, but workable sense of what this means – it means things like trials and leases and speeding tickets, or more generally, what lawyers, policemen, judges, litigants and legislators do. This view of the legal order is of course much *too* rough, and will have to be considerably refined before we can understand Weber's own, quite precise, concept of law. But since we have an intuitive, if unexamined, idea of what the law is, it makes sense to begin our inquiry with the second question: what distinctive method or approach does a sociologist adopt when he studies the law? Those unfamiliar with the writings of Weber and other sociologists of law are unlikely to have even a provisional answer to this second question; yet it leads directly, as we shall see, to the philosophical ideas that shape Weber's conception of the sociology of law and his understanding of legal phenomena.

Three ways of thinking about the law

Weber contrasts the sociological study of law with two other ways of thinking about legal rules and institutions, and the contrast he draws illuminates the distinctive features of the sociological approach. Although each has special properties which mark it off, in a logical sense, from the others, in actual experience they are frequently found in combination; for example, such a combination is characteristic, perhaps even definitive, of the way in which practising lawyers think about the law. These three attitudes or approaches to law should therefore be viewed as 'ideal types', exaggerated or one-sided descriptions that emphasize particular aspects of what is obviously a richer and more complicated reality, but whose very unreality aids us in disentangling the different elements that existing practices and institutions invariably contain.*

*For Weber's own account of the nature and utility of ideal types in the social sciences, see ' "Objectivity" in Social Science and Social Policy' and 'Critical Studies in the Logic of the Cultural Sciences,' both in *MSS*. Useful discussions of Weber's theory of ideal types may be found in T. Parsons, *The Structure of Social Action* (New York, 1937), pp. 601–10; Freund, *The Sociology of Max Weber*, pp. 59–70; W.G. Runciman, *A Critique of Max Weber's Philosophy of Social Science* (Cambridge, 1972), pp. 33–7; Hempel, 'Typological Methods in the Natural and Social Sciences' in *Aspects of Scientific Explanation* (New York, 1965); and J.W. Watkins, 'Ideal Types and Historical Explanation' in *Philosophy of Social Explanation* (A. Ryan, ed., Oxford, 1973). As Runciman points out, the construction and use of ideal types is not, by itself, peculiar to the social sciences. Since my concern here is to illuminate the special characteristics of sociological understanding, I have chosen to ignore the many interesting questions raised by the general theory of ideal types.

The moral attitude toward law

The first of these three ways of thinking about law I shall call the *moral attitude toward law.** The moral attitude can best be understood with a simple example. Suppose that our legal system contains a rule (statutory or judge-created) requiring the victims of contractual breach to mitigate their own damages whenever possible, and that sanctions their failure to do so by reducing the compensation to which they would otherwise be entitled. One question we can ask about such a rule is whether it is a good rule. We might conclude, for example, that a rule of this sort is a good one on the grounds that it is morally wrong for the victim of a breach to allow his own damages to pile up out of the vindictive desire to hurt the other party; or, we might conclude that a mitigation rule is bad because it hinders the economically efficient allocation of resources, something thought to be desirable either for its own sake or as a means to other, intrinsically desirable ends such as happiness and self-fulfilment.

To decide whether a particular legal rule is good, bad or morally neutral, we must first adopt a standard or criterion of some sort in terms of which the rule may be evaluated. The moral attitude toward law is distinguished by the fact that it employs standards of an *extra-legal* sort, standards whose normative force does not depend upon their being rules of law (although, in certain circumstances, they may be legal rules as well). To assess the moral goodness of specific legal rules (such as the one requiring disappointed promisees to mitigate their damages) is thus to adopt an evaluative standpoint outside the legal order itself.

In evaluating a particular legal rule from the moral point of view, there is, of course, room for disagreement about the proper standard of assessment (what normative principle should one adopt as a basis for evaluating the rule?) and also about the application of the standard to the case at hand (what does the standard require in this instance?). However, despite the possibility of disagreement on either score, moral judgments regarding the law all have the same logical structure. First, every judgment of this sort is *evaluative:* it states that a rule is either good or bad and, by implication, should be preserved or abandoned. Second, all such judgments rest upon the presumed validity of an *extra-legal* standard; since the standard in question purports to provide a basis for the normative assessment of conduct, it must contain an explicit or implicit 'ought' – for example, that the legal system ought to be designed in such a way as to reward virtue or maximize human happiness. Finally, all moral judgments of this sort are supported by a *chain of reasoning* (not necessarily a deduction in the logical sense) which links an extra-legal standard at one end with a particular legal rule or institution at the other.

Weber's conception of the moral attitude toward law implies a sharp distinction between legal standards and moral ones, the latter standing

---

*Weber himself calls this first attitude toward law the 'political' attitude but this term seems misleadingly narrow. See *CS*, 126–7.

wholly outside the legal order and providing a non- or extra-legal standpoint from which the moralist may evaluate the law itself. Now it might be objected that no such distinction exists, at least in the case of certain advanced legal systems such as the American. The American legal system rests upon a Constitution that incorporates ethical norms of an exceedingly general character; these norms are themselves capable of interpretation along the most diverse philosophical lines and cannot be applied in a meaningful way until they have been given some such interpretation. Consequently, one might argue, the American legal order contains *within itself* a requirement that its component rules – at least those embedded in the Constitution – be justifiable from a moral point of view, thereby rendering any distinction between their moral and legal validity ultimately meaningless. This line of thought has recently been developed and defended by Ronald Dworkin.[9]

The suggestion that the law may itself contain standards of an explicitly ethical sort does not, however, undermine Weber's conception of the moral attitude toward law. Weber himself acknowledged that the legal order contains standards of a moral or ethical nature. In his discussion of the modern law of contracts, for example, he remarks that ' "good faith and fair dealing" or the "good" usage of trade or, in other words, *ethical categories* have become the test of what the parties are entitled to mean by their "intention" '.[10] But even if a legal system contains norms with an explicitly ethical content (the requirement that contracting parties deal in good faith, or the constitutional guarantee of a right to equal protection under the laws), there are two quite different ways of viewing these norms themselves. In the first place, one may regard them as morally obliging solely in virtue of their content. On this view, whatever moral force the norms in question have is to be explained by their intrinsic merit and not by the fact that they also happen to be legal rules, that is, part of a legal system. Viewed in this way, the legal status of the norms – their legal form – neither adds to nor diminishes their moral force: they are extra-legal principles and any judgment which employs them to evaluate some aspect of the legal order will be a moral judgment in the sense defined above.

It is possible, however, to view these same ethical norms in the way judges frequently do – as imposing duties to act or refrain from acting in certain ways only because they happen to be rules in a legal system. Often, of course, the scope of such norms (what they require and forbid) cannot be determined without elaborating a moral theory of some sort, and to this extent the statement and defence of such a theory becomes a part of the judge's official task. But from the judge's point of view, the rule in question – whatever its content – is an evaluative standard which he must respect in the adjudication of disputes solely because it is a legal norm and because the interpretation of the law is the only aim he may legitimately pursue in his official capacity as a judge. It is entirely possible that a judge, faced with an adjudicative problem, may conclude that a particular legal rule – one which happens to have an explicit ethical content – can only be construed in a certain way and feel duty-bound to apply the norm even though he finds it personally abhorrent.* However, if he were to adopt a moral attitude toward the law, a dilemma of this kind could not arise. The ethical principles to which the moralist orients himself, and which he employs as criteria in evaluating the adequacy of the legal order, are, by definition, principles he takes to be binding because they have the content they do and (in his judgment) express the right view. It is of course conceivable that in a particular legal system a judge might be required, as one of his official responsibilities, to adopt the position of a moralist and evaluate the rules he applies in light of his own personal morality. But to describe the judge's role in such a system, and to distinguish this system from those in which the judge is not permitted to rely on his own, personal view of what is morally right and wrong, one needs the distinction between legal and extra-legal standards of evaluation which Weber's conception of the moral attitude toward law implies. This distinction is a useful one and worth preserving. The suggestion that the distinction cannot be maintained just because there are legal norms which state moral principles is misguided.

Dogmatic jurisprudence
A second way of thinking about the law is exemplified by the attitude of the judge in the hypothetical case described a moment ago, and also by the approach a legal scholar takes to his subject-matter. Weber has a technical term for this way of thinking about rules of law and legal institutions: he calls it 'dogmatic jurisprudence' or 'legal dogmatics'.[11]

Suppose a legal scholar sets himself the limited task of explicating the meaning of the rule requiring victims of contractual breach to mitigate their damages, without attempting to evaluate the moral attractiveness of the rule itself. To do this, he must interpret the rule and determine how it is to be applied in particular situations – for example, in contracts for the sale of goods, employment contracts and security transactions. In many cases (although not in all), this is precisely what a judge does when forced to apply an ambiguous rule in a novel setting; the judge attempts to discern the 'correct meaning' of the rule – its purpose and scope – and then applies the rule, so construed, to the case before him .

The scholar's attitude toward the rule he is interpreting (and the judge's, to the extent that he approaches *his* task in a similar fashion) has two distinguishing characteristics. First, unlike the moralist, a legal scholar seeking to clarify the meaning of a particular rule need not take an evaluative attitude toward the rule itself in order to accomplish his purpose, that is, he need neither approve nor disapprove the rule in order to expound its correct legal meaning. A scholar may, of course, have such views, but it is not a necessary condition of his scholarship that he do so – in contrast to the moralist, whose attitude toward the law is by definition an evaluative one. For a legal scholar

---

*This was exactly the predicament in which many abolitionist judges found themselves in the antebellum period. See R. Cover, *Justice Accused* (New Haven and London, 1975).

to do his work, it is not even necessary that he approve the idea of law in general: in one of his methodological essays, Weber remarks that an anarchist may be able to make an especially useful contribution to legal scholarship precisely because he is free of the value commitments which enter unconsciously into the work of most legal academics.[12]

The first characteristic of dogmatic jurisprudence distinguishes the scholar's orientation to the law from the moralist's. The second distinguishes it from sociological understanding: although he need not take an evaluative attitude *toward* the rule whose meaning he is expounding, a legal scholar necessarily *employs* the rule as an evaluative standard by using it to assess, as correct or incorrect, the behaviour of various actors in the legal system including, most obviously, the behaviour of those responsible for applying the rule in question. Suppose, for example, that a scholar sets himself the task of explicating the correct meaning of the mitigation rule – something he can do, according to Weber, despite the fact that he has no views regarding the ethical merits of the rule or even thinks the rule a bad one. In most cases, his interpretation of the rule will lead the scholar to approve some decisions construing its meaning or scope, and to disapprove others on the grounds that they are inconsistent with a correct view of what the rule requires. It is a defining characteristic of dogmatic legal scholarship that it results in – indeed, has as its object – evaluative judgments of precisely this sort. In this respect, the moral evaluation of a rule and its scholarly interpretation are similar to one another: both *end* in value judgments, judgments couched in the normative language of approval and disapproval. In the first case, however, the premise of the judgment is some extra-legal standard which the moralist himself personally approves; by contrast, the value judgments of the scholar are based upon his conception of the correct meaning of a rule that he need not personally approve but which he treats – for the sake of argument, as it were – as a standard for judging the correctness and incorrectness of the rule's application in various cases.

Sociological understanding
In addition to evaluating legal rules from a moral perspective and expli-
cating their correct meaning in a 'dogmatic' sense, it is possible to think about and study rules of law from a sociological point of view. How does this attitude differ from the other two? To begin with, when a sociologist studies law and legal behaviour, he does not assume an evaluative stance of the sort adopted either by the moralist or scholar engaged in dogmatic jurisprudence. He neither judges the ethical quality of the law nor seeks to expound its true meaning in order to evaluate the correctness of the conduct of various actors in the legal system. The sociology of law is not an evaluative discipline in any sense. Weber repeatedly describes the sociology of law as an *empirical* science, meaning by this that it aims at, and has as its characteristic product, judgments of fact (more specifically, causal propositions) which unlike the judgments of both the moralist and legal scholar, are not cast in the language of praise and blame.[13]

But this is only a negative description of the sociological attitude toward law. If his orientation is not an evaluative one, in either of the two senses already discussed, what is it that a sociologist does when he investigates the legal order? In his inquiry, the sociologist of law is interested in only one thing – the fact (and for him it is just a fact) that certain human beings view legal norms as evaluative standards, or expect them to be viewed in this way by others, and are led to modify their conduct in some observable way as a result. The sociologist seeks to describe how the behaviour of individuals is causally influenced by their own normative commitments to the law and by their beliefs regarding the similar commitments of others; his account of law-oriented behaviour is strictly factual – or *value free*, to use an important but ambiguous term of Weber's[14] – insofar as he neither passes judgment on the ethical quality of the legal rules to which the subjects of his inquiry are themselves committed, nor attempts to determine whether their conduct is correct or incorrect in a legal-dogmatic sense. From a sociological point of view, behaviour that is based upon what a scholar would consider an incorrect interpretation of the law is as relevant and interesting as correct behaviour. In short, even though the sociology of law does not itself seek to establish judgments of a normative sort, it is centrally concerned with what may be called the *phenomenon of normativity* – the fact that human beings are influenced in their behaviour by their commitment to evaluative standards, including those contained in the legal order.

Suppose, for example, that Jones unjustifiably breaches his contract with Smith who then takes steps to minimize his damages because he believes that the mitigation rule applies to him and that all rules of law – including this one – ought to be obeyed. A moralist asks whether the mitigation rule is a good one; a legal dogmatist asks whether Smith has acted in a legally correct manner in light of the rule's true meaning (perhaps Smith is mistaken, from a dogmatic point of view, in thinking the rule applicable in this particular case). The sociologist, by contrast, is only interested in the fact that Smith's normative attitude toward the mitigation rule – his conception of the rule as an evaluative standard for the assessment of conduct (in this case, Smith's own conduct) – has an observable influence on his behaviour which can be described in the form of a causal proposition.

Now consider a more complicated case. Suppose that Jones decides to breach his contract because he believes that Smith's own commitment to the mitigation rule will cause him to reduce his damages; suppose, in addition, that Jones himself thinks the rule a bad one and believes that in any event it is inapplicable to this particular contract. Is Jones's decision to breach an event which is of interest to the sociologist, an event which is, so to speak, cognizable from a sociologist point of view? For Weber, the answer is clearly yes. Although Jones is not committed to the mitigation rule himself, he is led to act in a certain way, to *do* something, because of his beliefs regarding Smith's normative commitments. Jones's conduct is therefore causally influenced by someone else's view that the mitigation rule represents an evaluative norm that must be respected in certain cases. It is true that the influence of Smith's normative commitment on Jones's conduct is an indirect one, being mediated, as it were, by Jones's own beliefs regarding Smith. The indirectness of the causal connection between normative commitment and conduct does not, however, alter matters in any fundamental respect; it is the existence of such a connection, however complicated and remote, which makes it possible to understand a particular event, such as Jones's breach, from a sociological point of view and that gives the event at least potential interest to the sociologist of law. Thus, even if we make the connection between normative commitment and conduct more remote by assuming that Smith himself does not think the mitigation rule ought to be obeyed, but nevertheless takes steps to reduce his damages because he believes, whether rightly or wrongly, that someone else – a judge, for example – *is* normatively committed to the rule and has the power to enforce it, Jones's decision to breach, insofar as it is based on Smith's expected conduct, can again be said to be influenced by someone's (namely, the judge's) normative commitment; although commitment and conduct are now mediated by *two* sets of beliefs – Smith's as well as Jones's – the one continues to be a causal determinant of the other making Jones's breach, even in this case, an event of sociological significance.[15]

This last example helps us to understand what, superficially at least, may seem paradoxical – that to a sociologist, even *illegal* behaviour constitutes a legal phenomenon. So long as a thief alters his behaviour (for example, by concealing his activity) because he believes he is violating rules that others consider binding and are prepared to enforce, his conduct is causally influenced by their normative commitment to the rules in question. Consequently, efforts to break the law and actions undertaken because of a misunderstanding as to what the law requires are of as much potential interest to the sociologist as conduct motivated by a desire to uphold the law correctly understood. This means, of course, that a vast range of human actions are possible subjects of investigation for the sociologist of law. Only the behaviour of a person who himself has no normative commitments to the law and is wholly uninfluenced by the commitments of anyone else – a kind of legal sociopath – necessarily falls outside the domain of the sociology of law.[16] The apparent breadth this gives the discipline raises a question concerning its limits and its relation to other branches of sociological inquiry. I shall return to this problem later in the chapter.

Before continuing, I should emphasize that the sociological attitude toward law is not restricted to social scientists studying the legal order from without for the purpose of acquiring knowledge regarding its characteristics, but is an attitude that may also be adopted by those performing certain roles within the legal order – that may, indeed, be definitive of these roles, at least in part. I have in mind the work of a practicing attorney. In preparing a case for trial or advising a client, an attorney must make an effort to predict how the behaviour of other actors in the legal system – judges especially – will be influenced by their own normative commitments to the law. The conclusions he reaches in this regard are judgments of fact, descriptive causal propositions no different from those offered by the professional sociologist in his account of law-oriented behaviour.[17] To this extent, a practising attorney must himself be a kind of sociologist. There is, however, a twofold difference between the attitude of an attorney and that of a professional (academic) sociologist. In the first place, the attorney's interest in sociological knowledge is intensely *practical*: he wants the knowledge as a means to a practical end – the promotion or defence of his client's interests. The professional sociologist, by contrast, seeks a descriptive causal understanding of law-oriented behaviour because he considers such knowledge valuable for its own sake. Unlike the attorney, a sociologist has no interest in using his knowledge for practical purposes (at least so long as he adheres to his professional role).[18]

Second, a practising attorney seeks sociological understanding because it will aid him in predicting particular outcomes in the context of a specific matter. A sociologist of law, on the other hand, has an independent interest in the formulation and verification of *general* propositions concerning the causal relationship between normative commitment and behaviour – propositions which, again, are merely a means to an end from the attorney's point of view. Nevertheless, despite these significant differences between the lawyer's attitude toward law and the sociologist's, elements of one are to be found in the other; being a good sociologist is often a prerequisite for (although by no means the same thing as) being a successful attorney.

Weber's theory of value

Dogmatism and detachment
The special characteristics of the sociological attitude toward law can best be brought out by considering, in more detail, how it differs from what Weber calls dogmatic jurisprudence. The term he uses to describe the latter way of thinking is itself striking. What is it about legal dogmatics that gives it its *dogmatic* character, and what contrast with the sociological attitude toward law does this term imply? In its ordinary meaning, a dogma is a belief or commitment on which other beliefs rest but which is not itself grounded on or deducible from anything else; a dogma is in this sense a fundamental belief. To call someone a dogmatist ordinarily implies that he has a commitment which he cannot or will not scrutinize critically because of the foundational role it plays in his entire system of beliefs. Thus, when Weber contrasts dogmatic jurisprudence with the sociology of law, as he does repeatedly, he is implying that the former rests upon a fundamental commitment of some sort which has no counterpart in the sociological study of legal phenomena. This same idea can be expressed in a negative fashion: in contrast to all forms of legal dogmatism, the sociological attitude is one which is characteristically *uncommitted*. The sociology of law is marked by a

kind of detachment or disengagement that sets it apart from the legal-dogmatic approach of both scholar and judge.

But detached or disengaged from what? There is one obvious sense in which sociological inquiry is detached. Unlike the practising lawyer, the sociologist seeks knowledge for its own sake; the sociology of law is a theoretical discipline detached from practical concerns of the sort that motivate the lawyer (and to some extent the judge as well). So detachment first of all means: an unconcern with practical ends. In this sense, however, most dogmatic scholars may also be said to approach their work in a spirit of detachment, since they, too, typically seek knowledge (of the law's true meaning) for its own sake, rather than some ulterior, practical purpose. Furthermore, both the dogmatic legal scholar and the sociologist refrain from passing judgment on the law, as the moralist does, and so are equally disengaged in this sense as well. In what respect, then, is one of these two ways of thinking about the law dogmatic and the other not?

Whether or not he approves of them on moral grounds, the dogmatic scholar treats legal norms as evaluative standards, criteria by which to assess the adequacy or correctness of human behaviour (for example, the correctness of a judge's decision in a particular case). By contrast, the sociologist merely describes the way in which a normative commitment to legal rules influences individual behaviour; he does not himself treat these rules in the way the subjects of his inquiry do, as evaluative standards for the assessment of conduct. The sociologist is therefore detached or disengaged from the value commitments of those whose conduct he studies. The normative attitudes they adopt are a matter of interest to him, but he investigates their causal influence on conduct without entering into – in the sense of endorsing or making his own – these attitudes themselves.

Of course, detachment of this sort is often very difficult to achieve, especially if the sociologist does share a common or overlapping set of values with the subjects of his inquiry, or, alternatively, finds their values objectionable and disturbing. Powerful psychological forces sometimes make it impossible for the sociological observer to disengage himself entirely from the normative commitments of the individuals he is studying, with the result that his descriptive work may be coloured by evaluative ideas in ways that are perhaps imperceptible to the sociologist himself. However, despite the psychological difficulty of maintaining a detached or value-free attitude in any inquiry that is centrally concerned with the values of others, Weber believed such detachment to be attainable to a meaningful degree in a wide range of cases and viewed it as an ideal which should guide the professional sociologist in his work.[19]

That detachment is a characteristic of the sociological attitude toward law or human action generally does not mean, however, that the sociologist's own value commitments play no role at all in the choice and definition of his specific task. Weber's view was quite the opposite, and he repeatedly emphasizes the extent to which the sociologist's own values *do* shape his inquiry in ways that Weber thought entirely appropriate, indeed inescapable.[20] In the first place, the sociologist's personal values are almost certain to influence his choice of subject-matter, what he decides to investigate and from which perspective, since this choice will depend upon what he finds interesting and valuable and therefore worth doing. Second, and more fundamentally, the decision to engage in sociological inquiry itself reflects a commitment to sociology as a discipline, a belief in the value of the special form of understanding which its practitioners strive to attain. This belief, as Weber himself points out, is a dogma in precisely the sense defined above: it represents a commitment that can neither be demonstrated nor disproven – any more than the value of science in general, or indeed *any* form of human endeavour, can be established by rational argument.[21] In both of these ways, then – in his initial choice of sociology as a vocation and in the more specific decisions he makes about what to study and how – the sociologist's orientation to his subject-matter is shaped by his own value commitments.

But the fact that the sociologist's own values necessarily influence his work in each of these two ways is not inconsistent with his being able to take a detached attitude toward the values of those whose conduct is the subject-matter of his inquiry. It is perfectly possible for a sociologist to withhold all approval or disapproval regarding the normative commitments of his subjects (and for his inquiry, in this sense, to be value-*free*) even though he has decided to study their behaviour from a particular perspective because he believes the results will be interesting (and for his inquiry, in this sense, to be value-*laden*). The sociologist's inquiry can be both value-free and value-laden because it is so in different respects or at different levels. In order to understand Weber's conception of sociological method, one must keep both aspects in view and resist the temptation to think that the sociologist's own values must either have no influence on his work whatsoever or else inevitably transform his inquiry into a normative one, similar to that of the moralist or legal dogmatist. The first suggestion ignores the limitations of sociological understanding; the second denies its special possibilities as an empirical science of human conduct.

The positivity of values

The sociologist studies law-oriented behaviour without himself being committed to the rules of the legal order. He is uncommitted in the twofold sense that he neither passes moral judgment on the rules in question nor employs them as criteria for determining what is, and is not, legally correct from a dogmatic point of view. But while the sociologist does not himself treat rules of law as evaluative criteria, he must be able to understand the normative commitments of those whose behaviour he is studying. He must be able, in other words, to empathize with the individuals who are the subjects of his inquiry, to see the world, and in particular the social world, from their perspective, as a field of experience ordered in accordance with the individuals' own normative commitments – their beliefs about what is morally good and bad, legally required or forbidden, and so forth.[22] Only if a sociologist can see the world from the perspective of *their* values, and appreciate what these values mean to *them*, can he explain how the behaviour of his subjects is influenced by the values they hold and construct an empirical causal explanation of the sort he seeks to provide. But although a sociologist must empathize with his subjects, he does not treat their values as normative criteria in his own investigation. He attempts to understand the normative commitments of those he is studying without, as it were, reproducing these same commitments in himself. This combination of empathy and detachment is characteristic of the sociologist's attitude toward all human behaviour, including behaviour that is causally influenced by a normative commitment to the legal order. How is the combination of such seemingly different elements to be explained – indeed, how is it possible at all?

One way of answering, or rather avoiding, this question is to deny that a detached understanding of another person's values *is* possible. Someone might argue, not unreasonably, that a sociologist will be unable to appreciate what another person's values mean to him unless he (the sociologist) feels a special sympathy for the values in question – which is possible only if they are his values as well. Put differently, it can be argued that genuine understanding presupposes the very commitment which the sociologist purports to withhold in conducting his inquiry and that understanding and normative belief therefore cannot be separated in the way that Weber's conception of sociological method assumes they can.

This is undoubtedly true in some cases, at least as a psychological matter. There are values so remote from our own that we have great difficulty in seeing what the world looks like from the vantage point of those who embrace them; indeed, if the values in question are sufficiently unfamiliar, we may not even notice their existence. In this sense, some degree of similarity between the values of the inquiring sociologist and the values of his subjects is almost certainly a precondition of sociological understanding. Weber himself suggested that this is likely to be so. He also thought, however, that to a varying degree and across a wide range of cases, it *is* possible for one person to empathize with another person's values while withholding his own commitment to these values themselves, a view that has intuitive plausibility and seems to be confirmed by a variety of everyday experiences. We often feel we understand the way in which another person's values influence his behaviour, without having judged his values in a moral sense or adopted them as critical, normative standards for the assessment of conduct. I am better able to understand my friend's unwillingness to attend a Friday night dinner party, for example, when it is pointed out that he is an orthodox Jew and believes it would be a violation of religious law to travel by automobile on the Sabbath. One need not oneself be a Jew, or have any religious convictions whatsoever, to find this explanation illuminating.[23]

In general, for the detached understanding of another person's values to be possible, evaluation – the use of a norm as an evaluative standard – must be distinct from knowledge or understanding of the norm, from an intellectual comprehension of what the norm requires and forbids and how it functions generally. If evaluation and understanding were the same, no one could understand another person's values without having made them his own. The distinctness of understanding and evaluation is therefore a necessary premise of Weber's theory of sociological understanding. This assumption may seem non-controversial. However, not all philosophers have accepted Weber's distinction between evaluation and understanding. One philosopher who denied the distinction was Socrates, judging from his views as they are presented in certain of Plato's early and middle dialogues. In these dialogues, Socrates defends the position that knowledge or understanding is a necessary and sufficient condition for virtue and hence for right conduct,[24] a view which implies the impossibility of detached understanding of the sort that Weber claims is characteristic of all sociological inquiry. A brief examination of the Socratic equation of knowledge and virtue will help to clarify, by opposition, the special and quite different assumptions on which Weber's distinction between evaluation and understanding is based. The juxtaposition of their views will also illuminate the extent to which Weber's distinction is embedded in a particular picture or conception of the human soul.

According to Socrates, we ought to think of virtue as a kind of craft or technique for living. This analogy – which one recent writer calls the 'craft analogy'[25] – is at the heart of Socrates' moral theory. The analogy implies two things about the nature of virtue. It implies, first, that virtue, like any craft, has a specific object or purpose, and second, that virtue constitutes the best or most appropriate method for achieving this object, whatever it might be.

The object of virtue, Socrates tells us, is to put the soul in a particular condition which he calls 'good' or 'admirable' and to attain the happiness that necessarily accompanies this condition. Socrates believed that the condition in question is both *determinate* and *universal* – that it consists in the soul's being in a specific and identifiable state which does not vary from one individual to the next but is the same for all men. According to Socrates, men have different conceptions of what this state is only because they are ignorant of its true nature. The goodness of the soul, in Socrates' view, is in no way ambiguous or indeterminate; consequently, when men acquire an accurate knowledge of its true nature, disagreements as to what it is or consists in are bound to disappear.

Ignorance also explains why men lead different sorts of lives and seek happiness in different ways. Everyone, according to Socrates, desires happiness but since men have different conceptions of what happiness is (some thinking it is pleasure, others equating it with honourable actions, others still finding it in the pursuit of wisdom) they are led to act in different ways. That is to say, what individuals find worthwhile and consider to be of value, depends on their conception of what it means for the soul to be in a good and therefore happy condition. It follows that if someone is leading a bad or unvirtuous life it can only be because he has a faulty understanding of the nature of happiness; to assume that he desires something other than happiness would, according to Socrates, be absurd. Consequently, once his ignorance has been removed, his conception of what is good and bad will necessarily be altered and his way of life reformed. It is unthinkable, in Socrates' view, that someone can know what true happiness consists in, and yet fail to act in the way best suited to put the soul in a happy state. In this sense, a person's knowledge of goodness is a necessary and sufficient condition for his having the values that he does – for his regarding certain things, and not others, as valuable or worthwhile. Thus, the ethical attitude which distinguishes the truly virtuous man is not something 'added on' to his knowledge, an attitude requiring an additional act of choice or judgment on his part, distinct from intellectual comprehension. On Socrates' view, a man cannot see the good and act badly; if he does act badly, this by itself conclusively demonstrates that he has not understood the nature of goodness but still suffers from a kind of ignorance or blindness in the mind's eye.

This view of the relationship between knowledge and values has lasting appeal and has had adherents in every age, including our own. There are, for example, important parallels between Socrates' view and Freud's theory of psychoanalysis. Although Freud does not insist, as Socrates does, that happiness is a determinate and universal condition of the soul which is the same for all men, he does assume that the knowledge a patient acquires regarding his own history makes it possible for him literally to re-evaluate his situation (for example, to rid himself of obsessive symptoms, thereby allowing new interests and desires to emerge with increased effectiveness). More importantly, Freud also suggests that insight unaccompanied by a re-evaluation of this sort, a 'turning about of the soul' as Socrates calls it in the *Republic*,[26] is not genuine insight at all – that the patient's self-knowledge, on the one hand, and his values and desires on the other, are indistinguishable in precisely the sense maintained by Socrates.[27]

Weber's theory of value rests upon a strikingly different conception of the relationship between knowledge and values. According to Weber, it can never be true that being committed to a particular value is equivalent to having knowledge of a certain sort. Weber does not deny that a person's knowledge – his experience and beliefs – may *influence* his values in both a negative and positive sense: commitment to a particular value may be psychologically impossible unless one also believes certain things about the world, and particular beliefs may predispose the person holding them (again, at least as a psychological matter) to adopt one value rather than another. Influence of both sorts can be described by saying that a person's knowledge or beliefs are sometimes a *necessary condition* of his values. But Weber strenuously denies the stronger claim, associated with the Socratic view, that a person's knowledge is also a *sufficient condition* for his having a particular value or set of values. According to Weber, a person *chooses* his values; whatever his knowledge or beliefs may be, an additional and distinct act of choice is always necessary to make the object of his choice – whether it be a limited principle of conduct or entire way of life – a value for the person involved.* On this view, every value owes its existence to the exercise of a power fundamentally different from cognition or understanding – the frightening power we all possess to affirm or disaffirm even those things we understand most clearly. Weber uses its traditional name to describe this power: he calls it the *will*.**

According to Socrates, knowledge is a kind of sight or vision which has as its object something that exists independently of the knowing person himself and which he sees more or less clearly depending upon the condition of his soul. On the Socratic view, a person acquires his knowledge of values, along with his knowledge of everything else, in this way, through an act of intellectual vision. And since, for Socrates, knowledge of what is right is a necessary and sufficient condition for virtue, i.e., for a commitment to *do* what is right, this act of intellectual insight is, on his view, the central event – and the power in the soul which it involves the central power – in the moral life of human beings. If one accepts Socrates' view, the basic task of moral life can only be conceived as the attainment of a certain clarity of vision. To achieve this goal, one must put his soul in the right condition by eliminating the ignorance that darkens his vision and limits his powers of comprehension. This may require an active effort over a long period of time; nevertheless, the goal itself should be conceived as an essentially *passive* state or condition in which the soul looks at the world in an unclouded way and, seeing what is true, finds itself disposed to do the right thing without an intervening act of choice.

For Weber, on the other hand, even the clearest knowledge of values – of what is right and wrong from the standpoint of different normative principles – can never be more than a preparation for the act of choice which alone makes such a principle a value for the person who holds it. According to Weber, all values are in some ultimate sense freely chosen; indeed, on his view, it is only through choice that values come into being. To this extent, Weber's theory of value requires us to think of values as having their foundation not in the world, as Socrates claimed, but in the choosing subject or, more precisely, in the faculty of choice which a person exercises when he

---

*'The fruit of the tree of knowledge, which is distasteful to the complacent but which is, none-theless, inescapable, consists in the insight that every single important activity and ultimately life as a whole, if it is not to be permitted to run on as an event in nature but is instead to be consciously guided, is a series of ultimate decisions through which the soul – as in Plato [!] – chooses its own fate, i.e. the meaning of its activity and existence.' *MSS*, 18.

**MSS, 54. Kant defines the will as 'a faculty of determining oneself to action *in accordance with the conception of certain laws.*' Kant, *Fundamental Principles of the Metaphysic of Morals* in *Critique of Practical Reason and Other Works* (trans. T.K. Abbott, London, 1873), p. 45. For a discussion of the neo-Kantian influences that shaped Weber's methodological views, see D. Henrich, *Die Einheit der Wissenschaftslehre Max Webers* (Tübingen, 1952). Weber's relationship to the tradition of German Idealism is discussed by Parsons in *The Structure of Social Action*, pp. 473–87. The lengthy introductions to *CS* and *RK*, both by Guy Oakes, also throw considerable light on the philosophical background against which Weber was writing.

commits himself to a norm by adopting it as an evaluative standard.*

Because he conceives every value a person holds to be the product or posit of an act of choice, Weber's theory of value may be called *positivistc*. We should be clear, however, as to what such a theory does and does not imply. To begin with, it does *not* imply that individuals are always free to choose their values from among an unlimited or even very wide range of alternatives; Weber recognized that a person's choices are in most cases narrowly circumscribed by historical, cultural, economic and personal factors. Nor does Weber's theory of value necessarily imply that an individual's choice of values is always, or ever, made in a fully self-conscious and deliberate manner: the values we have rarely seem to be the product of free choice in this sense. What Weber's positivistic theory of value *does* imply is that the status of a value, the fact that a particular norm happens to be a value for someone, can be accounted for conceptually only if we view the value in question as the product of an act of choice, no matter how unrealistic this may be in any given case.

Unlike Socrates' theory, which assigns the central role in moral life to our capacity for knowledge or understanding, Weber's positivistic theory of value assigns this same role to an entirely distinct power, to the will, the power of creative choice. In this sense, his theory of value entails a shift from what might be called a reason or intellect-centred conception of the moral dimension of personhood to a *will-centred* conception. The full implications of Weber's will-centred conception of moral personality will be developed in subsequent chapters. For now, it is enough to note its connection with his positivistic theory of value: Weber's claim that values are chosen or created, not discovered by passive intellectual contemplation, necessarily gives a prominence to the faculty of choice which it can never have in the Socratic conception of value.

How does Weber's theory of value help to explain the peculiar combination of detachment and empathy characteristic of all sociological inquiry? As we have seen, the sociologist deliberately abstains from entering into (in the sense of the making his own) the normative commitments of those whose conduct he is studying. If every value is the product of an act of will, as Weber's theory of value assumes, then this abstention on the sociologist's part can only mean that he refrains from willing the values of his subjects. But to refrain from willing is also an act of will, albeit a negative one, since the will cannot be suspended by any other power or agency than itself. If it is appropriate to represent the detachment required of the sociologist in this way – as a kind of negative act of will – then, assuming that willing and knowing are separate powers or faculties, the sociologist's willful abstention need not impair his ability to understand the rational structure of someone else's value commitments and the distinctive form they give his experience.

---

*'The fate of an epoch which has eaten of the tree of knowledge is that it must know that we cannot learn the *meaning* of the world from the results of its analysis, be it ever so perfect; it must rather be in a position to create this meaning itself.' *MSS*, 57.

Sociological detachment is achieved, then, by a deliberate act of abstention on the sociologist's part which has the effect of neutralizing the normative commitments of those he is studying.* Neutralizing their commitments in this way does not render them unintelligible, however; because our values are something we *add* to our knowledge of the world by making choices, by exercising a power wholly distinct from the power of comprehension, the sociologist can withdraw or suspend his own normative commitment to the values affirmed by his subjects – can, as it were, *subtract* his commitment through a counteract of will – without losing his ability to understand what these values mean, as ordering principles of conduct, to those who hold them. In short, the peculiar form of detached empathy which distinguishes sociological understanding from all forms of dogmatism is possible because (contrary to what Socrates taught) knowing and evaluating are not the same. His rejection of the Socratic claim that virtue is knowledge and his adoption, instead, of a theory of value that distinguishes knowing from willing and which treats the latter as the ground of all value, is the philosophical presupposition on which Weber's concept of sociological understanding is based.[28]

Purposive explanation and social action

The concept of a purpose

A sociologist of law seeks to describe the way in which an individual's behaviour is causally influenced by his normative commitment to legal rules and by his belief that others have similar commitments of their own. The sociological investigation of legal phenomena therefore results in causal judgments of the following general form: X (an individual) did or can be expected to do or refrain from doing something, to behave in a certain way, *because*, among other things, he considers himself normatively bound by a particular legal rule, or because he believes that some other individual or group of individuals is committed to the rule in this same sense.

According to Weber, causal judgments of this sort describe factual relationships and must therefore be cast in probabilistic terms, given the inherent complexity of human behaviour and inevitable limitations on the sociologist's powers of observation and verification.[29] Unfortunately, this makes for considerable awkwardness in the actual formulation of sociological propositions regarding legal behaviour, especially those that seek to describe complex institutions such as the state. It is nevertheless a striking characteristic of Weber's own work in the sociology of law that his causal

---

*This negative act of abstention corresponds, in many ways, to the suspension of the 'natural believing in existence involved in experiencing the world' that constitutes the critical step in Husserl's phenomenological method. See E. Husserl, *Cartesian Meditations* (trans. D. Cairns, The Hague, 1960), p. 20.

judgments – especially those which are meant to be technically precise – are frequently stated in probabilistic terms.*

The probabilistic character of these judgments underscores, again, the fundamental difference between the sociological and legal-dogmatic points of view. When a scholar or judge offers an interpretation of the correct meaning of a particular legal rule, he is not making a probabilistic causal judgment either about his own future behaviour or the behaviour of other actors in the legal order.[30] The dogmatic exegesis of legal concepts has as its goal the definitive statement of what constitutes correct legal behaviour; propositions of this sort are essentially normative and therefore cannot be formulated in probabilistic terms. By contrast, since every sociological investigation of legal phenomena seeks to establish and confirm factual truths its results may legitimately be cast in the form of probabilities. Weber's own deliberate use of probabilistic terms is meant to dramatize the difference between the sociological attitude toward law and all forms of dogmatic jurisprudence, and to remind us that sociology is an empirical science concerned with the causal explanation of human behaviour.

However, this definition of sociology – including the sociology of law – is not sufficiently precise. According to Weber, all sciences (with the possible exception of mathematics) are concerned with the knowledge of causes. This is true, on his view, of both the natural and social sciences.[31] What distinguishes the *sociological* explanation of human behaviour, including legal behaviour, from other forms of explanation (those, for example, that a physicist or biologist might offer of the same phenomena) must therefore be attributable to some special characteristic of the causal explanations the sociologist constructs. According to Weber, the sociological explanation of human behaviour always includes individual 'purposes' among the factors said to be causes of the behaviour in question and this, he claims, distinguishes the explanations offered by a sociologist from those advanced in the natural and biological sciences.[32] The concept of a purpose is a key one in Weber's theory of sociological method; its meaning, however, is unclear.

Many different activities or processes, non-human as well as human, have *ends* in the sense that there is some state or condition which we are inclined to view as their appropriate terminus, and which it is illuminating to think of as shaping the process in question and guiding it toward its conclusion – in Aristotle's words, 'that for the sake of which' the process exists.[33] However, for an activity to be a 'purposive' one as Weber uses that term, it is not enough that it have an end in this very general sense. An activity is purposive, according to Weber, only when the person engaged in it has in his mind an *idea* of the end toward which the activity is directed and when he is guided, in his conduct, by this ideational anticipation of the end and by a

---

*According to Weber, the central question of the sociology of law is, 'what *actually* happens in a group owing to the *probability* that persons engaged in social action, especially those exerting a socially relevant amount of power, subjectively consider certain norms as valid and practically act according to them, in other words, orient their own conduct toward these norms?' *ES*, 311.

rule or method for attaining it.* If the explanation of a human action attempts to make it intelligible merely by showing how it leads to a particular state of affairs (its end) – by showing, for example, that the behaviour in question tends to maximize the actor's welfare or chances for survival – the explanation is a *teleological* but not a *purposive* one. For it to be purposive, the explanation must treat the actor's own idea or mental representation of the end toward which he is striving as a (although not necessarily the only) cause of his conduct, irreducible to anything qualitatively different such as an organic state or genetic disposition. There are obviously many explanations of human behaviour which are teleological but not purposive in this sense – sociobiology offers a contemporary example[34] – as well as many that are neither.

Purposive behaviour, then, is behaviour that is consciously oriented toward an end of some sort, an end which is represented in advance of its attainment by an idea in the actor's mind and that is accompanied by the conception of a rule or method for attaining it. To describe such behaviour in a way that adequately expresses its purposive character, the idea of the end which the actor represents to himself and which he deliberately strives to attain must be treated as a determining cause of his behaviour. If it is not, the peculiar characteristic that distinguishes this kind of behaviour from unconscious processes that also have a discernible end in the general sense described above, will be obscured. It is, of course, possible and often illuminating to explain purposive behaviour in non-purposive terms; sociobiological and pharmacological explanations even of fully self-conscious human conduct can be quite instructive. But it is also always possible to explain purposive behaviour in a way that reflects its distinctive character. To do so, however, the explanation must treat ideas as primary causes – primary in the sense that they are not themselves to be explained, in turn, by something other than ideas. On Weber's view, this is precisely what distinguishes the sociological explanation of human behaviour from those causal explanations that a physicist or biologist might offer of the same phenomena.

Several things follow from Weber's concept of purposive explanation. First, there are obviously some events for which no such explanation can be given; these are events which do not have a purpose, the idea of an end, as one of their determining causes. It is possible, for example, to explain in causal terms why a star explodes or a thunderstorm occurs but one cannot give a purposive explanation of the same event (unless, in the latter case, the storm has been induced by cloudseeding for the purpose of producing rain). On the other hand, even those occurrences for which a purposive explanation *can* be given are also explicable in non-purposive terms. Every human action can also be viewed as a natural occurrence that is subject to the laws of physics or biochemistry. The domain of non-purposive explanations

*'From our viewpoint, "purpose" is the conception of an *effect* which becomes a *cause* of an action.' *MSS*, 83.

(more precisely, the domain of events that can be explained in this way) is therefore wider than and inclusive of the domain of purposive explanations.

Second, purposive explanations are necessarily individualistic – a point that some commentators have expressed by describing Weber as a methodological individualist.[35] By definition, every purposive explanation of an event includes among its determining causes one or more ideas and an idea, according to Weber, is something that can only arise in or be represented by the mind of an individual. Different individuals may have the same idea, and one person's idea may have as its content another person's ideas or behaviour. This is the case, for example, if I walk downtown in order to meet you at an appointed place, with the expectation that you will keep the appointment because you believe it is in your interest to do so. But whatever its *content*, an idea is always the product or representation of an individual mind. This is, so to speak, its unvarying *form*. According to Weber, there is and can be no such thing as a group idea, an idea grounded in something other than the consciousness of a single individual. Consequently, every purposive explanation, even of complex events and processes, must treat what it seeks to explain as a combination or series of distinct individual actions.

Third, and most importantly, the purposive explanation of an event makes it possible for us to understand it in what Weber called a 'meaningful' way – in contrast to the kind of understanding afforded by a mechanistic or teleological account of the same phenomenon. Our understanding of an event is 'meaningful' to the degree we are able to view it as the product of one or more purposive acts. This presupposes that the event can be brought into relation with a purpose. Since, for Weber, an event *has* meaning only when it is related to a purpose, our ability, in any particular case, to imaginatively construct such a relation will determine whether the event in question can be understood in a meaningful sense.

The meaningful explanation of an event (where such an explanation can be given) is satisfying in a special way. The appeal of such explanations derives from the fact that they render transparent what might be called the *internal* connection between the event that is to be explained and its causal ground.* Weber believed that every scientific explanation – whether of a meaningful sort or not – must be framed in causal terms. All causal propositions assert a connection between one event (the explanandum) and one or more temporally antecedent events (the explanans) which are claimed to be

---

*'Suppose that somehow an empirical-statistical demonstration of the strictest sort is produced, showing that all men everywhere who have ever been placed in a certain situation have invariably reacted in the same way and to the same extent. Suppose that whenever this situation is experimentally reproduced, the same reaction invariably follows. . . . Such a demonstration would not bring us a single step closer to the "interpretation" of the reaction. By itself, such a demonstration would contribute absolutely nothing to the project of "understanding" "why" this reaction ever occurred and moreover, "why" it invariably occurs in the same way. As long as the "inner", imaginative *reproduction* of the motivation responsible for this reaction remains impossible, we will be unable to acquire this understanding.' *RK*, 129.

its causal ground. This is just as true in physics and astronomy as it is in sociology. But every explanation which postulates something other than a purpose (in Weber's sense) as a causal ground, leaves obscure the nature of the connection between cause and effect. All explanations of this kind assert the existence of such a connection but do nothing more to illuminate it than Voltaire's principle of dormativity does to explain the sleep-producing powers of opium. Put differently, the causal connections that all non-meaningful explanations assert can only be understood from the *outside;* explanations of this sort leave us in the position of always being able to ask what the nature of the connection between cause and effect actually is, a question we are unable to answer, so long as purposes play no role in our explanation. Purposive explanations *do* provide an answer (of the only sort we can give!) to this last question, and thus enable us to understand at least certain causal connections from *within.* This gives purposive explanations a special kind of transparency or completeness and helps to explain why we find meaningful understanding so satisfying where we are able to attain it.

In the deepest sense, perhaps, the special transparency of purposive explanations should be attributed to the fact that every purpose, understood as the ideational representation of an as-yet unattained end, is a human creation and therefore uniquely intelligible to us in the way that Vico and Kant, among others, have suggested.* We can understand purposive behaviour from within because we are able, through an empathic identification with the actor, to view ourselves as its author. This is impossible where natural events are concerned; no one but God, the author of nature, can understand in a meaningful way the causal mechanism which produces an event in the natural order.** In short, only to the extent that we discover our own human purposes in the world can its causal regularities be grasped as meaningful relations whose inner connection is transparent to a human observer. This

---

*'A new light flashed upon the mind of the first man (be he Thales or some other) who demonstrated the properties of the isosceles triangle. The true method, so he found, was not to inspect what he discerned either in the figure, or in the bare concept of it, and from this, as it were, to read off its properties; but to bring out of what was necessarily implied in the concepts that he had himself formed *a priori*, and had put into the figure in the construction by which he presented it to himself. If he is to know anything with *a priori* certainly he must not ascribe to the figure anything save what necessarily follows from what he has himself set into it in accordance with his concept.' Kant, *Critique of Pure Reason*, Bxii.

**'In the night of thick darkness which envelops the earliest antiquity, so remote from ourselves, there shines the eternal and never-failing light of a truth beyond all question: that the world of civil society has certainly been made by men, and that its principles are therefore to be found within the modifications of our own human mind. Whoever reflects on this cannot but marvel that the philosophers should have bent all their energies to the study of the world of nature, which, since God made it, He alone knows; and that they should have neglected the study of the world of nations, or civil world, which, since men made it, men could come to know.' Vico, *The New Science of Giambattista Vico* (trans. T. Bergin and M. Fisch, Ithaca and London, 1948), § 331. See also K. Marx, *Capital* (S. Moore and E. Aveling trans., New York, 1906) p. 406n.

same idea underlies Weber's conception of modernity, as I shall attempt to show in Chapter 8.

Social action

According to Weber, sociology seeks to explain only certain purposive actions, those he calls 'social actions'; the latter represent a subset of all actions which are purposive in the broadest sense. A social action is an action having as one of its causes an individual purpose which 'takes account of the behaviour of others and is thereby oriented in its course', that is, a purpose framed with the expected conduct of other individuals in mind.[36] Suppose that a number of people on the street simultaneously put up their umbrellas at the beginning of a rain shower.[37] The identical behaviour of each individual may be viewed as a purposive act, causally influenced by the idea of an end (not getting wet), and therefore understandable in a meaningful way. But their actions, though identical, are not *social* actions since none takes the behaviour of the others into account in deciding to raise his umbrella. By contrast, the decision to pay a parking fine *is* a social action if, as is usually the case, the decision to pay it is motivated, in part, by an expectation that if it is not paid, other people – representatives of the state – will do things which the person who has been fined would prefer they not do (arrest him, impound his automobile, etc.). Here, the action in question (paying the fine) is a meaningful one, but unlike the act of raising an umbrella in a rainstorm, is informed by a purpose which has the expected behaviour of other persons as part of its content.

The sociology of law is concerned only with social actions. If an individual acts in a certain way because he considers himself normatively bound by a particular legal rule, he acts purposively (motivated by the idea of compliance with the norm) and his purpose is almost certain to take into account, even if only implicitly, the disapproval and other sanctions he can expect if he fails to observe the rule in question. In this sense, his action is oriented to the anticipated conduct of others. Likewise, if a person acts in a certain way because he believes that other people consider themselves bound by a particular legal rule, his own purposes, whatever they might be, take the (law-oriented) behaviour of others into account, making his action a social action in Weber's sense. (If he acts without regard to what others will think or do, but only because he believes the rule is ethically correct, his conduct is purposive but not *law*-oriented.)*

Although the sociology of law is concerned exclusively with social actions, it does not attempt to explain all actions even of this kind, but only those in which the actor's behaviour is importantly influenced by his orientation to

---

*Even a judgment of ethical (as distinct from legal) correctness will almost certainly make reference, at least implicitly, to the expected behaviour of other persons (their approval or disapproval, ostracism or comradeship, etc.). Thus, although it may not be law-oriented, behaviour which is motivated by a desire to do what is ethically correct does constitute social action in Weber's sense.

norms of one very particular sort, namely, those belonging to the legal order. Consequently, in order to understand what distinguishes the sociology of law from other branches of sociological inquiry (for example, the sociology of religion) it is necessary to clarify Weber's notion of a legal norm and, more generally, his concept of law.

The subject-matter of the sociology of law

We now have an answer to the first of our two questions: how does a sociologist of law study or investigate the subject-matter of his discipline? The sociologist of law seeks to explain law-oriented behaviour in causal terms. The explanations he offers are value-free; they do not provide a basis for the normative assessment of conduct, unlike the judgments of the moralist and dogmatic scholar. Moreover, because sociological explanations of human behaviour treat individual purposes as causes, they make it possible for us to understand human conduct in a meaningful way. Finally, the sociological attitude is characterized by a peculiar combination of empathy and detachment. The sociologist enters into the value-orientations of his subjects; only by doing so can he understand their behaviour in a meaningful way. At the same time, however, he abstains from making their values his own; without such abstention on his part, the sociologist's inquiry would cease to be value-free. In order for this kind of detached empathy (and hence for the discipline of sociology) to be possible at all, normative evaluation and judgment must be distinct from understanding. This distinction in turn requires us to assume that a person's values are established through the exercise of a creative faculty (the will) distinct from the power of rational insight.

We can now take up the second of the questions posed at the beginning of the chapter: what is the subject-matter of the sociology of law? The obvious answer is that the sociology of law studies conduct which in some important sense is law-oriented. But this only pushes the question further back: what, according to Weber, *is* law and how is it distinguished from other forms of social control?

Weber's concept of law

A legal rule is a norm, an evaluative standard for the critical assessment of human conduct,[38] and a legal system is an ordered collection of such rules. But this, of course, is insufficient to distinguish legal rules and systems from other normative regimes including, for example, morality and social convention. Legal rules must have some additional characteristic, other than their normativity, which marks them off from non-legal rules that also function as standards of evaluation. What did Weber believe this characteristic to be?

In answering this question, it is useful to begin with his formal definition of law. 'An order will be called *law*', according to Weber, 'if it is externally guaranteed by the probability that physical or psychological coercion will be applied by a *staff* of people in order to bring about compliance or avenge violation.'[39] The full significance of this definition can best be brought out by first considering three other ways in which one might attempt to distinguish legal from non-legal norms. To begin with, one might define law in terms of the types of conduct it seeks to regulate. This view assumes that certain aspects of human behaviour – for example, religious or moral behaviour and the internal affairs of the household – lie beyond the limits of legal control (although they may be subject to other, non-legal, norms). Weber emphatically rejects this view: there is, he claims, no area of human conduct which the law has not, at one time or another, attempted to regulate with greater or lesser success, no fixed domain of religious, moral or familial obligations whose content necessarily places them outside the scope of legal regulation.[40]

Second, a legal rule might be defined as a norm that is sanctioned in a particular way – by the use or threatened use of physical force. Every norm, legal or non-legal, is accompanied by a sanction of some sort, even if the sanction is only mild disapproval. An individual's failure to conduct himself in accordance with the norm cannot be a matter of indifference to those who consider it binding; if no one cares whether the rule is observed, it is not a social norm at all. Given this general fact, it is plausible to think that different kinds of norms ought to be distinguished from one another in terms of the sanctions typically associated with their enforcement.

Weber rejects this view as well. Legal rules, he claims, are enforced in many different ways; the sanctions that accompany them are by no means always physical in character but also include purely psychological methods of coercion.[41] By the same token, non-legal rules may be enforced by physical sanctions as well as psychological ones. Moral codes, for example, are enforced not only by encouraging a feeling of guilt in those who have violated its rules but also by more direct measures – including economic boycott and social ostracism – which are intended to hurt wrongdoers in a material sense. A particular moral norm may even be enforced by the threatened infliction of physical injury; the use of the duel as a means – an illegal means – of enforcing obligations of honour is an important example. Since both legal and non-legal norms may be enforced by a variety of sanctions, Weber felt that any effort to define the law in terms of one particular sanctioning mechanism would be hopelessly imprecise and necessarily underinclusive.

A third way of defining law is in terms of the method or procedure by which legal norms are established. One can define a legal rule, for example, as any rule promulgated by a sovereign authority, such as the Queen in Parliament. On this view, for a norm to be a legal norm, it must have been enacted by some determinate person or body of persons, or be derivable from some other norm that has been enacted in the specified manner.[42] Weber also rejects this way of defining law. According to Weber, the individuals subject to a legal norm need not view it as having had a particular genesis or even any genesis at all. Indeed, in some cases – those in which the legal system rests upon traditionalist attitudes – legal rules are considered binding precisely because they cannot be traced back to an original enactment or other norm-establishing event. In sum, Weber does not attempt to define legal norms in terms of their content, the nature of the sanction associated with them, or the manner of their establishment. Instead, in defining the concept of a legal norm and the related idea of a legal order, he attaches decisive importance to the way in which such norms are *administered*. According to Weber, legal norms are administered by a specialized staff, a determinate group of persons charged with exclusive responsibility for administering the norms in question. The existence of a separate, specialized enforcement staff of this sort distinguishes law both from convention and morality.* The rules that comprise each of the latter two orders do have sanctions associated with them; however, in the case of both moral and conventional norms, the authority to administer these sanctions and the power to do so resides not in a specialized staff,** but diffusely, in the community as a whole.

Normally, the existence of a specialized staff means that some identifiable subset of the community (the class of 'legal officials') has sole responsibility for enforcing its laws. At one point, however, Weber makes an interesting remark which suggests that his notion of a specialized staff – the key element in his definition of law – may have another and perhaps more fundamental meaning. According to Weber,

> [i]n marginal cases [the coercive apparatus associated with a legal order] may consist in the consensually valid chance of coercive intervention by all the members of the community in the event of an infringement of a valid norm. However, in that case one cannot properly speak of a 'coercive apparatus' unless the conditions under which participation in such coercive intervention is to be obligatory, are firmly fixed.[43]

The last sentence in this passage suggests that a legal system is distinguished from other normative orders not by the presence of a discrete subcommunity of legal officials but by the existence of a rule or set of rules that specify who is to punish infractions and what form the punishment is to take. On this view, a legal order differs from morality and social convention in that its sanctioning process is itself regulated by clear and widely accepted norms. Normative standards for the evaluation of conduct need not be accompanied by equally clear rules for the sanctioning process, the process by which infractions of first-order rules applying directly to conduct are identified and punished. This seems, in fact, to be the case in many (if not all) systems of morality which have not yet been legalized, that is, stamped

---

*'Convention . . . is characterized by the very absence of any coercive apparatus, i.e. of any, at least relatively clearly delimited, group of persons who would continuously hold themselves ready for the special task of legal coercion through physical or psychological means.' *ES*, 320.

**The analogous point is sometimes made that international law is not really law because of 'the absence from the system of centrally organized sanctions'. For a criticism of this view, and of the effort to define law in terms of its sanctioning mechanism, see Hart, *The Concept of Law*, pp. 211–15.

with the *imprimatur* of legal validity. In defining law as he does, Weber may mean to suggest that it is the existence of binding norms at the second or sanctioning level which distinguishes the law from other normative social orders.*

Legal phenomena

According to Weber, a norm is a rule of law and a set of such rules is a legal system if it is administered by a specialized staff enjoying exclusive powers of enforcement. As we have seen, there are other ways of defining law, but Weber rejects these, emphasizing, instead, the distinctive manner in which legal rules are administered or enforced. To some extent, of course, his definition is arbitrary, since law could be defined in any one of these other ways as well. Weber's own definition reflects his desire to define law in the broadest possible fashion so as to preserve the meaningfulness of distinctions that other concepts of law deny – for example, the distinction between made and unmade law, which becomes incomprehensible if the defining property of all legal rules is said to be their deliberate enactment by a sovereign authority. Weber's definition of law is sufficiently narrow to distinguish law from morality and convention but broad enough to encompass legal rules of the most diverse origin and content, thus allowing us to take account of distinctions that alternative definitions either ignore or obliterate.

However, even if one accepts Weber's definition of law as a useful heuristic device, it does not by itself provide an adequate basis for defining the subject-matter of the sociology of law. 'Law-oriented behaviour', behaviour which is causally influenced by a normative commitment to legal rules – whether the commitment be the actor's own or someone else's – obviously covers an extraordinarily broad field. As Weber himself points out, almost every social action is law-oriented in the sense that the existence of a legal order and the presence of a class of officials charged with its enforcement are among the background conditions of the action itself and causally influence the actor's behaviour to a greater or lesser degree.[44] Does the whole of this wide province form the subject-matter of the sociology of law, or only some smaller portion of it?

One way of restricting the scope of the discipline is to stipulate that it is only concerned with the behaviour of officials belonging to the specialized enforcement staff whose presence, according to Weber, gives the legal order its distinctive character. But this seems too narrow a definition, just as the totality of social actions having the actor's orientation to legal norms as one of their determining causes seems too broad. If we adopt the former, narrow

---

*See Hart's discussion of 'secondary rules' in *The Concept of Law*, pp. 91–2. One of the purposes of introducing such rules, according to Hart, is to remedy the defects of a regime in which 'punishments for violations of the rules, and other forms of social pressure involving physical effort or the use of force, are not administered by a special agency but are left to the individuals affected or to the group at large.' *Id.*

conception of the discipline, even such an indisputably legal action as the drafting of a conveyance will fall outside its limits; if we adopt the latter, wide conception, any explanation of an event which mentions the law as a causal factor of even the slightest importance must be considered a contribution to the sociology of law.

In general, there are two different ways in which one can define the class of legal phenomena (those social actions which have special interest or relevance for the sociologist of law and which constitute the distinctive subject-matter of his inquiry). It is possible, in the first place, to define such actions in terms of the nature, strength and importance of the actor's own orientation to legal norms. On this view, a particular action is a legal event if the actor's orientation to legal norms (his own commitment to them or his belief in the commitment of others) has a significant causal effect on his conduct, but not otherwise – if, in other words, his orientation to the law plays an important role in determining his behaviour and is not merely a background condition for other, more powerful motives and interests.

Any difference in the strength of the various causal factors influencing an actor's behaviour will always be a matter of degree. Nevertheless, the relative significance (in a causal sense) of the actor's orientation to legal norms does vary from case to case and provides a rough, but workable, basis for distinguishing legal phenomena from non-legal ones. To use one of Weber's own examples,[45] even the painting of the Sistine Chapel can be viewed as an event in the legal order, as a legal phenomenon, since one of its background conditions was the existence of a relatively stable legal system. But even supposing those involved in painting the Chapel could be said to have been causally influenced in their behaviour by their belief in the continued stability of the legal order, the importance of *this* causal factor, as compared with others of an economic, cultural or aesthetic sort, was obviously quite slight. When a businessman hires a lawyer to draft a form contract that will enable him to control the terms of his transactions with customers, on the other hand, legal norms – their existence, meaning and continued effectiveness – are likely to be uppermost in the minds of both lawyer and client, and to exert a significant causal influence on their behaviour. This makes it appropriate to classify the businessman's interaction with his lawyer as a legal phenomenon, while denying that Michaelangelo's artistic activities had a similar character. In the former case, the law is, so to speak, at the centre of attention; in the latter case, it is on the far periphery, at least if we look at things from the actors' own point of view.

This first way of demarcating the class of legal phenomena takes the content and strength of the actor's own motives as its touchstone. A second, and entirely distinct way of defining the subject-matter of the sociology of law is in terms of the sociologist's interests, the relative importance of *his* orientation to the legal order rather than the actor's. This second definition is the one that best accords with Weber's own work in the sociology of law, and with his general conception of sociological understanding.

In his methodological writings, Weber repeatedly states that every sociological investigation of human conduct approaches its subject from a distinct point of view, emphasizing only one particular aspect of the material in question, whether it be its legal, economic, religious, cultural or political significance.[46] Every inquiry of this sort is therefore necessarily one-sided. In any given case, according to Weber, the particular perspective from which a scientist views his subject-matter is determined by his own concerns and interests – what he thinks is meaningful, significant or worthy of emphasis. The scientist's own interests delimit the field of his investigation by bringing his subject-matter into focus from a distinct point of view. To this extent, even though they cannot be rationally justified or proven true in a scientific sense, the sociologist's personal interests are a necessary condition of his being able to do any scientific work at all.

Weber's affirmation of what might be called the 'interest-relatedness' of all scientific inquiry helps to explain how the sociology of law is distinguished from other branches of sociological research. In his investigations, the sociologist of law gives special emphasis to legal factors, and seeks to explain other aspects of cultural or social life from this point of view. He does so because *he* is interested, for whatever reasons, in drawing attention to the causal importance of legal norms. Thus, even if the norms in question appear relatively unimportant from the actor's own point of view – even if he merely takes them for granted as background conditions – the actor's behaviour constitutes a legal phenomenon if the inquiring sociologist *chooses to make it such*. For example, an investigation of the extent to which legally protected property rights establish a framework for economic exchange belongs to the sociology of law, even though the individuals actually involved in the exchange process rarely think about the legal conditions and consequences of their actions. On this view, differences between the various branches of sociology simply reflect what the practitioners of each choose to emphasize and make the organizing focus of their inquiry: the actors' orientation to legal norms in one case, their concern with eternal salvation in another, their desire to increase the extent of their control over material goods in a third, and so on.

In an important sense, then, the sociology of law does not have a 'natural' subject-matter – there is no sub-class of social actions that is marked out in advance, by their inherent content, as the exclusive subject-matter of the discipline. Every action has a legal component, which the sociologist is free to emphasize in his inquiry if he chooses to do so. The sociology of law therefore has a potential subject-matter as wide as the domain of social life itself and is distinguished from other branches of sociological research not by *what* its practitioners study (since any social action can be investigated from a point of view that emphasizes its legal relevance), but by *how* they study it – by the peculiar, organizing perspective which the sociologist of law adopts in his inquiry.

Weber's concept of interest-relatedness, and the use he makes of it to define the scope and subject-matter of the sociology of law, reveal, once again, his most basic philosophical commitments. The interests that a sociologist brings to his work and that give his investigations their distinctive direction, represent *ultimate value judgments* – judgments of worth, interest, value, importance and beauty which can be avowed or disavowed, chosen or rejected, but that cannot be proven true or false by means of rational argument alone. The scope of his inquiry is not determined by inherent characteristics of the actions he seeks to explain, but is freely established by the sociologist himself through the initial value judgments that he makes, judgments which bring certain features of social life into prominence at the expense of others. In this sense, the sociologist of law is as responsible for the definition of his discipline as he is for the creation of his own personal values: in each case, it is a question of actively inventing something which he can never acquire by a passive inspection of the world, no matter how great his powers of observation.*

Causal and exegetical explanation

We now have an answer, in general terms at least, to each of the two questions posed at the beginning of the chapter: what sorts of things does a sociologist of law study (which aspects of human behaviour fall within the special province of his discipline) and how does he study them (what distinguishes the method he employs and the kind of knowledge or understanding he seeks to acquire)? More importantly, we also have some idea of the way in which Weber's answer to both questions is shaped by his positivistic theory of value and the will-centred conception of the person associated with it.

In my account of Weber's methodological ideas, I have not yet mentioned, however, one of the most striking features of the *Rechtssoziologie:* its preoccupation with modern law. The *Rechtssoziologie* is concerned, above all else, with 'the development of those juristic qualities which are characteristic of [the law] today',[47] and throughout Weber's aim is to explain (in a twofold sense to be described in a moment) the ideas and institutions he considered definitive of the modern legal order. Whether he is discussing the law of contracts or the theory of juristic persons or the organization of the legal profession, Weber treats his subject from the point of view of its relevance for modern law. In this respect, the *Rechtssoziologie* reflects his general interest in the meaning and development of modern occidental civilization, an interest that represents the unifying theme of everything he wrote.

The *Rechtssoziologie* attempts to explain modern law in two very different ways. The first type of explanation that Weber offers is *causal*. Much of the *Rechtssoziologie* is devoted to explaining how and to what extent different

---

*'Science . . . presupposes that what is yielded by scientific work is important in the sense that it is "worth being known". In this, obviously, are contained all our problems. For this presupposition cannot be proved by scientific means. It can only be *interpreted* with reference to its ultimate meaning, which we must reject or accept according to our ultimate position toward life.' *FMW*, 143.

forces – in particular, economic forces – have contributed to the historical growth of the modes of thought and substantive doctrines characteristic of the law today. This problem of historical causation is related to, but distinguishable from, the more general question of causation addressed by every sociological investigation. Every sociological inquiry seeks to make the meaning of some aspect of human behaviour understandable by relating it to the actor's own ideas, beliefs and purposes – subjective states which are treated in the inquiry itself as the determining ground of his conduct. It is, however, always possible to ask how the ideas or beliefs that are invoked in any particular case to explain the actor's conduct have themselves been acquired, to ask what forces, conditions, events and institutions have contributed, in a causal sense, to *their* development. This represents what might be described as a second-order causal inquiry. At the first level, the aim is to make an observed bit of human behaviour understandable in a meaningful sense by relating it to some belief or purpose as its causal ground; at the second level, one takes this same belief or purpose as something to be explained, and attempts to provide a causal explanation of its existence by showing how the attitude in question has been determined either by other beliefs and purposes or by material forces of one sort or another.

Every sociological inquiry necessarily involves a first-order causal explanation of behaviour in terms of beliefs or purposes; if the sociologist then goes on to offer a second-order causal account of these beliefs or purposes themselves, he is engaged in a different inquiry, one that builds upon his earlier, first-order explanation. In the *Rechtssoziologie*, Weber attempts to provide an historical explanation of the modes of thought he considered most characteristic of the modern legal order and to account for the existence of certain beliefs or attitudes which could themselves be treated as causes of observed behaviour in a first-order inquiry; to this extent, the *Rechtssoziologie* is addressed to a second-order problem of causation, in the sense just described.

There is, however, another and entirely different way in which Weber attempts to explain the modern legal order. I shall call this second type of explanation *exegetical.** The model of all exegetical explanation is the interpretation of a written text, where the goal of the interpreter is to clarify the relations of meaning or significance that connect different aspects of the text and to deepen our appreciation of its unity as a meaningful whole. The

---

*For Weber's own views regarding the difference between causal and exegetical interpretation, which he sometimes refers to as the 'value-analytic approach', see *MSS*, 138–52. I use the term 'exegetical' instead of the more familiar term 'hermeneutical' to avoid directly linking Weber with the specific philosophical tradition which the latter term denotes. Weber was influenced by writers in the hermeneutical tradition, such as Burckhardt and Dilthey, but the extent of the influence is controversial. For a detailed exposition of the history and philosophical foundations of hermeneutical theory, see H. Gadamer, *Truth and Method* (trans. G. Barden and J. Cumming, New York, 1975). See also Z. Baumann, *Hermeneutics and the Social Sciences* (London, 1978), and J. Bleicher, *Contemporary Hermeneutics* (London, 1980).

relationships that exegetical interpretation seeks to establish are not relationships of antecedent cause and effect, but relationships of meaning. A relationship of this sort may be said to exist whenever different aspects of social life (single events, practices, formal institutions, etc.) express or reflect, even if only implicitly, a common set of purposive attitudes on the part of the individuals involved. Unlike causal relationships, which link successive states of affairs, relationships of meaning can be established between contemporaneous events and institutions. Understood in this way, exegetical explanation has a different goal and, where it is successful, produces a different kind of knowledge or understanding than causal explanation. These two forms of explanation are of course complementary, and the same phenomenon can often be explained in both ways, as the consequence of some antecedent cause and as part of a meaningful whole. The difference between them, however, is fundamental.

The *Rechtssoziologie* offers an exegetical explanation of the modern legal order as well as a causal one. To the extent he is engaged in exegesis, Weber's aim is to make manifest the common thread of meaning that links certain centrally important features of the modern legal order – including all those substantive and procedural aspects of modern law that he characterizes as 'formally rational', the distinctive type of contractual association which predominates in modern legal systems (the 'purposive contract'), and the conception of authority that underlies the modern state and its bureaucratic apparatus ('legal-rational authority'). One of Weber's principal objectives is to show how these techniques, doctrines and institutions fit together into a meaningful whole, forming a world with a characteristic and historically unique meaning of its own.

Finally, I should emphasize the important philosophical connection between Weber's theory of value and his exegetical explanation of the modern legal order. What links the various aspects of modern law and ties them together into a meaningful whole is their common rootedness in a positivistic theory of value. It is this idea, and the will-centred conception of personhood associated with it, which gives the modern legal order its unity as a world of meanings. More generally, it is the same theory of value that implicitly shapes all of the institutions that Weber believed to be characteristic of modern society. At this point, I can only assert the existence of a connection between Weber's methodological ideas and his modernism. One of my main aims, in the chapters that follow, will be to defend this claim in a systematic and detailed fashion by showing how the positivistic theory of value that underlies his account of sociological understanding is also implicitly presupposed by each of the institutions and modes of thought – legal, political, economic and religious – that he considered an essential component of modern occidental culture.

3
Authority

Why do individuals ever believe they are obligated to obey the law? Put differently, how does the legal order come to be viewed as a repository of normatively binding standards in the first place? Up to a point, the commitment an individual feels to one legal norm can be explained by his commitment to other higher-order norms of the same sort. It is, however, always possible to ask why these latter norms should themselves be regarded as binding. If we pursue this question far enough up the hierarchy of rules contained in the legal order, we inevitably reach a point where an answer can be given only by invoking something other than a legal norm, namely, the foundational belief on which an individual's normative commitment to the legal order *as such* is based[48] – his belief, for example, that a legal rule is binding if, and only if, it expresses an immemorial tradition, or represents the word of God as declared by one of His authentic interpreters, or has been deliberately enacted by a particular group of individuals commissioned to establish legal rules by those now being asked to obey. All behaviour that is motivated by a belief in the normative validity of specific legal rules ultimately presupposes a commitment to some such principle of legitimation.[49] Even where the commitment is unstated, it is anterior (in a logical sense) to a belief in the binding force of particular legal norms.

The aim of Weber's theory of authority is to describe these principles of legitimation – their general structure and main types. Because its subject is the legitimation of domination in all its forms and not merely those which could be described as 'legal' in a narrow sense, Weber's theory of authority is broader in scope than his sociology of law. His description of specific legal institutions and his analysis of the modes of legal thought cannot be adequately understood, however, apart from the more general account of legitimation contained in his theory of authority. Two features of Weber's theory of authority are of special importance for anyone who wants to understand the *Rechtssoziologie* and, in particular, its central, organizing concept – the concept of formal legal rationality. The first concerns his general notion of authority. What did Weber understand authority, in all its various forms, to be, and how did he distinguish authority from other ways of exercising power over human beings? The second concerns his famous division of the different forms of authority (or legitimate domination) into three so-called 'pure types' – legal-rational, charismatic and traditional. What did Weber conceive the essential differences between these three pure types to be, and why did he assign legal-rational authority a privileged position (in a sense yet to be defined) in his typology of authority relations?

The general theory of authority

Power and authority

Authority may assume different forms and rest upon the assertion and acceptance of different sorts of claims. Nevertheless, every authority structure (that is, every relationship between two or more human beings in which one person exercises authority over another) has certain features that are common to all relationships of this sort. What is the defining characteristic of authority *per se*, the characteristic which distinguishes this way of exercising power over human beings from every other?

Weber defines power, in the most general sense, as 'the probability that one actor within a social relationship will be in a position to carry out his own will despite resistance, regardless of the basis on which this probability rests.'[50] To be sure, in any particular case this probability may be significantly increased by the fact that the person seeking to impose his will is regarded by the other as an authority. But that is just to say that authority is one species of power; in other cases power may be attributable to brute force or to psychological factors entirely unconnected with the existence of an authority relationship (as, for example, in an erotic relationship where one partner is able to exercise power over the other solely in virtue of his or her sexual attractiveness).[51] Power refers merely to the fact of control, however achieved, and therefore includes but is not limited to those forms of control that depend upon the existence of an authority relationship between the person exercising power and the person on whom he seeks to impose his will.*

When does a relationship constitute an authority relationship, in Weber's sense? This question is made more difficult by the fact that Weber defines authority in slightly different ways at different points, and is less precise in his terminology than one might wish (for example, equating domination with authority at one point and using it in 'the quite general sense of power' at another).[52] The following definition, however, expresses the essence of Weber's concept of authority.

> *Domination* [or authoritarian power of command] will thus mean the situation in which the manifested will (*command*) of the *ruler* or rulers is meant to influence the conduct of one or more others (*the ruled*) and actually does influence it in such a way that their conduct to a socially relevant degree occurs as if the ruled had made

---

*The distinction between power and authority is a distinction that has been drawn, in one form or another, by every important political philosopher since Hobbes. See, for example, Hobbes, *Leviathan* Chapter 15 (Oxford, 1948); Rousseau, *The Social Contract* Book I, Chapter 8 (trans. C. Frankel, New York, 1947); Kant, *The Metaphysical Elements of Justice* Part I, Chapter 1, Paragraph 2 (trans. J. Ladd, New York, 1965); Hegel, *Philosophy of Right*, §45.

the content of the command the maxim of their conduct for its very own sake. Looked upon from the other end, this situation will be called *obedience*.[53]

In commenting on his definition, Weber acknowledges that it is an 'awkward' one, 'especially due to the use of the "as if" formula', but insists that the awkwardness cannot be avoided.[54] In his view 'the merely external fact of the order being obeyed is not sufficient to signify domination'; we must, in addition, take cognizance of 'the fact that the command is accepted as a "valid" norm' by the person to whom it is addressed.[55] In an authority relationship, one party (the ruler) issues commands to someone else (the ruled), commands supported by an appeal – implicit or explicit – to a principle of some sort which the ruler claims justifies him in issuing the command and which, in his view, obligates the ruled to obey. If the ruled himself accepts this claim, that is, if he considers himself bound by the principle invoked by the ruler in justification of the power he seeks to exercise, we may speak of the ruler exercising the power of *authoritarian* command and of the existence of an authority relationship between the parties, but not otherwise. Put differently, the hallmark of an authority relationship is the fact that it involves an exercise of power that is justified in the eyes of the person being dominated because he acknowledges the normative validity of the principle to which the party wielding power appeals as the warrant for his actions.[56] Of course, in most cases, the motives for obedience are likely to be mixed, the addressee of an authoritarian command typically obeying both because he believes it is in his self-interest to do so, and because he considers himself obligated to respect the justificatory principle to which the person issuing the command has appealed. But it is only if his conformity is motivated and therefore caused, at least in part, by a belief in the normatively binding quality of some principle to which the person exercising power makes – or may make – appeal, that the power relationship between the parties can be said to have an authoritarian character.

Although authority is merely one form of power, it is, according to Weber, the most stable and enduring form.

> An order which is adhered to from motives of pure expediency is generally much less stable than one upheld on a purely customary basis through the fact that the corresponding behaviour has become habitual. The latter is much the most common type of subjective attitude. But even this type of order is in turn much less stable than an order which enjoys the prestige of being considered binding, or, as it may be expressed, of 'legitimacy'.[57]

The claim that authority is the most durable form of power may seem surprising at first, since it implies that the strongest force in human society is not physical compulsion, but a belief in the binding quality of certain normative principles – which are, after all, only ideas. A king is able to exercise command over his people not because he possesses some extraordinary physical power that enables him to coerce their compliance and that insulates him from attack; he is able to exercise such control because those to whom he issues his commands (at least a sufficient number of them) think his orders rightful and consider themselves obligated to obey. Even if most of the king's subjects do not feel this way, there must be enough who do to compel the obedience of the rest through the (threatened) use of physical force. In a word, the real strength of the most important and lasting forms of domination depends on the ideas or beliefs of the dominated, and this is likely to seem puzzling to anyone used to thinking of ideas as relatively weak and fragile things compared with the robust reality of physical force. How are we to explain the important role played by ideas in the creation and maintainence of the strongest and most enduring power relationships?

Authority and the problem of meaning
Authority, in Weber's sense, is a uniquely human phenomenon. Animals exercise power over one another but they do not attempt to justify their use of power by appealing to normative standards that are claimed to be binding on those subject to the control of the more powerful individual or group.[58] Authority relationships by definition rest upon an appeal of this sort, and – so far as we know – exist only between human beings.

In fact, authority structures can be viewed as a response to a basic and uniquely human need, the need to see and experience the world into which we are born as a meaningful one, as something more than a concatenation of fateful accidents devoid of significance or purpose. According to Weber, this need is felt most acutely by the privileged or well-endowed, by those whom fate has treated kindly, who seem compulsively driven to justify or legitimate the advantages they enjoy.*

> The fates of human beings are not equal. Men differ in their states of health or wealth or social status or what not. Simple observation [!] shows that in every such situation he who is more favoured feels the never-ceasing need to look upon his position as in some way 'legitimate', upon his advantage as 'deserved', and the other's disadvantage as being brought about by the latter's 'fault'. That the purely accidental causes of the difference may be ever so obvious makes no difference.[59]

Each of us comes into a world he did not make, a world characterized by natural and social differences which are often of the greatest importance in determining an individual's life prospects. Even though some of these differences (differences in wealth and status, for example) are social artifacts, from the standpoint of the individual who has been born into an established and ongoing world, they are as much a part of his fate as his natural endowment (his health and intelligence).** In 'the distribution of fortunes among

---

*Weber's own view is similar, as he himself acknowledged, to Nietzsche's notion of the 'slave revolt in morality', although it differs from the latter in emphasizing the anxiety of the fortunate and well-to-do rather than the oppressed. Compare *FMW*, 170–1 with F. Nietzsche, *On The Genealogy of Morals* (trans. W. Kaufmann and R.J. Hollingdale, New York, 1967).

**[O]nce we are troubled by the influence of either social contingencies or natural chance on the determination of distributive shares, we are bound, on reflection, to be bothered by the

men', some obviously fare better than others – these are the lucky ones who are born to health and status and material well-being. Advantages of this sort, which can only be attributed to the inexplicable fact that an individual happens to be who he is rather than someone less fortunate, are all sources of power in Weber's broad sense, and according to Weber, there is a 'generally observable need of any [human] power, or even of any advantage of life, to justify itself'.[60] The well-off are never content merely to *enjoy* their good luck; they always want, in addition, to view their advantages as something other than an arbitrary piece of fate.

> The fortunate is seldom satisfied with the fact of being fortunate. Beyond this, he needs to know that he has a *right* to his good fortune. He wants to be convinced that he 'deserves' it, and above all that he deserves it in comparison with others. He wishes to be allowed the belief that the less fortunate also merely experiences his due. Good fortune thus wants to be 'legitimate' fortune.[61]

What is the source of this need to legitimate the 'fact of being fortunate'? Weber's argument implies that good fortune which has *not* been justified or shown to be deserved is always open to a powerful and universally accepted criticism, a criticism it is most natural to imagine being advanced by someone who has fared less well in the distribution of human fortunes: 'The advantages you enjoy, and the disadvantages under which I labour, are entirely attributable to the accidents of birth. There is no good reason why you should prosper while I suffer. As rational beings, we are obligated to respect the claims of reason, and you ought therefore to share your good fortune with me rather than keep its fruits entirely for yourself.' Every attempt to justify good fortune, to show that it is deserved and that its possessor has a *right* to its enjoyment, represents an effort to meet this criticism. Obviously, one reason for attempting to rebut the criticism is that the less fortunate may be more inclined to accept their situation if they receive what they consider to be a satisfactory answer. But the well-off feel a need to justify their advantages not only because they want to pacify those who are less fortunate by comparison. In addition – and this is the point Weber stresses – the well-off must persuade *themselves* that their fates are deserved and therefore rightful. The criticism that I put in the mouth of a dissatisfied plebian is in fact a criticism which the rich and honourable and physically robust implicitly address to themselves, and by attempting to meet it they are seeking to still a voice within as well as the sometimes louder but no more pressing voices without. Indeed, to the extent that he anticipates and understands the criticism of those who are less fortunate, the man of good fortune must already be a critic himself.

At the root, then, of all legitimating explanations is the demand, a demand felt by the fortunate and unfortunate alike, that there be a *reason* for these inequalities. Some human beings suffer, and others flourish – that is simply

---

influence of the other. From a moral standpoint the two seem equally arbitrary.' J. Rawls, *A Theory of Justice* (Cambridge, Mass., 1971), p. 75.

a fact, attributable in part to natural differences and in part to socially created ones. But it is not the fact of suffering, by itself, that human beings find intolerable; after all, men are prepared to tolerate the most exquisite torments if they believe their suffering has a meaning. Rather, it is the threatened meaninglessness of suffering and good fortune alike that is unacceptable.* The fact of suffering is redeemed and made tolerable by the meaning we give to it; what is quite literally unthinkable is the possibility that it may have no meaning at all. Like other living creatures, human beings do not wish to suffer; but beyond that, and more importantly, they do not wish their suffering or even the suffering of others to be pointless. Human beings generally, whatever their place in the distribution of fortunes, demand to live in a world that has reason and meaning. The fact that we all live under this unshakeable demand sets us apart from the rest of nature, and stamps each of our most important institutions, including every structure of authority, with its distinctive human character.

Legitimating explanations seek to justify the distribution of fortunes by showing that it conforms to a coherent normative conception of some sort, a conception which not only makes the differences in human fates intelligible but justifies them in an ethical sense as well. Put differently, every legitimation of good fortune attempts to justify the *fact* of suffering by imposing a specific *value* on it, or by incorporating the fact of suffering in an evaluative picture of the world. By being placed within the context of an evaluative scheme of this sort, suffering and good fortune are each assigned a specific value, either positive or negative, and thereby saved (redeemed) from the threat of meaninglessness. The fateful fact that human beings begin life from different natural and social starting points acquires meaning only when it is evaluated, when it is made the subject of a value-judgement.

Where do these value-judgements come from? It is at this point that we can begin to see the connection between Weber's theory of authority and the positivistic theory of value that underlies his methodological views concerning the nature of sociological understanding. According to Weber, the values that endow the facts of differential power and happiness with meaning are not themselves facts; they are not part of the world as men find it, already made and beyond their control. The values in question, whatever their content, must be invented or created by men themselves and imposed on the world – much in the way that an artist gives meaning to material that would otherwise have no aesthetic significance by deliberately imposing a form of one sort or another on it. We know, from Weber's methodological writings, that he believed every value to be the product of an act of will.

* '[M]an, the bravest of animals and the one most accustomed to suffering, does *not* repudiate suffering as such; he *desires* it, he even seeks it out, provided he is shown a *meaning* for it, a *purpose* of suffering. The meaninglessness of suffering, *not* suffering itself, was the curse that lay over mankind so far – *and the ascetic ideal offered man meaning!* . . . . In it, suffering was *interpreted*; the tremendous void seemed to have been filled; the door was closed to any kind of suicidal nihilism.' Nietzsche, *The Genealogy of Morals*, p. 162.

Those values that are posited or invented in order to pacify the problem of meaninglessness are no exception: they, too, are products of the will, the name we give to the faculty which empowers us to create our own commitments through acts of choice. Since the aim of every authority structure is to legitimate the fact of superior power and well-being, it, too, must be viewed as an artifact of the will, an institution that owes its existence to the human capacity to impose a freely created world of values on the universe of facts in which it is our fate to live.

This capacity to create values, like the need for meaning that it seeks to satisfy, is distinctively human. Only human beings experience the need to live in a meaningful – as opposed to a merely pleasant – world, and only they have the capacity to make it so by creatively elaborating values that transform the factual content of the world into something with normative significance. We solve the problem of meaning by imposing our values on the world, and one way in which we do this is by inventing authority structures to legitimate the superior power of those who have fared well in the distribution of human fortunes. This solution to the problem of meaning is of course a profoundly irrational one since no value that we impose on the world in order to give it meaning can ever be proven true in a rational or scientific sense. We give the world meaning only through our own choices and therefore cannot believe, except in bad faith or from a lack of self-awareness, that our values come to us as part of the world and are to be passively received rather than invented, freely and with a sense of responsibility. As we shall see, it is this simple idea which explains why legal-rational authority occupies the special place it does in Weber's typology of authority relations.

The three pure types of authority

Authority is a species of power, the kind of power one person exercises over another when he invokes a principle of legitimation which the person subject to domination himself views as a binding norm, whether or not he actually obeys the ruler's command. Every authority relationship rests upon an appeal to some such principle, and the acceptance of its validity by the person to whom the appeal is addressed. But although they all exhibit this same general structure, authority relationships (and the institutions associated with them) differ from one another according to the substance or content of the legitimating principle invoked by the ruler and relied upon as a justification for the exercise of power.* Weber identified three pure types of authority, each of which is based upon a distinct conception of legitimacy and establishes a different interpretive framework for the assessment of

---

*'[A]ccording to the kind of legitimacy which is claimed, the type of obedience, the kind of administrative staff developed to guarantee it, and the mode of exercising authority, will all differ fundamentally. Equally fundamental is the variation in effect. Hence, it is useful to classify the types of domination according to the kind of claim to legitimacy typically made by each.' *ES*, 213.

authority claims.* Naturally, these three types rarely appear in their ideally pure forms; actual authority structures typically include elements of two or even all three types in varying combinations. As logical categories, however, Weber's three pure types of authority exhaust the possibilities – or so he appears to have believed.

Traditional authority
According to Weber, authority is *traditional* 'if legitimacy is claimed for it and believed in by sanctity of age-old rules and powers.'[62] All authority of this sort is based upon 'piety for what actually, allegedly, or presumably has always existed',[63] upon the belief that authoritarian rule is (and can only be) justified by immemorial practices of one sort or another. Within a traditional regime, authoritarian commands are valid today, if they are valid at all, because they were so 'of yore.'[64]

Traditional authority has several distinguishing characteristics. In the first place, it is invariably modelled upon the relation between a 'traditional master' and his 'personal retainer' or servant or child. As a consequence, traditional authority relations are essentially relations between unequals and rest upon what Weber, following Nietzsche, calls the 'pathos of distance'[65] – the belief that men differ fundamentally in their natural endowments and social position and the conviction that these differences justify the domination of those 'designated according to traditional rules'[66] over their natural and social inferiors. In any traditionally 'stereotyped' authority structure, an individual's position – his right to rule or duty to obey – is ultimately determined by his 'status', by his possession or non-possession of certain natural and personal qualities (especially honour). Thus, patriarchalism – 'the most elementary type of traditional domination' – rests upon the 'personal devotion to, and personal authority of "natural leaders" '.[67] There are, of course, many complex variations on this elementary type, but in each the same basic relation of status-inequality can be observed, whether in 'the authority of the father, the husband, the senior of the house, the sib elder over the members of the household and sib; the rule of the master and patron over bondsmen, serfs, freed men; of the lord over the domestic servants and household officials; of the prince over house- and court-officials, nobles of office, clients, vassals; of the patrimonial lord and sovereign prince over the "subjects".'[68]

A second important feature of traditional authority is its association with routine economic activity and, more specifically, with one particular form of economic organization – that of the household.[69] According to Weber, tradi-

---

*At one point in *Economy and Society*, Weber lists *four* types of legitimacy, adding 'value-rational faith' to the other three (tradition, prophetic revelation, and legal rationality) (ES, 36). As an example of legitimacy based on 'value-rationality', Weber mentions 'natural law'. It is unclear what he means by this, or whether 'value-rationality' is indeed a distinguishable fourth type. Elsewhere, Weber speaks of *three* pure types (*ES*, 215) and this would appear to be his more settled view.

tional authority is a 'structure of everyday life', a form of social organization 'rooted in the need to meet ongoing, routine demands' and devoted to what he calls 'normal want satisfaction'.[70] By itself, however, the routine character of traditional authority does not distinguish it from its legal-rational counterpart, since 'both are permanent structures ... oriented toward the satisfaction of calculable needs with ordinary, everyday means'.[71] What does distinguish these two forms of authority is the *type* of economic organization with which each is associated. Traditional economies are organized on the basis of an 'orderly household' or *oikos* and are concerned with the satisfaction of wants; by contrast, legal-rational authority is associated with the 'rationally managed enterprise'[72] and hence with profit-making rather than want satisfaction (a distinction I explain more fully later in this chapter). As a general rule, traditionally stereotyped patterns both of production and consumption are based upon the principle of ' "natural" participation' that informs 'the household's social action.'[73] This principle not only determines the social status of the individual members of the household (their position in its authority structure), but fixes, as well, their role in the productive and consumptive activities that comprise its economic life. In this dual sense, the orderly household is, as Weber repeatedly states, the specific *locus* of all traditional authority.

Finally, all traditional authority is, to some degree, religious in nature. It 'is characteristic of patriarchal and of patrimonial authority, which represents a variety of the former, that the system of inviolable norms [on which it rests] is considered sacred; an infraction of them would result in magical or religious evils.'[74] Traditional authority is therefore at once religious and economic (in the sense of being oriented toward the routine satisfaction of recurrent needs); indeed, it is typical of all such authority structures that they treat the 'sacred' and 'everyday' dimensions of social life as essentially continuous.[75]

Legal-rational authority

Legal-rational authority (the second of Weber's three pure types) rests upon 'a belief in the legality of enacted rules and the right of those elevated to authority under such rules to issue commands'.[76] What distinguishes legal-rational authority from all authoritarian relationships based upon the 'eternal yesterday'[77] of tradition is the fact that it has at its basis 'a consistent system of abstract rules which have normally been intentionally established',[78] that is, 'a system of consciously made *rational* rules'.[79] Where legal-rational principles control, power cannot be justified by an appeal to the presumptive validity of what 'has always existed', but only by the formal process of enactment through which the norms invoked by the ruler have been promulgated or posited. Consequently, in a legal-rational regime, the validity of the rules that fix the limits of legitimate authority depends upon their form, their status as formally correct enactments, rather than their specific content; in a regime of this sort, 'any given legal norm may be established by agreement or by imposition'.[80]

While traditional forms of domination base an individual's position in an authority relationship on his possession of some natural or social quality – his status, as Weber uses that term – legal-rational relationships rest upon the more abstract notion of 'membership' in an 'organization'. Within a legal-rational authority structure, an individual has rights and duties 'only in his capacity as a "member" of the organization and what he obeys is only the "law" '.[81] Although a person's natural characteristics (his age, for example) may figure in the *description* of the rights and duties that constitute his membership in the organization, from a legal-rational point of view these characteristics have whatever juridical significance they do solely in virtue of the formal correctness of the legislative procedure by means of which specific legal consequences have been assigned to them, and not because they are thought to possess an intrinsic legitimating power of their own. It is this that distinguishes the concept of membership, and the related idea of citizenship, from the notion of status, a notion alien to every legal-rational regime.

A related feature of legal-rational authority relationships is their dependence upon what Weber calls the principle of 'formalistic impersonality'.[82] Insofar as they 'obey a person in authority', the members of a legal-rational organization 'do not owe this obedience to him as an individual, but to the impersonal order'.[83] This is true even of the highest official in such an organization, to the extent that he, too, is subject to the law. The officials in a legally-rational organization – those authorized by law to exercise power over others – carry out their responsibilities

> *sine ira et studio*, without hatred or passion, and hence without affection or enthusiasm. The dominant norms are concepts of straightforward duty without regard to personal considerations. Everyone is subject to formal equality of treatment; that is, everyone in the same empirical situation. This is the spirit in which the ideal official conducts his office.[84]

The impersonality which characterizes the relation between ruler and ruled in every legal-rational authority structure rests upon the acceptance, by everyone concerned, of the principle of 'formal equality of treatment'. Whether they give commands or follow them, the members of such an organization are all equal before the law, and represent, in Weber's terms, a uniform 'mass' whose homogeneity corresponds to the 'abstract regularity' of the rules which define their rights and duties.[85] The impersonality and formal equality of treatment characteristic of all legal-rational regimes reflect a 'horror of "privilege"', and the principled rejection of doing business "from case to case" ',[86] and inevitably result in 'a levelling of economic and social differences'. The members of a legal-rational organization all stand on the same social level – in contrast to traditionalism, which is everywhere premised upon relations of intrinsic inequality and an 'aristocratic sense of distance'.*

ES, 376. Nietzsche's critique of modernity, with which Weber felt some sympathy, was in part based upon a rejection of just this process of social levelling, the 'animalization of man into

Legal-rational authority is also distinguished from all forms of traditional domination by its insistence on the separation, in both a physical and legal sense, of official and private life. The sharp disjunction between these two domains is reflected most clearly in 'the modern organization of the civil service', which 'separates the bureau from the private domicile of the official and, in general, segregates official activity from the sphere of private life.'[87] By contrast, traditional authority, which is based upon a 'strictly personal loyalty' rooted in 'the master's authority over his household',[88] assumes an undifferentiated continuity between the public or official sphere and the private.

Finally, legal-rational authority is characterized by its tendency to penetrate and become rooted in 'the sphere of everyday economic routines'. In this respect, it represents the 'rational counterpart of patriarchalism'.[89] Unlike all traditional or patriarchal forms of economic organization, however, legal-rational authority has *its* specific locus in the rationally managed, profit-making firm rather than the household; indeed, a principled separation between household and firm – the analogue, in the economic sphere, of the separation between household and bureaucratic office – is the distinguishing characteristic of every economic activity organized on a legal-rational basis. Moreover, unlike the traditionally stereotyped economic routines of an *oikos*, the behaviour of a rational, profit-making firm is not conditioned by 'sacred norms' of any sort. Legal-rational economic action has no religious meaning as such, but reflects, instead, the exclusion of religious practices and beliefs from the sober world of 'workaday existence'. 'Today', Weber asserts, 'the routines of everyday life *challenge* religion.'[90] In this respect, legal-rational authority stands in sharp contrast to traditionalism which presupposes a union of the sacred and the everyday.

Charismatic authority
Authority is *charismatic*, according to Weber, insofar as it rests 'on devotion to the exceptional sanctity, heroism, or exemplary character of an individual person, and of the normative patterns of order revealed or ordained by him.'[91] The charismatic leader is distinguished by the possession of 'a certain quality' not accessible to the ordinary person, a special characteristic that sets him apart from other men, and in particular from his followers. The exceptional qualities of the charismatic leader can legitimate his claim to authority, however, only if the meaning he ascribes to them is accepted by his followers: 'it is recognition on the part of those subject to authority which is decisive for the validity of charisma.'[92]

To the extent it is based upon certain 'specific gifts of body and mind', the authority of the charismatic leader resembles that of the traditional master whose right to rule is also predicated upon his possession of certain natural

the dwarf animal of equal rights and claims', *Beyond Good and Evil* (trans. W. Kaufmann, New York, 1966), § 203.

qualities, namely, age and paternity; in fact, 'the external forms of [these] two structures of domination are often similar to the point of being identical.'[93] Nevertheless, there is an important difference between them. The 'naturally given' differences that condition the social action of the household and which provide the basic foundation for all forms of traditional authority are differences between *kinds* of men (primarily, between men and women on the one hand, and parents and children on the other). Within a traditionalist regime, the father of a family enjoys certain rights and privileges in virtue of a particular attribute (his paternity), but the attribute in question does not distinguish him from innumerable other fathers. The basis of his authority is a natural quality that he shares in common with the other members of a particular class of human beings. By contrast, the specific gifts that distinguish the charismatic leader from his followers and that legitimate his command always constitute a 'highly individual quality'. The difference between a charismatic leader and his followers is not a generic difference between two kinds of men; it is a difference between one unique individual and everyone else. Unlike the qualities that distinguish the traditional master, qualities rooted in the ordinary biological or metabolic routines of everyday life, the gifts that mark the charismatic leader off from his followers are typically regarded as supernatural both in character and origin, as the manifestation of an extraordinary calling which interrupts and challenges everyday routines. Consequently, although 'both charismatic and patriarchal power rest on [the] personal devotion to, and personal authority of, "natural" leaders, in contrast to the appointed leaders of the bureaucratic order, yet this basis is very different in the two cases.'[94]

Because his gift is unique and belongs to him alone, the authority of the charismatic leader always constitutes, in Weber's words, a 'personal mission'.[95] The bearer of a charismatic gift 'enjoys loyalty and authority by virtue of a mission believed to be embodied in him',[96] a mission which, from the leader's point of view, represents 'a "call" in the most emphatic sense of the word.'[97] Furthermore, because it is unique, the gift on which the charismatic leader bases his claim to rule is necessarily unrepeatable – a single, extraordinary quality or occurrence. The meaning of his gift, and hence the limits of the charismatic leader's authority, are therefore not 'bound to intellectually analysable rules';[98] charismatic domination, in contrast to both of the other pure types of authority, 'knows no abstract laws and regulations and no formal adjudication',[99] and is 'specifically irrational in the sense of being foreign to all rules.'[100] As a result, the relations between a charismatic leader and his followers cannot be subjected to regulation in a continuous and predicable manner and there are no limits (in principle!) to the claims that a charismatic leader may make on those who acknowledge his authority.

How, then, is the meaning of the leader's charisma established and the limits of his authority fixed? According to Weber, it is an essential feature of all charismatic authority that the leader freely determines these limits himself. 'Charisma is self-determined and sets its own limits'[101] and hence 'the mission and the power of its bearer is qualitatively delimited from within, not by an external order.'[102] This observation helps us to understand the sense in which charismatic authority is 'specifically irrational' and clarifies its logical relationship to the other two pure types. On the one hand, charismatic authority is founded upon certain observable differences among men (the gifts of mind and body that set the charismatic leader apart from his followers); in this respect, it resembles all forms of authority based on tradition. On the other hand, because the gift that distinguishes the charismatic leader and that legitimates his claim to authority is absolutely unique and unrepeatable, there can in principle be no objective rules for determining the meaning of his gift or fixing the limits of his right to rule. These must be established by an interpretation which only the charismatic leader himself can provide – an interpretation that is *free* or *unrestricted* in the sense that its content cannot be circumscribed in advance. In this respect, charismatic authority breaks with tradition, for although the traditional master enjoys considerable discretionary powers, these powers themselves are always defined and hence limited by rules which the master himself is not free to interpret as he wishes and which 'cannot be overstepped without endangering the master's traditional status'.[103] The freedom enjoyed by the charismatic leader in determining the nature and limits of his own authority more closely resembles the regime of deliberate enactment presupposed by all legal-rational authority. Nevertheless, despite this important similarity, charismatic and legal-rational authority are fundamentally different in another respect: the one accepts but the other rejects the principle of formal equality of treatment. Although the charismatic leader enjoys an unlimited freedom to determine the limits of his mission, he does so by virtue of the gift he possesses, a gift which distinguishes him from other men and makes him unequal to them. The right of a charismatic leader to establish the limits of his own authority through a kind of free enactment is therefore itself predicated upon the unique power or quality which constitutes his gift. To this extent, unlike the bureaucratic official, he remains a 'natural leader'. Because it is based upon a conception of legitimacy that combines, in a distinctive way, certain elements of each of the other two pure types, charismatic authority may be said to occupy a logically intermediate position between them. I shall develop this point more fully in the concluding section of the chapter.

Two further aspects of charismatic authority are worth noting. First, in contrast to both traditional and legal-rational forms of domination, charisma 'is specifically foreign to economic considerations',[104] to what Weber calls the 'orderly round of activities which procure the material means of want satisfaction'.[105] The needs the charismatic leader seeks to satisfy are themselves extraordinary, and thus quite literally 'transcend' the life of the household, the *locus* of all traditional authority. In this respect, 'charismatic want-satisfaction is a typical anti-economic force' which 'repudiates any sort of involvement in the everyday routine world.'[106]

Second, all charismatic authority is inherently unstable. Charisma is based upon the 'unique, transitory gift'[107] of an extraordinary individual; consequently, if the authority of the charismatic leader is not to be a 'purely transitory phenomenon', it must somehow be transformed into 'a permanent possession of everyday life'.[108] In its pure form, 'charismatic authority may be said to exist only in *status nascendi*. It cannot remain stable, but becomes either traditionalized or rationalized, or a combination of both.'[109] Weber calls the process by which charismatic authority is transformed into one of the other two pure types the 'routinization of charisma'.[110] In part, this process is attributable to the transitoriness of the special gift on which all charismatic authority rests; in part, it is due to the anti-economic character of charismatically led movements, and the need for every such movement eventually to make its peace with the workaday world of routine need satisfaction. From a historical point of view, it is the inherent instability of charismatic authority which constitutes the most important difference between it and the other pure types, for it is the instability of charisma that gives it its peculiarly dynamic character. Charisma is a truly revolutionary force (at times, Weber implies that it is the only such force) since it breaks up existing authority structures by introducing novel claims of legitimacy, an idea he was fond of expressing by quoting the biblical injunction, 'It is written, but I say unto you . . .'[111] At the same time, charisma is incapable of sustaining itself for an extended period, and thus, if it does not simply disappear, always undergoes a metamorphosis in the direction of either traditional or legal-rational authority. Charisma breaks up old forms of authority and gives rise to new ones in the course of its own disintegration.

The primacy of legal-rational authority

Preliminary remarks
In Weber's typology of authority relations, one type – legal-rational authority – enjoys a privileged position in the sense that it is taken to provide the standpoint from which the other two types are to be understood.[112] The conceptual primacy of legal-rational authority is one of the most striking, and most easily misunderstood, features of Weber's general theory of legitimate domination. What accounts for the special place which this form of domination occupies in his three-fold division of authority types?

It is tempting to explain the leading role Weber assigns legal-rational authority by the general importance he attaches to all distinctively modern institutions.[113] Weber's historical and sociological investigations are in large part devoted to explaining why the beliefs and institutions characteristic of the modern West developed as they did and what prevented their development in other parts of the world (for example, in the great civilizations of Asia). According to Weber, the social and economic organization of the modern West is distinguished by its high degree of rationality and, in particular, by the dominance of legal-rational bureaucracies and their economic analogue, the rationally managed profit-making firm.[114] Nowhere else have legal-rational authority structures emerged or taken root on anything like the scale characteristic of the modern West. Today, according to Weber, these structures are so firmly entrenched that we have difficulty even imagining them being replaced by anything fundamentally different. Indeed, the opposite line of development seemed more probable to Weber, who thought (or at least wrote as if he thought) that the legal-rational institutions of modern European civilization would strengthen their grip and extend their field of influence, until the whole of humanity, even socialist humanity, had been brought under their power and in this sense 'westernized'.[115] Given his choice of the modern West as a focal point for his various investigations, and his belief that the uniqueness of modern Occidental civilization is in large part to be explained by the prominence within it of legal-rational institutions, it is not surprising that Weber should also have assigned this form of authority a special position in his general theory of authority relations, and it might therefore seem unnecessary to inquire further as to his reasons for doing so.

This is not a very illuminating view, however, for it merely postpones, without answering, the question before us. So long as we do not know why Weber attached an overriding importance to the political and economic institutions of the modern West, and made their historical development the organizing theme of all his work, the leading role he assigns to legal-rational authority cannot be satisfactorily explained merely by pointing to its 'specifically modern' character. Indeed, this way of looking at things puts the cart before the horse since Weber's modernism was itself based upon his belief that the institutions of the modern West have a 'universal significance and validity',[116] a belief that cannot be justified, or even understood, without appreciating his reasons for taking legal-rational authority as a point of departure in analysing the other two forms of domination.

It is important to emphasize, at the outset, that Weber assigns legal-rational authority a privileged position in his typology of authority relations for strictly logical or conceptual reasons. In doing so, he does not mean to imply that this form of domination should be preferred over the others on ethical grounds (except, perhaps, in one very special and restricted sense that I shall describe shortly). Any judgment of the latter sort is a value-judgment which according to Weber has no scientific justification. Thus, it is perfectly possible to believe, without committing a scientific error, that traditional authority is on the whole better than its legal-rational counterpart – perhaps because it is based on warm and caring personal associations rather than the icy dispassion of bureaucratic duty – or hope for a resurgence of charisma because of a belief in its special redemptive powers. How one views legal-rational authority and, in particular, bureaucratic administration, from an ethical point of view – whether as a great achievement and a guarantor of individual liberty, or as an expression of spiritual emptiness, a 'shell of bondage' in which individuals are 'as powerless as the fellahs of ancient Egypt'[117] – ultimately depends on one's own value-preferences, and thus on considerations beyond the limits of scientific argument. As we shall see, Weber himself had deeply ambivalent feelings about the forms of social and economic organization associated with the principle of legal-rationality, an ambivalence poignantly expressed by his continual insistence on the 'fatefulness' of the historical development that has resulted in their dominance. However, Weber's reasons for according legal-rational authority a special place in his overall scheme of authority types have nothing to do with his own views regarding its ethical attractiveness, and in giving it a kind of conceptual primacy his intention is neither to applaud its historical triumph nor to urge its extension as a principle of social organization. For Weber, the pre-eminence of legal-rational authority is based exclusively on certain logical or conceptual considerations which justify the claim that this type of authority provides the key to *understanding* the other pure types (and, indeed, the structure of authority relationships in general) without implying that a civilization based on the idea of legal-rationality is *better* than one which is based, instead, on the authority of immemorial traditions, or the extraordinary experience of submersion in a charismatically inspired movement.

The self-consciousness of legal-rational authority

The features of legal-rational authority that account for the pre-eminent position Weber assigns it in his theory of domination can best be brought out by contrasting this type of authority with traditionalism, in many ways its polar opposite. All forms of legal-rational authority rest upon an appeal to norms which have been deliberately enacted and whose binding force is believed to derive from the very fact of their enactment in accordance with some agreed-upon practice or procedure. Implicit in this principle or method of legitimation is a specific conception of the nature and origin of norms, a theory of value as I have used that term. This theory is identical to the one presupposed by Weber's methodological views concerning the nature and limits of sociological understanding. Stated in simple terms, legal-rational authority rests on the assumption that norms are made, not discovered, and on the belief that it is this attribute, and this attribute alone, which confers on them their normative status as standards for the evaluative assessment of human conduct.

Traditional authority rests upon a conception of normativity that is exactly the opposite of this one. From the standpoint of all traditional forms of domination, the binding force of a norm is necessarily lost as soon as it comes to be viewed as a human invention, something deliberately made or created by human beings; traditional norms are uncreated and have a timeless validity that would be fatally compromised if they could either be established or undone by men. Traditional authority thus seeks to legitimate the exercise of power by appealing to norms that are assumed to be an inherent feature or component of the world itself, norms which do not owe their existence to human inventiveness and whose binding force can therefore neither be increased nor diminished by the deliberate actions of human beings. Legal-rational authority, on the other hand, is founded on the premise that binding social norms have no existence apart from those purposeful acts of human legislation that bring them into being, and hence cannot be viewed as an unalterable aspect of the world as it is given to men in experience – a 'fate' that human beings are powerless to avoid or change.

This fundamental difference between the conceptions of normativity underlying traditional and legal-rational authority structures has several important implications. To begin with, of the two, only legal-rational authority acknowledges the basic distinction between facts and values that is central to Weber's own theory of value. Traditional authority conflates 'is' with 'ought': from a traditionalist point of view, it is the age-old existence of a practice or institution which gives it legitimacy and normative force; every purely traditional justification of authority treats the norms to which it appeals as if they were an aspect of the world that could be discovered and described, in a relatively non-controversial way, like other facts.

By contrast, the attempt to legitimate a normative rule on legal-rational grounds must either establish that the rule itself has been enacted in accordance with an agreed-upon procedure of some sort, or show that it has been imposed pursuant to another rule which has in turn been promulgated in the specified manner. Any argument intended to establish the legitimacy of a particular rule from a legal-rational point of view must therefore appeal to the fact that it, or some other rule, has been enacted in the proper way. But this 'fact', unlike those invoked by all traditionalist justifications of power, has normative significance only because it is itself the product of, or more precisely, because it *consists in*, a deliberate and wilful act of norm-creation, an act of legislation. Legal-rational authority rests on the epistemological assumption that values can only be established in this way, and thus rejects the fundamental premise of all traditional domination – that there are certain facts which have an independent ethical meaning of their own, a meaning that has not (indeed, could not have) been given to them *by* men but which, quite to the contrary, is given *to* men as their ineluctable fate.

Traditional authority presupposes the essential identity or continuity of 'is' and 'ought'; legal-rational authority, by contrast, severs the connection between these two domains in a principled way by tracing the legitimacy of every binding norm back to its deliberate enactment – its imposition, by human beings, on an otherwise morally neutral world. Consequently, since Weber himself believed in the necessity – he calls it a 'logical' necessity[118] – of distinguishing between 'is' and 'ought', the legal-rational conception of legitimacy may be said to be consistent with his own theory of value in a way in which the traditionalist conception is not. It is this coincidence between Weber's own methodological theory of value and the principle of legitimation specifically associated with legal-rational authority which explains the primacy accorded this particular form of domination in his typology of authority relations.

In Weber's view, the meaning of the world is something that can only be established by an act of will, by the deliberate imposition of some meaning-giving value on the world (which considered by itself, constitutes an endless series of amoral occurrences devoid of normative significance). 'The fate of an epoch which has eaten of the tree of knowledge is that it must know that we cannot learn the *meaning* of the world from the results of its analysis, be it ever so perfect; it must rather be in a position to create this meaning itself.'[119] This fundamental epistomological principle is as applicable to traditional authority as it is to every other structure of domination. Every authority structure, regardless of the legitimating principle on which it is based, is the product of a normative evaluation whose aim is to justify the domination of some human beings by others and in this way satisfy the basic human need that suffering and good fortune be given meaning or significance.

But traditional authority does not itself rest upon an explicit *acceptance* of this principle, although like any authority structure, it may be said to *exemplify* it. Just the opposite is true: every traditionalist justification of power requires the ruled, the addressee of a command, to accept, at least implicitly, the claim that the world has an intrinsic normative significance which is discoverable through reason and experience. Thus, although a modern (Weberian) social scientist will necessarily view even traditional norms as the product of a wilful interpretation imposed by human beings on a morally neutral universe, this view is bound to conflict, in the most profound way imaginable, with the conception of normativity held by those who actually consider themselves bound by the claims of a traditional order.

If we assume that every value-system and therefore every authority structure is a human invention, then a form of authority which rests upon the belief that a norm has obligatory force only if it belongs to the pre-human natural order, may be said to rest upon an epistemological error. This same point can be expressed in another way by saying that every authority structure of this sort exhibits a peculiar lack of *self-consciousness or self-understanding*, reflected in the disjunction between what the participants in such a regime believe to be true about the nature of values and what we (critical, modern, Weberian) social scientists who accept the distinction between facts and values know to be the case.*

In the sense in which I am using the term, it is clear that legal-rational

---

*Compare Hegel's description of the disjunction between the standpoint of Consciousness and Science in the Introduction to *The Phenomenology of Spirit* (trans. A.V. Miller, Oxford, 1977). To begin with, consciousness takes something other than itself (the 'in-itself') to be the measuring-rod of its own knowledge; later, on the 'pathway of doubt', consciousness discovers that it is itself the instrument and medium by means of which the 'in-itself' is grasped. 'In pressing forward to its true existence, consciousness will arrive at a point at which it gets rid of its semblance of being burdened with something alien, with what is only for it, and some sort of "other", at a point where appearance becomes identical with essence, so that its exposition will coincide at just this point with the authentic Science of Spirit. And finally, when consciousness itself grasps this its own essence, it will signify the nature of absolute knowledge itself.' *Phenomenology of spirit*, pp. 56-7.

authority is characterized by a self-consciousness which traditional authority lacks. Legal-rational authority explicitly embraces the principle that norms must be created by men and rejects the idea that values are an inherent feature of what Weber calls 'the world process'. There is thus a convergence between the conception of normativity that defines this type of authority and the theory of value that Weber himself defends in his methodological writings and which he employs in his account of the general nature of authority relationships.

Weber's own account of sociological understanding rests upon a theory of value which asserts the positivity of all norms, regardless of their content. Among the various types of domination, only legal-rational authority is based upon an explicit endorsement of this same conception of normativity. Because legal-rational authority is the one form of domination whose fundamental principle of legitimation expresses what Weber considered to be the truth about values, he was bound to accord this form of authority a privileged place in his classification of the various pure types of domination. Legal-rational authority illuminates the actual foundation of *all* forms of domination by explicitly embracing the positivity of values as a principle of legitimation: it is this feature of legal-rational authority which gives it its peculiarly self-conscious character and which explains the priority Weber assigns it in his classificatory scheme.*

Legal-rational authority explicitly endorses a theory of value based upon what I have called the principle of positivity. Every form of authority exemplifies this principle (in the sense that all authority relationships rest upon humanly created norms) but only legal-rational authority employs the principle of positivity as the basis of legitimation. I have attempted to express this basic and important distinction by describing legal-rational authority as a peculiarly 'self-conscious' form of domination. It is worth emphasizing again, however, that even if one accepts my explanation of the logical primacy of legal-rational authority, it does not follow that this form of domination is better or more desirable than any other. A normative judgment of this sort can be defended only if one also accepts the controversial claim that self-consciousness is itself a value of overriding importance and believes that self-conscious principles and institutions should therefore be preferred to those which lack this characteristic, regardless of whatever other desirable consequences an absence of self-consciousness might have.

---

*Marx makes a similar point in the Introduction to the *Grundrisse* (trans. M. Nicolaus, London, 1973). 'Bourgeois society is the most developed and the most complex historic organization of production. The categories which express its relations, the comprehension of its structure, thereby also allows insights into the structure and the relations of production of all the vanished social formations out of whose ruins and elements it built itself up, whose partly still unconquered remnants are carried along within it, whose mere nuances have developed explicit significance within it, etc. Human anatomy contains a key to the anatomy of the ape. The intimations of higher development among the subordinate animal species, however, can be understood only after the higher development is already known. The bourgeois economy thus supplies the key to the ancient . . .' *Grundrisse*, p. 105.

Weber's own ethical evaluation of legal-rational authority and the formalistic mode of administration associated with it is, as I have noted, an
ambiguous one. At times, Weber seems to view the growing predominance
of legal-rationality as a great achievement and liberation – the triumph of
reason in human affairs. At other times, he speaks of the same phenomenon
in terms which suggest, instead, that legal-rationality – and in particular,
the modern bureaucratic order which he considered its highest
expression – inevitably leads to a kind of enslavement and stultification of
the spirit, a form of public life from which all passion and nobility have been
eliminated, an empty materialism that he described, with intense feeling, as
an 'iron cage'.[120] The ambiguity of Weber's ultimate judgment regarding
the ethical significance of legal rationality, indeed, the ambiguity of his judgment regarding modern European civilization as a whole, reflects an
underlying ambivalence on his part concerning the positivistic theory of
value presupposed by all legal-rational authority structures and the conception of personhood associated with it. What theory of value did Weber
juxtapose, even if only implicitly, to this one, and why did he imagine them
to be in conflict? I shall return to these questions in Chapter 8 when I take up
the most paradoxical idea in the whole of Weber's sociology – the idea of the
fatality of reason itself.

Impersonal domination
According to Weber, traditional authority is personal in nature; legal-
rational authority, by contrast, is characteristically impersonal.[121] What is
the meaning of this distinction, and how is it related to the difference
between conscious and unconscious principles of legitimation, as I have
used those terms? To begin with, although the distinction between personal
and impersonal forms of domination is a familiar one, it is more illusive than
might at first appear. At points, Weber equates the impersonality of legal-
rational authority with the condition or requirement that anyone exercising
such authority do so on the basis of a system of general rules whose validity is
entirely independent of the fact that it is *he* who happens to be invoking or
applying them, and which bind the officeholder just as much as they bind
those subject to his official power. This feature of legal-rational authority is
sometimes expressed by saying that it rests upon a rule of laws, not men. But
in a formal sense, at least, this is also true of traditional authority. The
patriarch, like the bureaucrat, bases his claim to authority on a system of
rules which are: (1) valid apart from the fact that it is he, rather than
someone else in the same position, who happens to be invoking them in
support of his claim to authority; (2) binding on the patriarch himself, as
well as those subject to his command; and (3) general in nature, that is,
stated in such a way as to be applicable to all similar cases – for example, all
disputes among siblings regarding the division of family property on their
father's death. Weber in fact emphasizes each of these three features of
traditional domination, especially when he is contrasting traditional and
legal-rational authority with authority based upon personal charisma, which

he describes as a peculiarly irrational – in the sense of ruleless – form of domination. To the extent that it, too, exhibits these three characteristics, traditional authority may therefore also be described as a rule of laws, not men, and hence as an essentially impersonal form of domination.

Indeed, when viewed abstractly, the authority claims made by a bureaucratic officeholder appear formally identical to those made by the master of a household, the prototype of all traditional authorities. Each says, 'I claim authority by virtue of being something or someone' (in the first case an official vested with specific responsibilities and in the second, a father or husband or feudal lord). In both cases, the claim in question will be accepted if two conditions are satisfied, if (1) the addressee of the claim accepts the principle of legitimation invoked by the person asserting a right to rule and (2) the factual premise of the claim is true – the person making the claim *really is* an officeholder or father, the incumbent of a position to which certain powers of legitimate domination are attached. The second condition is an empirical one whose satisfaction depends entirely upon whether the person claiming authority does or does not possess a particular attribute (the attribute of being a properly appointed official in one case and that of being the natural father of the person over whom a right of rule is claimed in the other). I shall call the attribute in question, whatever it may be, an *authority-generating attribute*.

From one point of view, the relevant authority-generating attribute can in both cases be thought of as defining a particular role or position which any given individual may or may not happen to occupy. But if this is the correct view of the matter, an individual's authority – whether he be a bureaucratic official or traditional master – would seem to be a function of his position in the social order and thus to be equally impersonal in both cases. On the other hand, if we view an authority-generating attribute as a property or characteristic of the person who possesses it, then both forms of domination may just as appropriately be described as personal in nature. It seems possible, therefore, to characterize legal-rational and traditional authority as equally personal or impersonal but not to distinguish betweem them in these terms. What is it, then, about these two forms of authority that Weber means to emphasize by describing one as personal and the other as impersonal?

In either a traditional or legal-rational regime, the assertion of a right to rule will be recognized only if the individual in question possesses a particular authority-generating attribute; there is, however, a fundamental difference in the nature of the attribute that a ruler must possess in the two cases and it is this difference which the distinction between personal and impersonal domination is meant to express. Consider, first, authority claims of a traditionalist sort. According to Weber, the archetype of all traditional domination is the domestic authority of the patriarch, the master of a household. The authority of the patriarch is decisively determined by two things – his age and sex: those who are younger necessarily stand under his authority, as do the non-male members of the household (wives and female children). These two attributes fix or specify the patriarch's relation to the other members of the household community and, in a traditional regime, legitimate his right to rule. Now the most striking thing about these attributes – age and sex – is that they are characteristics over which one has no control. A person's age, at any given moment in time, depends upon when he was born, and thus upon the occurrence of an event that he was powerless to cause or prevent. A person's sex is likewise a kind of fateful fact for which the person himself is not responsible, and which he is free to alter in only the most limited, and essentially negative, ways. In short, patriarchal authority is based upon given, natural characteristics that cannot plausibly be viewed as the product of a deliberate choice on the part of the person who happens to possess them.*

To be completely accurate, this last statement must be qualified in one important respect. Although some relations between the members of a household community – for example, those between parents and children or between siblings – may be said to exist by nature, there are other traditional authority relations, which Weber also associates with the household community, that do not have the same natural character. These latter relationships form a large and heterogeneous group including, for example, those between husband and wife, patron and client, lord and vassal, master and apprentice; each is a relation of service and support between individuals who are biologically unrelated, a relation that typically owes its origin, in part at least, to the agreement of the parties (or their representatives) and in this sense contains a consensual element missing in the biological relations that constitute the core of the household as a natural community. Nevertheless, as Weber points out, the creation of these artificial relationships almost always involves the attempt to suppress their own voluntarist origins and to endow them with an essentially natural character (something the parties seek to accomplish through various magical techniques, such as the mixing of blood or spittle).[122] This is an important fact for it demonstrates that in a purely traditionalist regime, all authority relations, including those which, strictly speaking, have been voluntarily created, must be *patterned after* and *assimilated to* one or another of the natural relations existing in the biological household, relations defined in terms of age, sex and common parentage – characteristics over which the individuals involved have no control and which they must accept as a fixed condition of life. Underlying this strenuous effort at assimilation is the belief that only a natural characteristic can ever legitimate one individual's right to rule another, a belief at the root of all traditional forms of domination. These quasi-natural relationships, about which I shall have more to say in chapter 5, may therefore be regarded as exceptions that prove the rule.**

*'In the case of domestic authority the belief in authority is based on personal relations that are perceived as natural. This belief is rooted in filial piety, in the close and permanent living together of all dependents of the household which results in an external and spiritual "community of fate".' *ES*, 1007.

**'No doubt, when with our modern ideas we contemplate the union of independent communities, we can suggest a hundred modes of carrying it out, the simplest of all being that the

If we compare the authority claims of a bureaucratic officeholder with those of a traditional master, one important difference now stands out. Although the bureaucrat justifies his right to rule by pointing to a particular fact about himself – the fact that he happens to be the incumbent of an office with a legally defined jurisdiction – this attribute, unlike those on which traditional forms of domination are based, is not in any sense a natural or biological destiny which the individual in question is powerless to control; on the contrary, his incumbency is an attribute which the officeholder has himself deliberately acquired by entering a *contract* with the state. The achievement of office is within the control of a bureaucratic officeholder in a way in which his age and sex and the identity of his parents are not, and this marks a fundamental difference in the nature of the authority-generating attributes whose possession is a prerequisite for the exercise of traditional and legal-rational forms of domination respectively.

The fact that in many bureaucratic regimes appointment to office follows as a matter of course from performance at a specified level on certain examinations or from the successful completion of a particular course of study, does not require us to qualify this last statement in any fundamental respect. Even if a given level of expertise is a necessary condition for appointment to office, the expertise in question must be acquired in a deliberately regulated and systematic fashion – at least so long as it is not thought to arise inevitably, in the course of time, from the ordinary experiences of life itself. The latter view is characteristic of traditionalist regimes, which typically justify the rule of old men on the grounds of their greater experience and superior life-wisdom; but wherever expertise is not simply equated with the practical wisdom of those who have lived a long time, it must be acquired, in a deliberate way, by undergoing a process of instruction. This is the case in every bureaucratic regime of a modern – that is to say, legal-rational – sort.

Naturally, in acquiring the expertise that he must have in order to be eligible for appointment to office, the aspiring bureaucrat is likely to be assisted or hindered by his native intelligence and talents, and these represent, to an important extent, attributes of the person that are fixed at birth and over which he has little control. But in a bureaucratic regime, although an individual's natural gifts may *affect his chances* of success in the competition for office they do not themselves *legitimate* his right to rule and hence are not the source or ground of his authority. In a legal-rational regime, the mere fact that an individual possesses certain natural qualities is

individuals comprised in the coalescing groups shall vote or act together according to local propinquity; but the idea that a number of persons should exercise political rights in common simply because they happened to live within the same topographical limits was utterly strange and monstrous to primitive antiquity. The expedient which in those times commanded favour was that the incoming population should *feign themselves* to be descended from the same stock as the people on whom they were engrafted; and it is precisely the good faith of this fiction, and the closeness with which it seemed to imitate reality, that we cannot now hope to understand.'
H. Maine, *Ancient Law* (London, 1917), p. 77.

no guarantee that in the course of time, barring unforeseen accidents, he will come to occupy a position of authority; whether or not he does eventually become the incumbent of an office to which authoritative powers are attached depends on what he chooses to do with his natural abilities and the career he pursues. To be sure, in a very general sense, the authority of both the modern bureaucrat and the traditional patriarch is explained by the fact that each occupies a well-defined position – an office – in a social arrangement of some sort. In the latter case, however, occupancy of this position is *equated* with the possession of certain natural characteristics and its attainment determined by biological processes over which the individual has little if any control; in the former case, the officeholder's natural characteristics are neither the source of his official powers (these spring, instead, from his contractual relationship with the state) nor a guarantee of his succession to office. In these respects, legal-rational authority differs sharply from all forms of domination based on traditionalist premises.

In all traditional regimes, authority claims are personal in the sense that they are based upon attributes which the individual claiming authority has not himself deliberately acquired and which cannot be added to or detached from his person at will: it is this quality of non-detachability that distinguishes the attributes on which traditional authority claims are based. By contrast, in the case of legal-rational authority structures, there is not this same indissoluble link between the person claiming authority and the particular attribute that legitimates his right to rule; to a significant extent, the attribute in question – the fact that he happens to be the incumbent of a particular office with a defined jurisdiction – is a characteristic that can be added to or subtracted from his person as he chooses. Put differently, although in both traditional and legal-rational regimes it will always be a contingent fact that a particular individual possesses the authority-generating attribute needed to legitimate the exercise of power over others, the source of the contingency is different in the two cases: in one it is attributable to the fatality of nature and in the other to voluntary choice.

The patriarch governs by virtue of circumstances beyond his control: it is his personal fate to rule. By the same token, the rules that define and circumscribe his authority are themselves conceived, from a traditionalist point of view, as an unalterably given aspect of the world, timeless and hence uncreated, one part of an inherently normative world-process that conditions all human action and presents itself to men as their fate. The idea of fate or choicelessness – the absence of freedom – thus links the principle of legitimation on which traditional domination is based to the personal attributes that ultimately ground every traditional ruler's claim to rightful authority. By contrast, the bureaucratic official acquires *his* authority-generating characteristic voluntarily, by his own deliberate action, and appeals to a principle of legitimation which traces the binding force of the rules he must apply back to their voluntary enactment. Here, it is the idea of voluntariness, of creative free choice, which links the underlying conception of legitimation to the special attribute on which the bureaucrat's claim to authority is based. Put differently, both the principle of positivity and the idea of impersonal domination (as I have construed it) reflect the *devaluation of the natural* – the separation of facts and values – that characterizes legal-rational authority and distinguishes it from its traditionalist counterpart. Just as the idea of fate provides a common element or theme connecting the different aspects of traditional authority, so its opposite, the idea of freedom, plays a similar role in the case of legal-rational domination.

The household
The original locus of all traditional authority is the household; complex traditional regimes merely reproduce, on a larger scale, relationships and authority structures of an essentially domestic sort. By contrast, legal-rational authority, in its purest form, is associated with the bureaucratic office and its economic counterpart, the rational profit-making firm, both of which are characterized by a complete separation, in law and fact, from the private households of those who staff or administer them. The separation of the household from both firm and office represents a distinctive feature of modern European civilization,[123] and is a principal cause of its sharp division between public and private life. Traditional authority structures, rooted as they are in the sphere of domestic action, do not exhibit a division of this sort and thus possess a kind of unity or continuity antithetical to everything Weber considered specifically modern.

As a form of social association, the household has certain distinguishing characteristics, two of which are especially important for Weber's theory of authority. In the first place, unlike a modern bureaucracy, a household is a natural community, a form of association based on natural relationships (as Aristotle observed long ago).[124] A household comes into being when a man and a woman, or a group of men and women, establish a permanent association for the maintenance of themselves and their children. The relations that exist between the members of even the simplest household, and which provide the pattern for those quasi-natural relationships characteristic of more complex forms of domestic association, are all natural relationships in the sense that each has a powerful – indeed defining – biological component. Even the most rudimentary household is of course not a spontaneously natural phenomenon in the same sense that sexual union and reproduction are; these can and often do occur outside the household, which must therefore be viewed as something added to or imposed upon the most elementary aspects of our natural, and especially sexual, life. Nevertheless, it is the principal aim of the household to provide a regular and stable framework for the process of sexual reproduction and although it may be thought of as an institution imposed upon underlying, and more basic, biological functions, the family derives its essential character from the fact that its purpose is to establish a protective sphere within which these functions may be carried out. To this extent, the household necessarily partakes of the naturalness of the biological relations it helps to stabilize, and thus comes to be identified with them. Consequently, relations among the members of a household community are significantly shaped by the same unalterable facts of age and sex that determine what role an individual plays in the biological process of reproduction itself; for this reason, the household has always been regarded as a sphere of unfreedom in which the actions of individuals and their relationships with one another are importantly constrained by biological conditions beyond their control.

By contrast, the various social relations created and legitimated by a modern bureaucracy – those between officeholders and citizen-clients as well as those that exist among the officeholders themselves – lack a similar biological foundation. The position an individual occupies in a regime of this sort is not determined by the relatively fixed role he is required to play in the elementary process of sexual reproduction (understood broadly to include the nurturing of children) but is, to a degree impossible in the family, defined by voluntary contractual arrangements that the individual makes for himself. Family relations may, of course, have a contractual dimension – marriage is the most obvious example – and an individual's position in a bureaucratic organization can be importantly influenced by fixed natural characteristics such as his native intellectual endowment. But despite these superficial similarities, a legal-rational bureaucracy is not a natural community in the same sense that a household is. The relationships established by a bureaucratic regime are not relationships of blood, nor do they rest upon mutual sexual attraction; in this respect, they are distinguished from the bonds of kinship and marriage, the basic constituents of family life, which reflect in a more direct and immediate way the elementary biological conditions of human reproduction.

The household is a natural association: this is its first and most striking characteristic. A second distinguishing characteristic of the household community is its constitution as a form of economic organization. According to Weber, every economically oriented association seeks to produce or acquire goods capable of satisfying some human need; this is as true of the household as it is of a profit-making firm. Weber draws a fundamental distinction, however, between those economically oriented associations whose aim is to satisfy the needs of their members, and those whose goal is the generation of a surplus or profit.* What distinguishes one from the other is the *purpose* for which the activity in question (the production or acquisition of want-satisfying goods) has been undertaken. Thus, a profit-making firm may be defined as an association that is engaged in economic activity for the sole purpose of increasing its worth or value: the defining aim of all profit-making is to increase the total value of the firm's assets. At the beginning of every period of economic activity, a profit-making firm has assets worth a certain amount. The value of its assets provides a benchmark by which the firm's success in the following period is to be measured; only if the firm

---

ES, 86–94. Marx draws a similar distinction, emphasizing that pre-capitalist forms of production all aimed at the production of 'use value' rather than 'exchange value'. See *Grundrisse* pp. 483–516.

concludes the period with assets of greater value than those with which it began can it be said to have made a profit and thus to have achieved its end or purpose. To the extent that it remains engaged in profit-making, the now increased value of the firm's assets can only serve as a fresh benchmark by which to measure its success in the next period of economic activity – a benchmark that must in turn be superseded if the firm is to continue to be a profit-making one. In this sense, although the firm's growth may be halted, and its profit-making brought to an end for any one of a number of different reasons, its defining goal does not require – indeed, it does not permit – the firm to terminate its economic activity at any particular point. Put differently, the activity of profit-making does not itself have a determinate end of any sort but must be conceived, instead, as an effort to overcome or exceed whatever is given as fixed at the outset (the value of the firm's assets at the beginning of each production period). Profit-making thus entails a process of economic expansion which, at least in principle, is limitless in the sense that it has no fixed end beyond which further economic activity would be pointless.[125]

Economic organizations oriented toward want-satisfaction – of which the household is the oldest and most important example – are fundamentally different in character. The purpose of every organization of this sort is to satisfy the wants of its members; once their wants have been satisfied, further economic activity is purposeless in the literal sense. The wants in question, even if they have a significant status component (that is, are wants which derive from and are defined by the social status of the individual involved) are fixed at the outset, and establish a determinate end which the organization then strives to attain through economic activity of one sort or another. Of course, many needs – for example, the need for physical nourishment – are periodic in nature, and the activities that seek to satisfy them must therefore be repeated over and over again, so that even want-satisfaction becomes an endless activity,[126] although in a sense quite different from the activity of profit-making whose endlessness results from the indeterminacy of its basic goal. It is also true that wants themselves change over time, often becoming more refined and difficult to satisfy; but this obvious fact does not undermine the distinction between want-satisfaction and profit-making either. Even if needs change, the goal of every economic activity aimed at want-satisfaction is to satisfy certain given needs, not to replace or overcome them; if the needs in question are altered or refined, it is because of changes which have taken place outside the process of want-satisfaction, strictly defined. By contrast, every profit-making activity has as its aim the transcendence of the starting point from which it begins, and therefore by definition seeks to alter its own conditions in a way in which want-satisfaction does not.

According to Weber, the fundamental aim of the household, viewed as an economic association, is to satisfy the needs of its members. To be sure, a household may engage in profit-making activity, but so long as it remains a household, it does so only as part of some larger scheme of want-satisfaction.

A household exploits opportunities for profit-making in order to generate the revenue needed to satisfy its members' needs; in this sense, it seeks profit only as a means to a quite different end. The reverse is true of a profit-making firm: although an entrepreneur must use some of his resources to satisfy his own needs, from the point of view he adopts as an owner or manager of the firm, this represents merely another capital expense that must be incurred to successfully complete a profit-making venture. As an entrepreneur, he eats in order to make a profit; as a householder he pursues profit-making activities in order to eat.[127]

The first characteristic of the household (its rootedness in the biological process of reproduction) is importantly related to its second characteristic (its orientation to the end of want-satisfaction). Both reveal, in different ways, the extent to which the household is an association based upon necessity, an association in which the roles of individuals and their relations with one another are, to a degrees uncharacteristic of other forms of social organization, shaped by circumstances beyond their power to create or change. This is obviously true of domestic authority relations insofar as they are based upon the sexual identity, age and blood relations of those involved. It is equally true of the economic life of the household which, as an association oriented toward want-satisfaction, is defined and therefore limited by the given needs of its members. In each of its aspects, the household is distinguished by the fact that its organizing principles assign determinative significance to what the individuals involved are likely to view as the fixed or given conditions of their existence.

By contrast, both the modern bureau and the profit-making firm (the two forms of social organization that Weber most frequently contrasts with the household) downplay the normative importance of the given and reflect, in different ways, the concept of freedom which underlies the principle of positivity. Bureaucratic organizations do this by substituting contractual ties for the biological ones that hold the members of a family together, and by explicitly adopting the principle of positivity as the sole basis of legitimate domination. The profit-making firm does something similar when it adopts as its defining goal an increase in the worth of the firm's assets – the transcendence of their given value at any moment in time – thus committing itself, in principle at least, to a process of expansion with no fixed or determinate end. In different but analogous ways, the types of administrative and economic organization characteristic of modern European civilization break with the age-old belief in the normative power of the actual; each therefore represents a fundamental departure from the household which, whether viewed as an authority structure or a form of economic organization, is decisively shaped by the identification of what exists with what has value.

The idea of separation as a theme in Weber's theory of authority

One recurring theme in Weber's theory of authority is what I shall call the idea of 'separation'. Properly understood, this idea links the three central features of legal-rational authority discussed above – its impersonality, non-domesticity, and self-conscious endorsement of the principle of positivity. In each respect, legal-rational authority separates what traditional regimes regard as continuous.*

To begin with, in distinguishing legal-rational bureaucracies from pre-modern forms of administration, Weber stresses the fact that a modern officeholder is separated from ownership of the means of administration, that he does not *own* the office he occupies. This separation has a legal meaning: however great his power, the modern bureaucrat does not have a legally recognized entitlement – a property right – to his office and hence it does not form part of his private estate (in contrast to the salary he is paid, which does belong to him, and which he is free to use for whatever personal ends he wishes). Patriarchial and patrimonial forms of administration rest upon the opposite premise. In regimes of this sort, an officeholder typically owns his office and may dispose of it as he would any other item of personal property – for example, by selling it or bequeathing it to his children.

In emphasizing the separation of the modern bureaucrat from ownership of his office (the 'means of administration') Weber means, of course, to remind the reader of Marx's similar formulation of the juridical basis of capitalist production and to suggest that Marx's formulation may be applied, more broadly, to political and other phenomena as well.[128] In Weber's view, non-ownership of the instrument or means for carrying on a particular activity is a characteristic not just of capitalist enterprise but of modern society as a whole. This is a point he underscores by using the same formulation to describe social phenomena as different as warfare (the modern soldier is separated from the ownership of his own equipment)[129] and scholarship (the contemporary scholar, unlike his predecessors, performs his work in laboratories and libraries which he himself does not own).[130] In short, the separation of the officeholder from ownership of his office is a characteristic feature of all legal-rational bureaucracies and one which they share in common with a broad range of other modern institutions.

This characteristic of modern bureaucracies is related to another – their impersonality. Today, an officeholder rules impersonally, which means that his right to rule is not based upon the possession of a fixed natural attribute. Impersonal rule also means that the bureaucrat's personal affairs – his own interests and feelings – must be excluded, insofar as is humanly possible, from the performance of his official duties; the ideal modern officeholder is one who rules '*sine ira et studio*, without anger or passion, and hence without affection or enthusiasm'.[131] Impersonality, in each of these senses, implies a kind of separation. Understood in the latter sense, it implies a separation between the bureaucrat's own estate and emotional life, on the one hand,

---

*The theme of separation is stressed repeatedly in the opening sections of the *Rechtssoziologie*. Weber asserts that the modern legal order is characterized by the separation of: public and private law; formal adjudication and administration; criminal and civil law; and (within the field of civil law) tort and contract. In each case, pre-modern law is characterized by the union of what we today regard as fundamentally distinct. *ES*, 641–51; *LES*, 41–56.

and his official tasks on the other. Understood in the former sense, impersonal rule assumes a separation, at least in theory, between the legal identity of the person who rules and his natural attributes. These may influence his chances of obtaining office but have no bearing on his right to rule. Since a bureaucrat's natural attributes do not themselves legitimate his claim to authority, the basis of his right to rule must be independent of, and in this sense separate from, the attributes in question.*

No such separation exists in the case of traditional regimes. The fact that his authority is personal means, first of all, that a traditional ruler draws no line between the respect and material support he is owed as a private individual and the powers he may rightfully claim as the incumbent of an office. The latter belong to him, form part of his estate, and it would therefore be meaningless to say that he should rule without regard to the effect his decisions have on his private affairs, as a modern bureaucrat must. 'Personal' authority also means that the traditional ruler rules in virtue of certain natural qualities that distinguish him as a particular kind of human being and set him apart from other members of the species. These constitute the legitimating ground of his right to rule; a fundamental conceptual distinction between official and personal action, or between the individual viewed as an officeholder and the same individual considered as the possessor of distinctive personal qualities, is as unthinkable in a traditionalist regime as it is unavoidable in a legal-rational one.

Finally, the idea of separation also underlies Weber's emphasis on the non-domestic character of legal-rational authority, and his equally strong insistence on the domestic origin of all forms of traditional domination. Modern bureaucracies presuppose the spatial separation of home and office, as well as their juridical distinctness. Traditional authority, by contrast, assumes the identity of official and domestic spheres in both a factual and legal sense.

In general, then, legal-rational authority demands that we separate what traditional authority assumes to be inseparable. This basic point is confirmed by recalling the first and most important distinction between these two types of domination. All legal-rational authority rests upon the principle of positivity, a principle which presupposes – or more accurately, which expresses – a sharp conceptual distinction between facts and values. Traditional authority, by contrast, identifies 'is' and 'ought'; from a traditionalist point of view, the world is assumed to contain the values that endow human life with whatever meaning and purpose it has. This presumed identity of facts and values is the source of what I have called the unself-consciousness of traditional authority, and represents the single most important difference between this form of domination and its legal-rational counterpart. Thus, it is the idea of separation (of facts and values) which links the

*'Between an individual and his office there is no immediate link. Hence, individuals are not appointed to office on account of their birth or native personal gifts. The *objective* factor in their appointment is knowledge and proof of ability.' Hegel, *Philosophy of Right*, § 291.

self-consciousness of legal-rational authority to the other aspects that Weber emphasizes (its impersonality and non-domesticity). The separation of facts and values expresses, in the most direct fashion, the devaluation of the natural which these other characteristics of legal-rational authority reflect as well. From whichever point of view we consider it, legal-rational authority denies to the given circumstances of human life the inherent normative significance they are accorded in every traditional regime. This is what the idea of separation means and what ultimately explains the primacy of legal-rational authority in Weber's typology of authority relations.

The intermediate nature of charismatic authority

Of the three pure types of domination, charismatic authority is in many ways the most complex.[132] Its distinguishing features can, I believe, best be understood if it is viewed as an authority structure of a logically intermediate sort, a form of domination that shares certain features in common with each of the other two, but which combines them in a unique and peculiarly unstable fashion.

Charismatic authority, it will be recalled, rests on 'devotion to the exceptional sanctity, heroism or exemplary character of an individual person, and of the normative patterns of order revealed or ordained by him.'[133] The charismatic leader is exceptional insofar as he possesses 'a certain quality' which is 'not accessible to the ordinary person';[134] it is the possession of this quality that legitimates his right to rule. In a broad sense, the quality in question is a personal attribute of the charismatic leader, an attribute which forms part of his character and distinguishes him as an individual with identifiable, concrete characteristics. To the extent that it is based on personal qualities, charismatic authority resembles traditional forms of domination and may be contrasted with legal-rational authority.

Putting the matter this way, however, obscures a fundamental difference between charismatic and traditional domination. The quality or attribute on which charisma rests is always an exceptional one. This means that it is uniquely possessed by the leader claiming a right to rule. By contrast, the qualities or attributes on which traditional authority is based (most importantly, age and paternity) are *un*exceptional: they are attributes possessed by many different individuals at the same time, attributes rooted in the biological life of the species and hence in those experiences and relationships which are precisely the most routine. All traditional authority structures implicitly ascribe normative significance to biological characteristics which are displayed most prominently and have their greatest importance within the sphere of natural necessity, the household-centred domain of activity whose principal aim is the maintainence and reproduction of human life.

This difference in the personal qualities on which traditional and charismatic leaders base their claim to rule has important consequences. To a considerable extent, the natural attributes that traditional rulers invoke as the ground of their authority appear (but only appear!) to have a straight-forward, even self-evident significance of their own, and consequently do not seem to require an interpretation of any sort to establish their meaning.* The facts of age and sex fix an individual's role in the reproductive process in a way that appears to have inherent ethical validity: reproduction is accomplished through the sexual union of men and women, and so it is *good* that men and women form associations for the purpose of having and raising children; the young are necessarily, for a period of time, in the care of their elders, and so it is *right* that they obey them and follow their commands. It may, in fact, be the seemingly self-evident significance of these natural characteristics that explains the conflation of factual and normative proposi-tions on which all traditional forms of authority rest. Since they appear to have a transparent meaning of their own, an inherent normative significance that does not require an interpretation in order to be understood, these characteristics (or, more precisely, the attitude we take toward them) tend to obscure what for Weber is a fundamental epistemological truth – that every norm, no matter how obvious and non-controversial, is the product of an interpretive evaluation.

The exceptional qualities on which claims to charismatic authority are based do not possess a similarly self-evident meaning of their own and in this respect differ from the familiar biological distinctions around which the reproductive life of the species is organized. Consequently, the unique attri-bute on which the charismatic leader seeks to ground his claim to rule *does* require an explicit interpretation of some sort before its normative meaning can be established; since the attribute in question is by definition something out of the ordinary, it is likely to have a mysteriousness and ambiguity which, unlike the more routine facts of age and sex, demands to be explained. The would-be charismatic leader attempts to provide an expla-nation of this sort by interpreting his gift as the 'sign' of a supernatural mission which justifies the claims he makes on his followers.

This aspect of charismatic authority brings the interpretive foundation of values into view in a way that is impossible within the horizon of every tradi-tionalist conception of legitimacy. Unlike a father's paternity or superior age, the extraordinary gift of a charismatic prophet requires a self-conscious interpretation before a meaning can be assigned to it or ethical consequences deduced from its possession; in this respect, charismatic authority marks a break with traditional forms of domination [135] and represents a step toward legal-rational authority which, as we have seen, explicitly embraces the idea that every value is a posit – the principle of positivity.

Charismatic authority stops short, however, of actually acknowledging

---

*'It is by way of conventional rules that merely factual regularities of action, i.e. usages, are frequently transformed into binding norms, guaranteed primarily by psychological coercion. Convention thus makes tradition. The mere fact of the regular recurrence of certain events somehow confers on them the dignity of oughtness. This is true with regard to natural events as well as to action conditioned organically or by unreflective imitation of, or adaptation to, external conditions of life.' *ES*, 326.

the positivity of values. Ultimately, every charismatic claim to authority rests upon an attribution of supernatural significance to the leader's gift, and despite the fact that it must be interpreted to be understood, his gift represents a unique personal destiny that has neither been chosen nor created by the leader himself. Indeed, just the opposite is true: for both the charismatic leader and his followers the gift that legitimates the leader's claim to rule represents a fate or destiny imposed upon him by inhuman powers beyond his control. To the extent it founds the leader's right to rule on the possession of a fateful gift, charismatic authority more closely resembles traditional domination than its legal-rational counterpart and exhibits a similar tendency to endow the given circumstances of human life with inherent normative significance; * in this sense, it, too, rejects the most basic premise of all legal-rational regimes – that values are created by men, not given to them as their fate, and that nothing may be counted a value unless it can be shown to have originated in a deliberate act of human will.

The charismatic leader is burdened by a fateful gift thrust upon him by divine or supernatural powers. The meaning of his gift is uncertain, however, and hence must be established through a self-conscious act of interpretation. It is an essential presupposition of all authority claims based upon personal charisma that only the prophet himself, the possessor of the gift, has the power to interpret its meaning and hence to decide the scope of his own mission. The authority which his gift confers upon the prophet includes, most importantly, the sole right to determine the meaning of the gift itself. Indeed, once the prophet's interpretive monopoly is recognized, all his other powers are secure; because no one else is qualified to challenge the prophet's interpretation or offer a competing interpretation of his own, the prophet's interpretive freedom is theoretically unlimited – a point Weber expresses by saying that the prophet's charisma is based upon a quality or attribute whose ethical significance can only be fixed by means of an interpretation that is wholly self-determined (with the important *caveat* that he must first persuade his followers to accept his interpretive monopoly).[136]

But while the prophet enjoys a limitless freedom in this regard, it is only he who does so since he alone possesses the relevant quality and is therefore entitled to speak. Consequently, although charismatic authority introduces the idea of free legislation and – in contrast to traditional authority – assigns it an important role in the process of legitimation, it does so in a profoundly undemocratic way. From this point of view, legal-rational authority represents a more egalitarian conception of legitimacy since it assumes everyone to be equally endowed with the power of evaluative interpretation, the power to create binding norms through legislation, which the charismatic prophet seeks to monopolize for himself. Legal-rational authority

---

*'Both charismatic and patriarchal power rest on personal devotion to, and personal authority of, "natural" leaders, in contrast to the appointed leaders of the bureaucratic order, yet this basis is very different in the two cases.' *ES*, 1117.

transforms the privilege of the prophet into a democratic franchise. It is able to do so, however, only because it rejects the assumption, central to all authority claims based upon personal charisma, that the power of evaluative interpretation is itself merely the adjunct of some natural quality possessed by a few extraordinary human beings.

The logically intermediate position of charismatic authority – attributable to its distinctive combination of the ideas of fatefulness and free legislation – also helps to explain its characteristic instability. Generally speaking, traditional and legal-rational authority structures tend to be stable and resistant to change. There are many different reasons why this is so. One especially important reason is that both forms of domination represent what Weber called structures of 'everyday life', structures that can be, and typically are, made to serve the routine economic demands of day-to-day existence. By contrast, charismatic authority represents a profoundly anti-economic force in the sense that it eschews all permanent forms of social organization aimed at an ongoing and planful satisfaction of ordinary needs; from the standpoint of those interested primarily in 'making a living', charismatic movements are always viewed with fear and suspicion. This principled opposition to all forms of routine economic activity contributes to the instability of charismatic authority by preventing it from taking root in that sphere of human life which has the greatest permanence and is least subject to dramatic, revolutionary change.[137]

The uniqueness of the gift on which the leader predicates his claim to rule also contributes to the instability of charismatic movements. If his gift is truly unique, there can be no successor to the charismatic leader, and his movement must therefore expire with him. Consequently, if the leader or his followers hope to maintain the movement he has inspired, a successor must be found. But in order to locate a successor, it must be assumed that the gift of the leader is shared by others, at least so long as his successors attempt to justify *their* right to rule on charismatic grounds as well. This obviously creates a problem, not only because it is inconsistent with the belief that the original leader's gift was unique, but more importantly, because the limitless interpretive freedom which any genuine charismatic leader enjoys necessarily tends to impede the formation of fixed and widely accepted criteria by which the claims of competing aspirants to the leader's role may be assessed. As a consequence, every charismatic movement is almost certain to experience a succession crisis in its early stages (before it has been traditionalized or transformed into a legal-rational structure of some sort).[138]

A third source of instability in charismatic movements derives from a conceptual tension inherent in the principle of legitimation on which charismatic leadership is based. Traditional authority rests on the assumption that the world of the 'is' – the world of factual experience – is an inherently meaningful one, with a self-evident normative significance of its own. Legal-rational authority rests on the opposite premise: the world, as it is given to us in experience, is entirely devoid of intrinsic significance and acquires an ethical meaning only insofar as it has been deliberately assigned one by human beings. Each of these contrary assumptions, whether or not it is true in some ultimate epistemological sense, represents a coherent and internally consistent view of the relation between facts and values. This makes for a kind of conceptual stability in the principles of legitimation based upon these assumptions, and thus, indirectly, for stability in the authority structures associated with them.

In contrast to the other two types, charismatic authority is based upon an ambiguous – indeed, inconsistent – conception of the relation between facts and values. Every charismatic authority claim rests on the assumption that certain facts (the observable qualities that constitute the sign of the leader's calling) do possess an inherent meaning, but only because they stand in some determinable relation to non-observable, supernatural powers of one kind or another. But the nature of this relation is not self-evident; it can therefore only be established by means of an interpretive explanation of some sort. However, since the relation between the prophet's sign and the invisible powers it signifies is, and is bound to remain, problematic, no definitively correct interpretation of the relation is possible. Every such interpretation is therefore always in jeopardy, subject to being ousted by a competitor in a contest with no fixed rules. Put differently, every charismatic claim is based upon an interpretation of certain factual states of affairs which purports to be the *true* interpretation (in contrast to competing views which are necessarily those of false prophets). To claim that one's interpretation is true, however, assumes the existence of a yardstick against which the truth and falsity of different interpretations can be assessed. But in the case of charismatic authority, no such yardstick exists or is even conceivable – which is what Weber means when he says that 'charisma is self-determined and sets its own limits', limits that are fixed by the bearer of the gift himself, 'from within, not by an external order.' In this sense, charismatic legitimation presupposes what, by its own assumptions, it makes impossible: a determinate, interpersonal standard of truthfulness by which the claims of the prophet may be judged. This gives the principle of legitimation on which charismatic authority is based an intellectual incoherence that is reflected, inevitably, in the instability of charismatic movements. Like each of its other main characteristics, the transience of charisma is to be explained by a tension in the principle of legitimation on which it rests, a tension that can best be understood by seeing the ways in which this form of authority occupies a logically intermediate position between the other two.

4

Formal legal rationality

This chapter, and the next three, explore a number of related themes in Weber's *Rechtssoziologie*. My basic aim throughout will be to show that Weber's positivist theory of value and the will-centred conception of person-hood associated with it play a central, organizing role in his analysis of legal phenomena, connecting the main elements of the *Rechtssoziologie* in a supris-ingly unified and coherent fashion.

I shall begin by examining the concept of formal legal rationality. According to Weber, formal rationality is a characteristic of law and legal thinking that has acquired unique prominence in certain modern European legal systems.[139] Weber was interested in identifying the factors – religious, political and economic as well as legal – that have promoted the develop-ment of formally rational law in the West and retarded its growth elsewhere; he was also interested in determining the extent to which formal legal rationality has contributed to the growth of market capitalism, a mode of economic organization that in its developed form is also unique to the modern West. A large part of the *Rechtssoziologie* is addressed to one or the other of these two questions. Without understanding what Weber meant by formal legal rationality, these questions, and the answers he gives to them, can make little sense.

The concept of formal legal rationality is the best known of Weber's jurid-ical categories. It is also the least understood; to a considerable degree, the idea of formal legal rationality has become a codeword or slogan, devoid of analytic content. But if the concept has not always been employed with theo-retical precision, this is not just because those using it have failed to read the *Rechtssoziologie* as carefully as they might. Weber himself, as we shall see, employs the idea of formal legal rationality in a confusing way, using it at different points to describe different, though related, features of various pro-cedural arrangements and substantive legal doctrines. Part of the blame for the continuing obscurity of this concept must therefore be placed on Weber himself.

In the first section of the chapter, I describe four distinct senses in which Weber uses the concept of formal legal rationality. In the second section, I trace the confusion which these multiple meanings introduce into his analysis of the so-called 'basic categories of legal thought' – Weber's famous division of the various types of legal thinking according to whether they are formal or substantive, rational or irrational. Having located the source of this confusion, I attempt to demonstrate, in the next three sections of the chapter, that the different meanings he gives the concept of formal legal rationality are nevertheless linked in ways that reveal a unity or coherence in the concept which his terminological carelessness belies.

Four senses of rationality

Although the term 'rational' is one of the most frequently used and important in the *Rechtssoziologie*, Weber employs it in a surprisingly careless fashion. Depending upon its setting, the term may refer to any one of four different (but related) characteristics of law and legal thinking.

In the first place, Weber often uses the term 'rational' to mean simply governed by rules or principles. This, he asserts, is the most elementary sense in which a body of substantive doctrine or a procedural arrangement may be said to be rational.[140] For a legal order to be rational in this sense, it is only necessary that the rights and obligations of individuals be determined by principles having some degree of generality and that the principles in question be identifiable. The closer a legal order comes to being a collection of idiosyncratic judgments or decrees, each tailored to a particular case and incapable of being subsumed under a limited number of identifiable rules, the less rational it is in this first sense. Weber sometimes uses the term 'formal' to express the same idea – for example, in those passages in which he is contrasting formal and non-formal (i.e. ruleless) types of adjudication.[141] Often, however, he employs the idea of formality in another way – to distinguish between what he calls formal and substantive types of legal thinking – and when he does, formality means something entirely different, as we shall see.

Although Weber frequently uses the term 'rational' to mean simply rule-governed, he also uses it in a second and seemingly distinct sense to designate the systematic character of a legal order.[142] According to Weber, a legal order is a legal system and hence rational in this second sense to the extent it 'represents an integration of all analytically derived legal propositions in such a way that they constitute a logically clear, internally consistent, and, at least in theory, gapless system of rules, under which, it is implied, all conceivable fact situations must be capable of being logically subsumed lest their order lack an effective guaranty.'[143] This conception of a legal system is a peculiarly modern one and has had a special influence on the European reception of Roman law; its highest expression, Weber claims, is to be found in the 'legal science of the Pandectists'.[144]

A particular legal order may be both rule-governed and systematic, and hence rational in each of the two senses identified so far. These characteristics are not always conjoined, however. Rationality, in the first and most general sense, necessarily involves some degree of legal analysis (the formulation of general rules through a 'specification and delimitation of the potentially relevant characteristics of the facts').[145] The analysis of legal concepts is also required for the construction of a legal system. System-building, however, involves an additional task which legal analysis by itself does not: the construction of a comprehensive, gapless and internally consistent body of rules deliberately arranged so as to give every actual or conceivable event a determinate legal meaning. According to Weber, legal analysis may achieve considerable refinement without resulting in a legal system; it is therefore possible, in his view, for a 'very high degree of sublimation in analysis' to be correlated with a relatively low level of systematization.[146] The formulation of general rules – legal rationality in Weber's first sense – thus constitutes a necessary but not sufficient condition for the construction of a legal system.

To generate a legal system (or even the idea of one) a particular type of legal analysis is required. Legal analysis is in general a two-step process. To begin with, those characteristics of events or states of affairs that are 'potentially relevant' from a legal point of view must be distinguished from the infinity of other characteristics lacking legal significance. Once they have been properly identified, 'the potentially relevant characteristics of the facts' must then be assigned a specific juristic meaning through the construction of legal rules or propositions.[147] But while the identification of 'those ultimate components [of the facts] which are regarded as relevant in the juristic valuation'[148] is a necessary precondition for the formulation of any general legal propositions whatsoever, there are, according to Weber, two entirely different interpretive principles that one may adopt in the specification of these 'ultimate components' themselves. On the one hand, legal analysis may proceed on the assumption that the 'legally relevant characteristics are of a tangible nature, i.e. . . . are perceptible as sense-data.'[149] Alternatively, it may rest on the assumption that the legally relevant characteristics of the facts can only be identified through what Weber calls 'the logical analysis of [their] meaning'.[150]

Although he never explains this distinction as clearly as one might wish, Weber does assert, quite emphatically, that the 'specifically systematic task' of constructing a comprehensive, gapless and internally consistent set of juristic propositions can only be accomplished if legal thinking is based upon the second of these two interpretive principles. Where legal thought is shaped by the first assumption, no system of law, as that concept is understood by 'present-day legal science',[151] can emerge. Under such circumstances, the most that can be expected is the growth of 'highly comprehensive schemes of legal casuistry' based upon a 'merely paratactic association' of 'extrinsic elements', schemes which lack what Weber calls 'logical sublimation'.[152] In short, 'only that abstract method which employs the logical interpretation of meaning allows the execution of the specifically systematic task, i.e. the collection and rationalization by logical means of all the several rules recognized as legally valid into an internally consistent complex of abstract legal propositions.'[153]

In addition to the two meanings we have already noted, Weber also uses the term 'rational' to describe this method of legal analysis – analysis based upon the 'abstract interpretation of meaning' – and to distinguish it from those forms of legal thought that are marked by a dependence on what he variously calls 'externally tangible formal characteristics', 'extrinsic elements', or 'sense-data characteristics'.[154] Although he emphasizes that the adoption of a rational method of legal analysis is necessary for the systematization of the legal order, Weber never adequately explains the connection between these ideas. It therefore seems best to view his repeated references to the special rationality of that type of legal thinking which is based upon 'the logical interpretation of meaning' as a third and distinct use of the concept of legal rationality, albeit one which forms a kind of connecting link between the first two: only if they are analytically derived through the logical interpretation of meaning can legal rules be arranged in a truly systematic fashion.

To the three senses of rationality identified so far, a fourth must be added. A considerable portion of the *Rechtssoziologie* is devoted to the analysis of primitive legal institutions. According to Weber, primitive law is distinguished by two characteristics, its formality and irrationality. The extreme formality of primitive law is a consequence of its adherence to rigidly prescribed procedural rules; its irrationality is attributable to the fact that primitive mechanisms for the resolution of disputes typically employ magical means which, in Weber's words, 'cannot be controlled by the intellect'.[155] In his discussion of primitive law, Weber uses the term rational, by way of contrast, to describe techniques of dispute resolution which *are* subject to intellectual control. Thus, in addition to meaning (1) rule-governed, (2) systematic and (3) based upon the logical interpretation of meaning, the term 'rational' also connotes, for Weber, (4) control by the intellect.

This last sense in which the term is used is, in some ways, the most obscure of the four. Weber does offer a few hints as to what he means – a procedural arrangement, for example, is said to be controllable by the intellect if 'logical or rational grounds'[156] are given for individual decisions, and if the procedure in question is 'regulated so as to aim at the relatively optimal chance of finding the truth'[157] – but these hints are never developed in a careful and systematic fashion. As a result, the import of Weber's assertion that primitive legal techniques are not controllable by the intellect remains unclear.

Despite its ambiguity, the meaning of the term 'rational' can usually be ascertained, in any given case, from the context in which Weber uses it. His terminological inconstancy nevertheless creates the impression that he has no, or at least not a well thought-out, concept of legal rationality and introduces a number of ambiguities into his fourfold division of the basic types of legal thought.

The basic types of legal thought

In the opening section of the *Rechtssoziologie*, Weber presents a typology of the basic forms of law-making and adjudication. It is unclear from the text whether he intended this scheme to be an exhaustive one covering every imaginable type of legal thought, or meant it to be merely a heuristic aid for the comparative analysis of certain legal institutions he considered particulary important. Whatever the intended scope of his typological scheme, the four categories of legal thought that Weber identifies are employed throughout the *Rechtssoziologie* and provide a conceptual framework for much of what he has to say. Indeed, it is his frequent and pointed use of these four categories that gives Weber's essay its apparent intellectual structure; without them, the connection between the different subjects treated in the *Rechtssoziologie* would be even more difficult to discern.

Weber's typology is based upon two distinctions, each of which contrasts a pair of seemingly opposite characteristics of legal thinking. The first contrasts those types of legal thought which are *rational* with those that are *irrational*; the second contrasts *formal* and *substantive* types of legal thinking. Taken together, these two distinctions yield a fourfold classification of law-making and adjudication.[158] The scheme in question can be represented by the following diagram:

	rational	irrational
substantive	substantively rational	substantively irrational
formal	formally rational	formally irrational

From the way in which he uses these four categories, it is relatively clear what qualities or characteristics of legal thinking Weber means to emphasize in each case. Consider, first, *formally irrational* adjudication, a type of legal thought that according to Weber is exemplified by primitive procedures for deciding disputes on the basis of oracular pronouncements. Law-making of this sort employs means that cannot be controlled by the intellect; it is this aspect of oracular adjudication that Weber means to emphasize by describing it as irrational. At the same time, oracular techniques for resolving disputes typically require meticulous observance, by the litigants or their representatives, of very detailed rules regarding the formulation of the question to be decided by the oracle. A failure to comply with these rules, in even the most trivial respect, usually nullifies the entire proceeding; the 'fundamental principle characteristic of all primitive procedure once it has become regulated by fixed rules' is that 'even the slightest error by one of the parties in his statement of the ceremonial formula will result in the loss of the remedy or even the entire case . . .'.[159] It is this aspect of oracular adjudication that Weber has in mind when he speaks of its formalistic character.

The clearest example of *substantively irrational* law-making is what Weber calls 'khadi-justice'[160] (after the judge presiding in a Moslem *sharihah* court) – adjudication of a purely *ad hoc* sort in which cases are decided on an individual basis and in accordance with an indiscriminate mixture of legal, ethical, emotional and political considerations. Weber offers, as examples, the justice dispensed by popular courts in Attic Greece and by the English justice of the peace.[161] Khadi-justice is irrational in the sense that it is peculiarly ruleless; it makes no effort to base decisions on general principles but seeks, instead, to decide each case on its own merits and in light of the unique considerations that distinguish it from every other case. The characterization of khadi-justice as a substantive form of law-making highlights another of its qualities, namely, its failure to distinguish in a principled fashion between legal and extra-legal (ethical or political) grounds for decision. It is the expansiveness of this form of adjudication – its willingness to take into account all sorts of considerations, non-legal as well as legal – which gives it its substantive character; the idea of a limited and self-contained 'legal' point of view is foreign to all true khadi-justice.

The third type of legal thought that Weber identifies – the *substantively rational* – is exemplified by certain priestly or theocratic legal systems and by what he calls 'the patriarchal system of justice'.

> A peculiar special type of rational, though not juristically formal, legal education is presented in its purest form in the legal teaching in seminaries for the priesthood or in law schools connected with such seminaries. Some of its peculiarities are due to the fact that the priestly approach to the law aims at material, rather than formal, rationalization of the law. . . . The legal teaching in such schools, which generally rests on either a sacred book or a sacred law fixed by a stable oral or literary tradition, possesses a rational character in a very special sense. Its rational character consists in its predilection for the construction of a purely theoretical casuistry oriented less to the practical needs of the groups concerned than to the needs of the uninhibited intellectualism of scholars. Where the 'dialectical' method is applied it may also create abstract concepts and thus approximate rational, systematic legal doctrine. But like all priestly wisdom, this type of legal education is bound by tradition. Its casuistry, inasmuch as it serves at all practical, rather than intellectual needs, is formal in the special sense that it must maintain, through re-interpretation, the practical applicability of the traditional, unchangeable norms to changing needs. But it is not formalistic in the sense that it would create a rational system of law. As a rule it also carries with it elements which represent only idealistic religious or ethical demands on human beings or on the legal order, but which involve no logical systematization of an actually obtaining legal order.[162]

Concerning the 'patriarchal system of justice' (law-making by a prince or other ruler aimed at the implementation of an ethically based 'welfare policy'), Weber remarks, rather cryptically, that although such a system 'can well be rational in the sense of adherence to fixed principles, it is not so in the sense of a logical rationality of its modes of thought but rather in the sense of the pursuit of substantive principles of social justice of political, welfare-utilitarian, or ethical content.'[163]

These passages are by no means free from obscurity; nevertheless, Weber's basic thought seems relatively clear. The types of law-making that he has in mind have two defining characteristics, and it is the combination or conjunction of these that distinguishes this type of legal thinking from the other three. First, both 'the priestly approach to law' and the 'patriarchal system of justice' refuse to recognize a boundary of any sort between law and ethics, but aim, instead, at the realization of certain ethical, political or religious ideals – in Weber's words, at a 'material, rather than formal, rationalization of the law'.[164] It is this characteristic which gives these types of law-making their substantive character and which distinguishes them from every type of legal thinking that acknowledges a difference between legal and extra-legal norms. The second characteristic of both priestly and patriarchal law-making, at least insofar as they aim at the construction of a doctrinal system of some kind (even if it is only a casuistical one), is their adherence to fixed principles. This characteristic distinguishes law-making of both sorts from all substantively irrational forms of adjudication (khadi-justice) and explains Weber's remarks that they are 'rational, though not juristically formal'.[165]

The modern civilian codes derived from Roman law and based upon the teachings of the Pandectists present the best example of *formally rational* legal thought, Weber's fourth basic type. In fact, according to Weber, only the modern code systems 'developed out of Roman Law' and 'produced through the legal science of the Pandectists' reflect, to any really significant extent, attitudes and methods of a formally rational sort. The uniquely high degree of formal rationality which these codes exhibit is to be explained by the fact that they are based upon 'the logical interpretation of meaning' and are highly systematic in nature, adhering to the following five 'postulates':

> first, that every concrete legal decision be the 'application' of an abstract legal pro-position to a concrete 'fact situation'; second, that it must be possible in every concrete case to derive the decision from abstract legal propositions by means of legal logic; third, that the law must actually or virtually constitute a 'gapless' system of legal propositions, or must, at least, be treated as if it were such a gapless system; fourth, that whatever cannot be 'construed' rationally in legal terms is also legally irrelevant; and fifth, that every social action of human beings must always be visualized as either an 'application' or 'execution' of legal propositions, or as an 'infringement' thereof, since the 'gaplessness' of the legal system must result in a gapless 'legal ordering' of all social conduct.[166]

In his description of the modern code systems inspired by the juris-prudence of the Pandectist school, Weber often uses the concepts of formal-ity and rationality interchangeably to refer to their systematic character, their rule-governedness, and to the fact that they have their 'point of departure in the logical analysis of meaning'.[167] He also, however, uses the notion of formality to describe another characteristic of these same legal systems – the extent to which they are based upon a principled 'separation of law from ethics' and constitute 'self-contained' legal orders.[168] In the many passages in the *Rechtssoziologie* dealing with formally rational legal thought, the concept of formality is used in all these various senses, some of which seem to be only another way of describing the same quality or characteristic of legal thinking that Weber elsewhere designates as its rationality. As we shall see in a moment, this confusing ambiguity in Weber's notion of formality is a by-product of the corresponding ambiguity in his concept of rationality.

It is fairly clear which features of his four main types of legal thought Weber means to emphasize by describing them in the way he does, and the differences he identifies are important ones. He nevertheless introduces considerable confusion into his scheme by using the distinction between rational and irrational types of legal thought, on the one hand, and formal and substantive types, on the other, to express different ideas in different contexts. Thus, for example, when he is describing formally irrational methods of adjudication, Weber most often employs the notion of rationality in its third and fourth senses and (by implication) in its second sense as well. When he characterizes these same techniques as formalistic, he is using the notion of formalism as a synonym for rationality in its first and most elementary sense – rationality as rule-governedness.[169] By contrast, when he is describing the difference between substantively rational and irrational types of law-making, Weber for the most part employs the concept of rationality in its first sense, to mean what the term 'formal' means in other contexts (although he does hint at a connection between this sense of rationality and the others that I have identified); and when he contrasts formally and substantively rational modes of legal thought, he uses the idea of formality to describe something other than mere rule-governedness, namely, what he calls the 'self-contained' nature of a legal system – its recognition of a principled distinction between legal and non-legal norms of an ethical or political sort. Again, Weber hints at a connection between this sense of formality and the other meaning he gives the term when he asserts that a legal order based upon substantive ethical or religious postulates will also tend toward formlessness in adjudication (khadi-justice). But why this should be so is never made entirely clear; Weber addresses the question explicitly only once, and although he offers an answer of sorts, it is one that leaves much to be desired in the way of precision and clarity.[170]

What is the source of the conceptual confusion in Weber's classification of the main types of legal thought? The confusion is, I believe, attributable to the fact that he attempts to draw three different sorts of distinctions between the various types of legal thinking that he describes, but uses only two pairs of contrasting qualities or characteristics to do so. At various points, Weber emphasizes: (1) the difference between those forms of law-making which are particularistic in the sense that adjudication is based on the unique factors of the individual case and those which, in one way or another, are governed by general rules or principles; (2) the difference between those legal systems that are based upon the logical interpretation of meaning and those which rest, instead, upon an 'adherence to external characteristics of the facts' and are, as a result, not subject to control by the intellect; and finally, (3) the difference between those legal orders which assume a principled distinction between legal and extra-legal norms and those that exhibit what Weber calls 'a featureless conglomeration of ethical and legal duties, moral exhortations and legal commandments . . .'.[171] When he calls khadi-justice substantively irrational, Weber is using the term irrational to mark a difference of the first sort. When he describes primitive law as formally irrational, however, he is using the same term to identify a difference of the second kind, and the concept of formality to describe a difference of the first sort; and when he contrasts formally and substantively rational types of legal thought, the concept of formality is meant to describe a difference of the third kind. The slippage in Weber's use of these two terms is the inevitable result of his effort to describe three distinct variables using only two linked pairs of descriptive terms. In order to account for all the differences in juristic thinking that he considers relevant, Weber must necessarily employ his basic analytic categories in an equivocal fashion.

Once the terminological ambiguities in his classificatory scheme have been exposed, it is natural to wonder what, if anything, the different meanings Weber assigns to the concept of legal rationality have in common. In the next three sections, I attempt to give a fuller account of the second, third and fourth senses of legal rationality identified earlier and to show that they are, in fact, importantly connected. In the concluding section of the chapter, I shall return to the problem of legal formality and attempt to show that here, too, the different senses in which Weber employs this concept are connected, although in a way that is not immediately obvious.

The irrationality of oracular adjudication

In a legal order in which 'recourse is had to oracles', the decision of cases rests ultimately with certain 'magical powers'. These powers must be addressed or invoked by means of a 'magically effective formula', even a slight deviation from which 'renders the whole transaction void'.[172] It is this feature of oracular adjudication that gives it its rigorously formal character.

> The presence of the magical element in the settlement of disputes and in the creation of new norms results in the rigorous *formalism* so peculiar of all primitive legal procedure. For, unless the relevant question has been stated in the formally correct manner, the magical technique cannot provide the right answer. Furthermore, questions of right or wrong cannot be settled by any magical method indiscriminately or arbitrarily selected; each legal problem has its own technique appropriate to it. We can now understand the fundamental principle characteristic of all primitive procedure once it has become regulated by fixed rules, viz., that even the slightest error by one of the parties in his statement of the ceremonial formula will result in the loss of the remedy or even the entire case . . . [173]

Oracular adjudication is formal because it is rule-bound. It is therefore rational in the first of the four senses identified earlier. At the same time it is irrational because, according to Weber, it relies upon a method for resolving disputes that is not 'subject to control by the intellect'. What does he mean by this?

The beginning of an answer is suggested by the contrast Weber draws, at several points, between a 'primitive system of magically bound proof', on the one hand, and procedural techniques that aim at what he calls 'the disclosure of the real truth' or at least at the 'relatively optimal chance of finding the truth', on the other.[174] Unlike adjudication by oracle, techniques of the latter sort require the parties to a lawsuit to resolve their dispute by proving the truth or falsity of certain propositions through the introduction of evidence and the testimony of witnesses. In the case of oracular adjudication, 'no proof [is] offered to show the allegation of a particular fact to be either "true" or "false". The issue [is] rather which party should be allowed or required to address to the magical powers the question of whether he was right and in which of the several ways this might or ought to be done.'[175] It is this aspect of oracular adjudication – its indifference to the factual basis of the parties' claims – that gives it its 'thoroughly irrational character'.

Weber's assertion that primitive law employs means which are not controllable by the intellect implies that its techniques are peculiarly ill-adapted to the task of disclosing or discovering the 'real truth'. It would be wrong to conclude, however, that oracular adjudication is indifferent to the truth, that it is unconcerned with what is 'actually' true so long as the appropriate magical technique has been executed in a 'formally correct manner'. Oracular adjudication is not a form of what has been called 'pure procedural justice',[176] a procedure for resolving disputes (like rolling dice to see who should go first in a game) whose results are fair by definition so long as they have been arrived at by following the procedure in question. When two litigants put their dispute before an oracle they are attempting to have the *truth* of their respective claims established. The magical procedure which they follow is – from their perspective – merely a means to this end. Weber does not claim that oracular adjudication is unconcerned with truth-finding, but only that it is a method which is ill-suited to this task, or rather which appears ill-suited from what he repeatedly characterizes as 'our' point of view.[177] If adjudication by oracle 'discloses the real truth', it does so, according to Weber, in an accidental and hence arbitrary fashion.

Oracular adjudication also appears arbitrary because of its relative unpredictability. To be sure, even an oracular procedure is predictable in certain respects. The parties to a particular dispute are likely to know, for example, which oracle to address and what procedure to follow in doing so. Certainty in these respects does not, however, enable them to predict the outcome of their contest – except in the unhelpfully general sense that each knows that the one who swears to a falsehood will lose.

According to Weber, the unpredictability of oracular adjudication is attributable to the fact that the oracle, or rather the 'magical power' which speaks through it, gives no reasons for its decisions. In this respect, a jury – which simply announces its verdict without offering a supporting justification – resembles an oracle.[178] Where disputes are resolved by an arbiter who gives reasons for his decisions, his past decisions provide a basis for predicting how he will decide disputes in the future. In the case of an oracle, past decisions, unsupported by reasons, provide only minimal guidance in predicting the outcome of future litigation. Even assuming that like cases will be treated alike, a judgment that is not accompanied by supporting reasons gives little information to the prospective litigant who wishes to know how his own case will be decided.

This helps us to understand the special assumptions that must be made in order to view oracular adjudication as a method for discerning the truth rather than a technique of pure procedural justice. The goal of every oracular procedure is to decide which litigant is in the right; this is achieved by putting the question to a divine power that presumably is able to determine which of them is telling the truth. Deciding cases in this way makes sense, however, only if there is a rational justification for the decision expressed in the oracular result, a justification which is known to the divine power that speaks through the oracle even though it is not given along with the decision itself. That such a justification exists and is known to the power responsible for the decision is an article of faith on which all oracular adjudication rests; but because the actual justification remains unstated, oracular methods for deciding disputes give the appearance of being groundless (unsupported by reasons) and hence arbitrary or irrational.

Two related considerations help to explain why oracular decisions are not accompanied by reasons. First, an adequate statement of the reasons supporting such a decision is likely to be too complex or subtle for human beings to grasp given their limited capacity for understanding. If this were not the case, there would be no need to put the question of the truthfulness of the parties' claims to a divine power in the first place. Though a god with superhuman wisdom and insight may appreciate the full complexity of a case and give every consideration its appropriate weight, it does not follow that he can explain his decision in a way that will make it intelligible to human beings with their finite powers of comprehension; if he cannot, an adequate statement of the reasons that justify the oracular outcome will be impossible. Second, even if an explanation of this sort could be understood by human beings, it would be unnecessary since there is no reason to doubt the wisdom or ethical propriety of the decision itself – the divine power responsible for the decision possesses a wisdom and beneficence greater than that of any human being.

These explanations are closely related and depend upon a common assumption: both assume that the power which speaks through the oracle is unlike us in some fundamental respect. Either his intelligence transcends our own, or his capacities for wisdom and goodness are greater than ours, or he exceeds us in all these respects. Whichever is the case, it is the essential incommensurability of the power that resolves the dispute and the litigants who stand before him which explains the absence of reason-giving in oracular adjudication.

A human being who resolves disputes can of course claim that he speaks for God or some other transcendent power.[179] In this case, there may be little pressure for him to give reasons for his decisions – he is in effect an oracle himself. But where this is not the case, where a human judge is prevented from claiming an oracular status for his own pronouncements, there is likely to be a demand that he produce reasons to support his decisions. Human beings are limited, and often err. The likelihood of detecting an error is increased if the potentially mistaken party exposes his reasoning process to public scrutiny. Thus, where human beings rather than oracular powers decide cases, there is a strong practical need for reason-giving. And since the mind of a human judge works in the same way as the minds of the litigants, it is fair to assume that he can frame a justification which will be intelligible to the disputants themselves. In this sense, an adjudicatory process in which human beings are responsible for deciding cases not only introduces a need for reason-giving – it makes reason-giving possible.

Reason-giving, and the increased predictability that accompanies it, may therefore be viewed as an important consequence of what Weber terms the 'disenchantment' of the law, the elimination from law-making and law-finding of all divine powers of adjudication and their replacement by human beings who claim no more for themselves than ordinary human powers of understanding amplified, at most, by professional expertise.[180] The establishment of a rational system of proof designed to promote the 'disclosure of the real truth' through the testimony of witnesses and the introduction of evidence should also be regarded as an aspect of this same process. According to Weber, the idea of a 'rational procedure' aimed at the adjudicative proof of facts can emerge only after the 'irrational powers' which control the course of oracular law-finding have lost their authority.[181] The distinctive feature of a rational proof procedure is that each party uses it to establish the truth of his claim by analysis and argument – instead of exposing himself to 'divine wrath' after having sworn a magically conditioned oath – and these are likely to be viewed as appropriate means for discovering the truth only if those participating in the process believe that the truth of a legal judgment is most convincingly demonstrated by displaying the reasons that support it. Predictability, reason-giving, the establishment of a system of rational proof and the disenchantment of the law – the transfer, so to speak, of judicial power from divine to human authorities – are related phenomena and it is not surprising that Weber emphasizes each in his account of the formal irrationality of oracular adjudication. Nor is it surprising that he attributes the irrationality of such procedures to the fact that they are not 'controllable by the intellect'. What Weber means is control by the human intellect, and for this kind of control to be possible, human beings must be responsible for the decision of cases in a way they cannot possibly be in any truly oracular regime. It is only with such responsibility that a need for reason-giving arises and only with reason-giving that predictability of a meaningful sort becomes possible.

Rationality and the logical interpretation of meaning

The juristic analysis of a fact or event always implicitly presupposes that only certain of its characteristics are, or can be, relevant from a legal point of view. Only 'those ultimate components [of the fact or event] which are regarded as relevant in the juristic valuation' possess legal meaning.[182] But while this is generally true of all legal analysis, there are two different ways in which the relevant characteristics of the facts may be identified or defined: either certain 'external' characteristics are isolated as the ones relevant for purposes of legal analysis, or, alternatively, 'the legally relevant characteristics of the facts [are] disclosed through the logical analysis of meaning.'[183] The latter approach 'substitutes attitude-evaluation as the significant element [of legal analysis] for assessment of events according to external criteria' and seeks 'to construct the relations of the parties to one another from the point of view of the "inner" kernel of their behaviour.'[184] Weber associated the first type of legal analysis with primitive law and the common law of England and the second with the civilian code systems of modern Europe. How is this distinction to be understood and what gives the latter form of legal thought its peculiar rationality?

According to Weber, primitive legal thought locates the juristic meaning of events in what he calls their 'external' or 'extrinsic' or 'tangible' characteristics, in those aspects of an occurrence which have a determinate physical presence and can therefore be sensed by human eyes and hands (a point he underscores by referring to attributes of this sort as 'sense-data' characteristics). From a primitive point of view, an event has the legal significance it does because it possesses certain external characteristics; these give the event juristic meaning not because they are thought to evidence or embody some other, intangible aspect of the situation – one which lacks a physical presence and thus cannot be directly apprehended by human sense organs – but because they are considered legally significant in their own right, because, in other words, they are regarded as having an intrinsic juristic meaning of their own. It is this belief in the inherent meaningfulness of 'concrete factual characteristics' which lies at the basis of all primitive legal thought.

The logical interpretation of meaning, a type of legal analysis which provides 'the point of departure' for the 'specifically modern form of systematization',[185] rests upon an entirely different premise. Unlike primitive legal thought, this method of defining the 'legally relevant characteristics of the facts' ascribes no inherent significance to external sense-data. Whatever juristic meaning observable events have from this point of view, they have because they are thought to express or reflect human purposes and intentions. The logical analysis of meaning is a method of juristic interpretation which rests upon the assumption that tangible sense-data acquire legal significance only by being related to purposive human attitudes. In a legal order based upon the logical analysis of meaning, external characteristics merely provide an evidentiary basis for asserting the existence of such attitudes; it is the latter which constitute the 'ultimate components' that give observable events their juristic significance. To be sure, purposes and intentions cannot be seen or felt directly: their existence must be established through the interpretation of sense-data which *are* directly apprehensible. These same sense-data acquire juristic significance, however, only by means of such an interpretation. In contrast to primitive legal thinking, the logical interpretation of meaning ascribes the juristic significance of events to human attitudes which are never fully reducible to the tangible characteristics that evidence them; it therefore necessarily denies what all primitive law assumes – the inherent meaningfulness of external sense-data.

The difference between these two types of legal thinking may be illustrated by comparing primitive and modern notions of liability for wrongdoing.

> The [primitive] procedure for obtaining composition either shows no trace at all or at most the mere beginnings of the distinction between felony that calls for vengeance, and tort that merely requires restitution. Furthermore, the absence of a distinction between actions for what we call 'civil' redress and criminal prosecution aiming at punishment, and the subsumption of both under the single category of atonement for wrong imparted, is connected with two peculiarities of primitive law and procedure. There is a complete unconcern with a notion of guilt, and, consequently, with the idea of degrees of guilt reflecting inner motivations and psychological attitudes. He who thirsts for vengeance is not interested in motives; he is concerned only with the objective happening of the event by which his desire for vengeance has been aroused. His anger expresses itself equally against inanimate objects, by which he has been unexpectedly hurt, against animals by which he has been unexpectedly injured, and against human beings who have harmed him unknowingly, negligently or intentionally.*

In the primitive law of obligations, it is 'the existence of a state of affairs objectively regarded as unlawful'[186] which gives rise to liability. Primitive law is primarily concerned with the deed (i.e. the fact of harm to the victim). If the deed has been done – whether intentionally or not – the doer is liable. There is no need to inquire into the doer's state of mind; once the 'objective' existence of the deed has been established, its legal consequences are fixed (typically through a stereotyped schedule of compensatory payments). Modern criminal law, by contrast, begins with the assumption that the legal meaning of an act can be determined only by locating the act within a framework of purposes or intentions. Before an actor's criminal liability can be

---

*ES, 647–48; LES, 51. Holmes's view is similar in some respects, although he stresses that criminal law and the law of torts, having 'started from a moral basis', are 'continually transmuting these moral standards into external or objective ones, from which the actual guilt of the party concerned is wholly eliminated.' *The Common Law* (Cambridge, Mass., 1963), p. 33. It would be a mistake, however, to think that the objective standards Holmes has in mind are indistinguishable from primitive standards of liability that emphasize the juristic significance of sense-data characteristics.

established, his deed, the *actus reus*, must be related to a mental state or intention. It makes no difference how the content of this mental state is defined; the important point is that our modern criminal law includes, in the description of nearly every crime, a reference to some intentional attitude or other. In this way, it 'substitutes attitude-evaluation as the significant element [of legal analysis] for assessment of events according to external criteria'.

The same can be said of the modern law of negotiable instruments, which might appear to be a remnant of primitive thinking in the modern legal order. As Weber himself observes, the extreme formalism of negotiable instruments law gives it an archaic appearance. Today, however, no one believes that the extrinsic characteristics of an instrument actually possess an inherent magical power of their own. We simply find it useful for a variety of reasons (including, most importantly, our desire to stimulate economic exchange by increasing the liquidity of obligations) to downplay the significance of intentions in determining an instrument's legal meaning. As Weber recognized, there is a tremendous difference between this attitude (which may be described as policy-oriented formalism) and any genuine ascription of magical power to extrinsic facts – of the sort, for example, which characterized the ancient formalities from which the modern law of negotiable instruments is in part derived.[187]

Although the phrase 'logical analysis of meaning' may suggest that Weber believed this type of legal thinking to be the only one concerned with the *meaning* of events or relationships, this is obviously not the case. According to Weber, primitive legal thought also seeks to specify the meaning of events. What distinguishes these two types of legal thinking is the different conception of juristic meaning on which each is based. Primitive legal thought finds inherent significance in the world of tangible sense-experience; the logical analysis of meaning, by contrast, assumes that a factual state of affairs acquires legal significance only by being related to a human purpose or intention.

Now we already know that Weber himself believed the latter conception of meaning to be the true one, and based his theory of sociological understanding on it. According to Weber, values do not inhere in facts and an individual cannot acquire his values by knowledge alone: he must create them, must legislate them into existence, by imposing his will on a morally neutral world. The normative significance of a factual occurrence can therefore never be equated with the sense-data characteristics of the occurrence itself – for the same reasons that a fact can never be a value.

This view, which represents Weber's own theory of value, is reflected in the type of legal thinking that rests upon what he calls the logical analysis of meaning and the special rationality he ascribes to this form of juristic analysis is his way of emphasizing the coincidence between it and the theory of value that he considered epistemologically correct. In this respect, the logical analysis of meaning occupies a position in Weber's typology of the forms of legal thought analogous to the position that legal-rational authority occupies in his theory of the three pure types of legitimate domination. Like legal-rational authority, the logical analysis of meaning assumes that sense-data characteristics have no inherent significance of their own, and embraces a conception of meaning based upon the principle of positivity; each, moreover, is explicitly contrasted with a form of analysis or principle of legitimation that conflates what they separate – facts and values, natural and authoritarian relations, sense-data characteristics and juristic valuations.

These considerations help us to see the connection between Weber's third sense of legal rationality, on the one hand, and his methodological views and theory of authority on the other. But what is the connection if any, between this sense of legal rationality and rationality understood as control by the intellect? Intellectual control of the legal order is impossible so long as decisions are not accompanied by reasons and the incentive to provide reasons becomes irresistably strong only when human beings take responsibility for the results of the adjudicatory process by assuming the position which in all oracular forms of law-making is occupied by a magical or divine power of some sort. This assumption of responsibility by human beings transforms the law from an inexplicable revelation of divine wisdom into an intelligible product of human manufacture: only when the law ceases to be considered the oracular pronouncement of a divine power and comes to be viewed, instead, as a product of deliberate human legislation, can the problems of its organization and content be regarded as ones that human beings are competent to solve. In a similar way, the logical analysis of meaning also places human beings at the centre of things by assuming that facts have legal significance only insofar as they are related to purposive human attitudes. This type of legal thinking belongs to the same general process of humanization or disenchantment that Weber associates with the attainment of intellectual control over the legal order itself. In each case, it is the self-conscious acknowledgement of human authorship that distinguishes rational from primitive law-making. The idea of disenchantment, an idea Weber uses to signify the assumption by human beings of powers previously reserved for the gods, provides a connecting link between his third and fourth senses of legal rationality. Ultimately, these are only different aspects of the same Copernican revolution in legal thought.

Rationality and the idea of a legal system

The conclusion that intellectual control and the logical interpretation of meaning are importantly related ideas appears inconsistent, however, with Weber's own discussion of the English common law. The common law system of adjudication based upon precedent requires the judge deciding a case to state the reasons for his decision in an accompanying opinion. Weber contrasts this method of adjudication with oracular law-making (although he also emphasizes the oracular character of jury verdicts and offers reasons to explain the continuing importance of the jury in the common law system as a whole). Because it is based upon reason-giving, common law adjudication tends to make the legal order more calculable; indeed, unless we assume that opinion writing and the rule of *stare decisis* increase the predictability of legal results in a meaningful way, it is difficult to explain the positive contribution made by the English legal system to the development in that country of a rational capitalist economy based upon market exchange, a form of economic organization which, according to Weber, demands the predictable application of a stable set of legal rules. To this extent, Weber seems to have viewed the common law as a rationalizing force whose distinguishing characteristics – reason-giving and the resulting increase in calculability – set it apart from all primitive, oracular forms of adjudication.

Weber also draws a contrast, however, between the common law method of legal reasoning, which he claims is based upon a 'merely paratactic association' of 'extrinsic elements', and the logical analysis of meaning characteristic of the modern Pandectist codes – by comparison with which the common law appears highly irrational. In England, according to Weber, 'legal practice did not aim at all at a rational system but rather at a practically useful scheme of contracts and actions, oriented towards the interests of clients in typically recurrent situations.'[188] The result, he claims

> was the emergence of what had been called in Roman law 'cautelary jurisprudence', as well as of such practical devices as procedural fictions which facilitated the disposition of new situations upon the pattern of previous instances. From such practices and attitudes no rational system of law could emerge, nor even a rationalization of the law as such, because the concepts thus formed are constructed in relation to concrete events of everyday life, are distinguished from each other by external criteria, and extended in their scope, as new needs arise, by means of the techniques just mentioned. They are not 'general concepts' which would be formed by abstraction from concreteness or by logical interpretation of meaning or by generalization and subsumption; nor were these concepts apt to be used in syllogistically applicable norms. In the purely empirical conduct of legal practice and legal training one always moves from the particular to the particular but never tries to move from the particular to general propositions in order to be able subsequently to deduce from them the norms for new particular cases. This reasoning is tied to the word, the word which is turned around and around, interpreted, and stretched in order to adapt it to varying needs, and, to the extent that one has to go beyond, recourse is had to 'analogies' or technical fictions.[189]

The type of irrationality that Weber has in mind is illustrated by the classical common law pleading system. Suppose that two businessmen enter into a new arrangement of some sort, whose legal effects are as yet unknown (because no one has ever asked what they might be). If this agreement collapses, and one of the parties involved sues the other, a question is bound to arise as to the juristic meaning of the arrangement they have devised. In the common law pleading system, at least during its formative period, this question could only be answered by accommodating the new event (the businessmen's arrangement) to the procedural framework established by the forms of action. For an event to be legally cognizable, it had to be brought within the compass of one or another of these procedural forms. And since each form of action was, in essence, a formula requiring the recitation of a standard or stereotyped set of facts, whenever it was necessary to determine the legal significance of a new event, the decisive question was always: what facts need to be alleged, in the pleadings, in order to bring the event in question within an established form of action? The question was *not*, what were the purposes and intentions of the parties?, but rather, what observable factual characteristics does this event possess that make it like or unlike other events for which a fixed legal meaning already exists? Thus, even if a common law judge were aware of the purposes which the arrangement in question was intended to serve, and wanted to help the parties (and others like them) accomplish their end, he would find himself prevented from doing so in a direct and explicit fashion by the requirement that he fit the arrangement into a system of procedural forms stereotyped on the basis of what Weber calls 'external criteria'. Consequently, even though common law judges (and lawyers) were especially concerned to make the law workable from a practical point of view, they had to do so covertly, through the use of fictions. Because of its emphasis on external characteristics as an ordering principle, the formulary system of common law pleading made it impossible to achieve this same end more directly through the logical analysis of meaning.

In sum, Weber's view of the English common law is a mixed one. At times, he emphasizes the rational features of the common law (for example, when he is contrasting the rule of *stare decisis* with truly oracular forms of adjudication); at other times, he emphasizes its irrational characteristics (primarily, the great importance attached in common law reasoning to external considerations and its consequent lack of systematic organization). It would thus appear, from Weber's own discussion of the common law, that a legal system may be calculable and in this sense subject to intellectual control but at the same time rest upon a type of analysis that he repeatedly characterizes as primitive and irrational. One might therefore conclude that Weber saw no close connection between the calculability of a legal order and its reliance on that type of legal thinking which has its 'point of departure' in the logical analysis of meaning. This conclusion would be mistaken, however, for Weber himself repeatedly asserts that these are related phenomena. To better understand the nature of the connection between them, it is important to see how both calculability and the logical analysis of meaning are related to a third idea, the idea of a legal system.[190]

Weber's idea of a legal system is based upon two related concepts – the concepts (as I shall call them) of comprehensiveness and organizational clarity. A legal order is *comprehensive* only if there are, in principle, no social actions beyond its reach – actions to which a legal meaning cannot be assigned – and if it contains no internal gaps or omissions. In a true legal system, 'every social action of human beings must always be visualized as either an "application" or "execution" of legal propositions, or as an "infringement" thereof, since the "gaplessness" of the legal system must result in a gapless "legal ordering" of all social conduct.'[191] A legal order has *organizational clarity* if the principles in accordance with which it has been constructed are themselves transparently clear and self-consciously applied.

In Weber's view, the more completely a legal order realizes the ideals of comprehensiveness and organizational clarity, the more calculable the consequences of every social action become (other things equal). As the range of occurrences that a legal order purports to cover narrows, as its internal gaps widen and become more numerous, as its own organizational principles become more difficult to discern, uncertainties regarding the application of the law to novel situations and inconsistencies in its application to familiar ones are bound to increase. Of course, as the English common law demonstrates, some calculability – perhaps even a significant degree – can be attained without the construction of a true legal system. Maximum calculability, however, cannot be achieved until the rules of the legal order have been arranged in a comprehensive and conceptually transparent fashion; no matter how great its calculability, a legal system can always be made more predictable by being systemized.

According to Weber, a genuine legal system can only emerge where legal thinking is based upon the logical analysis of meaning. The type of primitive legal thought that emphasizes tangible sense-data and treats them as juristically significant in their own right can never lead to a comprehensive and organizationally clear legal system, but at most, to a collection of particular rules and decisions connected in often ingenious but essentially external ways, lacking any inner unity of a conceptual sort (through what Weber calls 'casuistry' or 'cautelary jurisprudence'). There is, after all then, a connection between calculability and the logical analysis of meaning: the latter is the only type of legal thinking that leads, even potentially, to the systematic organization of the law and it is only through its systematization that the legal order can achieve a maximum degree of calculability.

A question remains, however: why does Weber assume that legal thinking based upon the logical analysis of meaning is a necessary condition for the construction of a legal system? His train of thought – never made explicit – would seem to be as follows. A collection of concrete rules and decisions, no matter how numerous, can never produce a comprehensive legal system. To achieve comprehensiveness, principles having a high degree of generality must be employed; only in this way can a legal order acquire the scope needed to cover all imaginable situations in a gapless fashion. These general principles are themselves the products of a process of abstraction or 'reduction', as Weber calls it; they are arrived at by reducing 'the reasons relevant in the decision of concrete individual cases to one or more "principles", i.e. legal propositions.'[192] Consequently, if a type of legal thought discourages abstraction, it must also impede the formulation of those general principles that a true legal system requires for its construction.

According to Weber, primitive forms of legal thinking that emphasize the importance of sense-data characteristics have anti-systematic consequences for exactly this reason. To see why this is so, it will be helpful to reflect, for a moment, on the nature of abstract thinking itself.[193] All abstract thought has what may be termed an imagistic or symbolic character. To use a famous example, if I am thinking about the properties of triangles in a general way – that is to say, if I am thinking about triangularity as an abstract concept – and I draw a triangle to help me puzzle through a particular problem, the actual triangle that I draw functions as an image or symbol of the abstract concept I wish to explore. I am not interested in the drawn triangle for its own sake, but only because its features may, for certain purposes, be taken to illustrate or represent what I am really interested in – the concept of triangularity, the properties which all triangles, and not merely the one that I have drawn, exhibit. The same is true, although not always in such an obvious way, of abstract reflection on non-mathematical subjects as well; indeed, it is a defining characteristic of all abstract thought that it treats concrete particulars as the representation, reflection, image or embodiment of something which they themselves are *not* – namely, an immaterial concept of one sort or another. Put differently, abstract thinking is not interested in concrete particulars for their own sake, but treats them, instead, as symbols or signs for something else, something that the mind's eye sees represented in or by what the body's eye physically apprehends.

Where this symbolizing attitude is absent, or where it is prevented from becoming self-conscious, abstract thought can develop only to a limited extent, if at all. This is precisely what happens when legal thought assigns juristic significance to events on the basis of their sense-data characteristics. As we have seen, this type of legal thinking treats the external, tangible aspects of an occurrence as if they had an inherent significance of their own. By its very nature, however, an image or symbol performs a representational function that cannot adequately be depicted as something wholly contained in the concrete object or event which happens to be functioning in a symbolic capacity. This is not to say that primitive legal thought is unsymbolic; throughout the *Rechtssoziologie*, Weber emphasizes the symbolism of primitive legal techniques and it would be impossible to imagine any type of legal thinking (or indeed any type of thought whatsoever) that was not symbolic to some extent. What is distinctive about primitive legal thought is that it denies the symbolic nature of its own intellectual processes by ascribing inherent meaning to sense-data characteristics; inevitably, therefore, these processes remain hidden from those who are engaged in them. In this sense, primitive legal thought, like traditional authority, is characterized by a kind of unself- consciousness. Just as authority structures based upon an appeal to tradition implicitly involve a creative positing of norms that is inconsistent with the conception of value on which such structures rest, so primitive legal thinking, insofar as it assigns any juristic meaning to the world at all, does so by means of a symbolic representation whose norm-creating role is implicitly denied by the assumption that external sense-data characteristics have an intrinsic legal significance of their own.

So long as legal thinking lacks self-consciousness in this sense, juristic analysis – no matter how subtle or detailed – is unlikely to result in the construction of a genuine legal system. Before law-makers can view its construction as their goal, the *idea* of such a system must first have occurred to them. But this idea is itself an abstraction of a very high order and is not likely to become a dominant and guiding concept in legal analysis until the logic of juristic abstraction, which must be exploited in a self-conscious fashion in order to create a true legal system, has itself been understood.

By discouraging the kind of abstract thinking required for the systematization of the law, the unself-consciousness characteristic of primitive legal thought inhibits the development of a legal order with greater overall calculability. A maximum of calculability can be achieved only where the law has been systematized by means of highly abstract rules generated through what Weber calls the 'logical generalization of abstract interpretations of meaning'.[194] Consequently, the 'growing logical sublimination [of the law] has meant everywhere the displacement of dependence on externally tangible formal characteristics by an increasingly logical interpretation of *meaning* in relation to the legal norms themselves as well as in relation to legal transactions.'[195]

There is, however, a tension between this form of legal thought and the very systematization it promotes. Because the logical interpretation of meaning (in contrast to all primitive, magical forms of legal analysis) seeks to give effect to the purposes and intentions of individual actors, it introduces an 'individualizing' factor into legal thinking which, according to Weber, cannot be 'defined with formal certainty'.[196] As an example, Weber cites the modern use of the concept of good faith in commercial law. The requirement that businessmen deal in good faith is imposed in order to give effect to 'the "real" intentions of the parties', to the attitudes and expectations of actors in the relevant commercial setting. However, because it involves considerations of 'an essentially factual nature', the good faith requirement cannot be translated into a set of abstract legal propositions; its application therefore necessarily involves some 'evaluation by the judge', which in turn encourages case-by-case adjudication, often on the basis of extra-legal (ethical or utilitarian) considerations – a result that tends to weaken the overall formality of the legal order.[197] Thus, although 'the rationalization of the law substitutes attitude-evaluation as the significant element [in legal analysis] for assessment of events according to external criteria', this form of legal thinking itself has certain anti-rationalistic consequences (understanding rational in its first sense to mean governed by general rules). The logical analysis of meaning is therefore both a necessary precondition of legal systematization and – to a degree – inevitably in conflict with it.

Legal formality and substantive justice

As we have seen, Weber uses the concept of formality to describe two different aspects of law and legal thinking. Sometimes he uses this concept to mean simply 'governed by general rules or principles'. At other times, he uses the concept of formality to describe a different property of legal systems – what might be termed their independence or self-containedness.

A legal order lacks formality, in this sense, if it does not recognize a distinct line between legal principles and non-legal ones. According to Weber, this is most likely to be the case where the entire legal order is geared toward the realization of certain political or ethical goals. To the law-makers in a legal order of this sort, 'the self-contained and specialized "juridical" treatment of legal questions is an alien idea, and they are not at all interested in any separation of law from ethics.'[198] Where no such separation exists, the law becomes a 'featureless conglomeration of ethical and legal duties', and ceases to be perceived as an independent or autonomous normative order.

Are these two senses of formality connected? Weber's own account of substantively rational (priestly or patrimonial) law-making seems to suggest that they are not, for legal analysis of this sort is both rule-governed and hence formal in the first sense, and yet strongly oriented toward extra-legal goals of a political or religious nature and thus non-formal in the second sense. Since it is possible for a legal order to combine these different properties, one might reasonably conclude that Weber's two senses of formality are only nominally connected. There are, however, several passages in the *Rechtssoziologie* which suggest that a legal order aimed at satisfying 'substantive demands of a political, ethical or affective character'[199] will also tend to favour the *ad hoc* decision of cases in a purely individualistic fashion; these passages hint at a more significant connection between the different characteristics described by the concept of formality. What is the nature of the connection?

The following passage contains Weber's most explicit answer to this question.

Formal justice guarantees the maximum freedom for the interested parties to represent their formal legal interests. But because of the unequal distribution of economic power, which the system of formal justice legalizes, this very freedom must time and again produce consequences which are contrary to the substantive postulates of religious ethics or of political expediency. Formal justice is thus repugnant to all authoritarian powers, theocratic as well as patriarchic, because it diminishes the dependency of the individual upon the grace and power of the authorities. . . . In all these cases, formal justice, due to its necessarily abstract character, infringes upon the ideals of substantive justice. It is precisely this abstract character which constitutes the decisive merit of formal justice to those who wield the economic power at any given time and who are therefore interested in its unhampered operation, but also to those who on ideological grounds attempt to break down authoritarian control or to restrain irrational mass emotions for the purpose of opening up individual opportunities and liberating capacities. To all these groups nonformal justice simply represents the likelihood of absolute arbitrariness and subjectivistic instability . . . . Above all, those in possession of economic power look upon a formal rational administration of justice as a guarantee of 'freedom', a value which is repudiated not only by theocratic or patriarchal-authoritarian groups but, under certain conditions, also by democratic groups. Formal justice and the 'freedom' which it guarantees are indeed rejected by all groups ideologically interested in substantive justice.[200]

In this dense and difficult passage, Weber appears to be saying the following. A legal order composed of general, abstract rules – a legal order that is formal in his first sense – can be either defended or criticized from an ethical point of view, depending upon the normative criterion one adopts. If one places a high value on the ability of individuals to control their own lives in a deliberate and planful way, and believes that their power to do so will be significantly increased if the consequences – in particular, the legal consequences – of their actions are known to them in advance, a legal system which promotes calculability is likely to seem preferable, on moral grounds, to one that does not. On this view, legal calculability has moral significance because, in Weber's words, it opens up individual opportunities and liberates capacities, that is, promotes self-determination and helps to 'guarantee' individual freedom.[201]

Of course, by increasing the freedom of individuals the law makes it easier for them to exploit whatever material resources or economic power they possess. A legal order that seeks to promote individual freedom by guaranteeing a maximum degree of calculability will therefore inevitably work to the advantage of those who possess economic power and to the disadvantage of those who do not – will, in other words, sharpen and stabilize existing disparities in the material well-being of different individuals and classes in society. However, if one places a very high value on individual freedom and legal calculability, these distributional consequences may be morally acceptable – especially to those who stand to gain as a result.

If one adopts a different normative perspective, however, calculability may well seem less important. Someone who believes, for example, that the only thing that matters from a moral point of view is whether an action increases the total amount of happiness in the world, or who thinks that the most significant moral issue facing any society is whether its resources have been distributed in a fair way, will, other things equal, be readier to sacrifice calculability where it interferes with the attainment of his desired goal than the person who values individual freedom and regards calculability as a means for achieving it. Put differently, if one attaches great importance either to realizing a particular conception of the good or to achieving a just distribution of resources and gives little weight to the protection of individual freedom – the right of individuals to determine for themselves which opportunities they shall exploit and who they shall become – the moral justification for enhancing the calculability of the legal order is significantly weakened. If individual freedom is thought to be of only slight importance from an ethical point of view, there is no obvious reason why *ad hoc* or particularistic forms of adjudication should be avoided where they can contribute to the achievement of one's ultimate normative goal.* Indeed, in Weber's view there is an 'inevitable conflict between an abstract formalism of legal certainty and the desire to realize substantive goals',[202] a conflict which explains the 'indifference or aversion to formalism' and the 'primacy

---

*This is one of the reasons for thinking that the only consistent form of utilitarianism is 'act-utilitarianism'. See D. Lyons, *The Forms and Limits of Utilitarianism* (Oxford, 1965).

of concrete ethical considerations' in priestly and patrimonial legal systems.[203] Because 'the rationality of ecclesiastical hierarchies as well as of patrimonial sovereigns is substantive in character', they do not seek to realize 'that highest degree of formal juridical precision which would maximize the chances for the correct prediction of legal consequences and for the rational systematization of law and procedure. The aim is rather to find a type of law which is most appropriate to the expediential and ethical goals of the authorities in question.'[204]

Throughout the *Rechtssoziologie*, Weber uses the term 'substantive' to describe forms of law-making whose fundamental aim is either to promote distributive justice or to realize a particular conception of the good. 'Juridical formalism', on the other hand, is described as a type of law-making that 'enables the legal system to operate like a technically rational machine'; by doing so, it guarantees 'to individuals and groups within the system a relative maximum of freedom, and greatly increases for them the possibility of predicting the legal consequences of their actions.'[205] As this last remark makes clear, the idea of a formal legal system has, for Weber, both a positive and negative meaning. Negatively understood, a formal legal system is one that eschews all ethical ideals based either upon a conception of the good or considerations of distributive justice; positively understood, a formal legal system is one that seeks to guarantee individual freedom – to open opportunities and liberate capacities – by maximizing the predictability of the legal order itself. Understood in the latter, positive sense Weber's concept of a self-contained legal order predicated upon a principled distinction between legal and extra-legal norms may itself be said to embody a commitment to a particular ethical ideal, the ideal of individual freedom, and thus to rest upon what he calls a 'substantive postulate'.[206] The difference between a substantive and formal legal system is not that one has an ethical orientation of some sort and the other none at all; the distinction between them is to be explained, instead, by a difference in their basic normative premises, the first seeking to realize some conception of the good or scheme of distributive justice and the second a 'relative maximum' of individual freedom.

When this difference in normative orientation is taken into account, it is easier to see why Weber believed that substantive types of law-making are likely to have anti-formalistic consequences, and why he also thought that a self-contained legal order tends to discourage particularism in adjudication (khadi-justice). The two meanings he gives to the concept of legal formality are indeed connected. Like the related concept of legal rationality, this one, too, has greater coherence than Weber's own text, with its terminological ambiguities, might suggest.

5

The forms of contractual association

According to Weber, 'the most essential feature of modern substantive law, especially private law, is the greatly increased significance of legal transactions, particularly contracts, as a source of claims guaranteed by legal coercion. So very characteristic is this feature of private law that one can *a fortiori* designate the contemporary type of society, to the extent that private law obtains, as a "contractual" one.'[207] Weber's characterization of the modern legal order as distinctively contractual echoes the similar claim of other writers including Durkheim, Marx and Maine.[208] Moreover, like each of these other three, Weber associated the growing importance of contracts as a source of legal rights with the expansion of the market as a form of economic organization. There is, he asserts, 'an intimate connection between the expansion of the market and the expanding measure of contractual freedom or, in other words, the scope of arrangements which are guaranteed as valid by the legal order or, in again different terms, the relative significance within the total legal order of those rules which authorize such transactional dispositions.'[209] By contrast, 'in an economy where self-sufficiency prevails and exchange is lacking, the function of the law will naturally be otherwise: it will mainly define and delimit a person's non-economic relations and privileges with regard to other persons in accordance, not with economic considerations, but with the person's origin, education, or social status.'[210]

More of the *Rechtssoziologie* is devoted to the subject of contractual association than to any other single topic. However, this part of the essay is unusually dense, filled with historical detail and concerned, in large part, with extremely technical problems (including, for example, the development of the institution of the notary, the history of the law of negotiable instruments, the legal status of associations in Roman and English law, the effect of contractual agreements on the rights of third parties and the relative freedom of testation under different legal regimes, both ancient and modern). The variety and technicality of the problems that Weber addresses in his discussion of contract law obscure his main ideas on the subject and make it difficult to see the relationship between this and other aspects of the *Rechtssoziologie*.

In this chapter, I examine Weber's account of the forms of contractual association and attempt to show that its principal themes are related, in important ways, both to his theory of authority and his concept of legal rationality. Weber's analysis of contractual association is based upon a distinction between what he terms 'status' and 'purposive' contracts. It is the latter type, he claims, that predominates today and the former that was most prevalent in pre-modern legal systems. The main aim of the present chapter is to explicate this distinction.

Contractual association and modern society

In the most elementary sense, a contract is an agreement between two or more individuals that creates legally enforceable rights and duties for the individuals involved (and sometimes, as Weber emphasizes, for third parties as well). The entitlements that a contract establishes do not exist before the contract is made; in this sense, a contract 'creates law for the parties' and represents, in a phrase that Weber quotes with approval, a 'decentralization of the law-making process'.[211]

Generally speaking, freedom of contract may be said to exist 'exactly to the extent to which' the legal order 'grants to an individual autonomy to regulate his relations with others by his own transactions';[212] the wider the range of relationships subject to autonomous control by the individuals involved, the greater the freedom of contract they enjoy. This suggests what might be called a quantitative interpretation of Weber's remarks concerning the contractual character of modern society. It is appropriate to describe modern society in this way, one might argue, because an individual's social relationships are today more broadly subject to his own autonomous regulation than in any earlier period.

In no legal order, however, is freedom of contract 'unlimited in the sense that the law would place its guaranty of coercion at the disposal of all and every agreement regardless of its terms.'[213] Only some agreements will be contracts, and 'a legal order can indeed be characterized by the agreements which it does or does not enforce.'[214] Consistently with this last remark, Weber associates the contractual character of modern society not with a generalized expansion of freedom of contract in all areas of life but with its growth in one particular sphere, that of economic exchange. 'The present-day significance of contract', he claims, 'is primarily the result of the high degree to which our economic system is market-oriented and of the role played by money. The increased importance of the private law contract in general is thus the legal reflex of the market orientation of our society.'[215] By the same token, some aspects of an individual's social life that in the past were subject to contractual regulation are no longer so. 'Freedom of contract once existed in spheres in which it is no longer prevalent or in which it is far less prevalent than it used to be.'[216] In short, modern law is not characterized by an unambiguous expansion of freedom of contract, but by its expansion in some respects and retraction in others.

The simple, quantitative assertion that greater freedom of contract exists today than in the past fails to express the important qualitative difference between the type of contractual association that predominates in the modern legal order and those that have been known in the past but are no longer legally recognized. To see what gives modern private law its distinctive character, we must therefore examine more closely the peculiar nature of the market-oriented exchange contract that Weber considered the paradigmatic form of contractual association in contemporary society.

Weber associates modern contract law with the process of economic exchange and the growth of the market, and asserts that 'in an economy where self-sufficiency prevails and exchange is lacking, the function of the law will naturally be otherwise.' This functional difference is to be explained by the nature of the household as a form of economic organization. According to Weber, the household is oriented toward want-satisfaction and rests upon attitudes that he characterizes as communistic. A household is both a producer and consumer of goods and insofar as it aims at self-sufficiency, it seeks to coordinate its own productive and consumptive activities, producing for itself all that its own members require.[217] To the extent this ideal cannot be realized, economic exchange with outsiders becomes necessary, as does production of the surplus required to finance such exchange. And where they go beyond simple barter, economic relations with outsiders in turn necessitate agreements of some sort – exchange contracts of a more or less formal nature. Within the household, economic relations between individual members – those governing the division of productive tasks as well as the distribution of goods – are not established through formal agreement; they derive, instead, from a traditionally stereotyped pattern of claims and obligations that is determined, in large part, by the relative neediness of particular individuals. In a society in which most economic activities are carried on within households that are largely self-sufficient, formal exchange with outsiders is likely to be a peripheral and episodic phenomenon and as a result there will be little pressure for the development of a set of legal rules designed to regulate such exchanges, i.e. a law of contracts.

Contract law begins where the household ends and has its foundation in the ancient 'dualism of legal relations within the kinship group and between different kinship groups'.[218] Only in interactions between individuals who are not members of the same sib or household community are formal rules and adjudicative procedures required; within the group, disputes are decided by means of informal patriarchal arbitration. When the number and frequency of such interactions increase, as they are bound to in an exchange economy where the goods individuals consume are for the most part produced by strangers, a law of contracts becomes indispensible. The importance of contract law in modern society thus reflects the demise of the self-sufficient household as the basic form of economic organization and its replacement by what Weber calls 'the market community', a community that represents 'the most impersonal relationship of practical life into which humans can enter with one another', and which is therefore 'an abomination to every system of fraternal ethics'.[219]

This contrast between the contractual form of association characteristic of

the market community and the non-contractual fraternal relationships existing within the household is reinforced by another observation that Weber
makes regarding the increased importance of contracts as a source of rights
in modern society.

> From the legal point of view, the juridico-economic position of the individual,
> i.e., the totality of his legitimately acquired rights and valid obligations, is
> determined on the one hand by *inheritance* based upon a legally recognized family
> relationship, and, on the other hand, by contracts concluded by him or for him in
> his name. The law of inheritance constitutes in contemporary society the most
> important survival of that mode of acquisition of legitimate rights which was
> once, especially in the economic sphere, the exclusive or almost exclusive one. In
> the case of inheritance the operative facts generally occur independently of the
> interested individual's own conduct. These facts constitute the starting-point for
> his further legally relevant activities; a person's membership in such a group as a
> given family is based upon a natural relationship, which is socially and
> economically regarded as a special and intrinsic quality and is attributed to him by
> the law independently of his own acts of consocation.[220]

In pre-modern societies, an individual's legal rights were largely determined
by his family membership and hence by a natural quality or attribute belonging to him 'independently of his own acts of consocation'. By contrast, the
rights an individual acquires through his contractual associations with
others are attributable to his own choices: he creates these rights for himself
rather than inheriting them by virtue of his birth into a particular natural
community. As we have seen, the distinction between naturally acquired
and deliberately created characteristics is critical to understanding Weber's
concept of personal domination and to explaining the difference between
traditional and legal-rational authority. His remarks concerning the
distinction between contract and inheritance as modes of acquiring legal
rights thus establish a first link between Weber's theory of contractual
association, on the one hand, and his analysis of the three pure types of
authority on the other.

Having described the importance of contractual agreement as a source of
rights in modern private law, Weber observes that in public law as well 'the
role of contractual transactions is, quantitatively at any rate, by no means
slight.'[221] Today, for example, 'every appointment of an official is made by
contract and some important phenomena of constitutional government,
especially the determinations of the budget, presuppose in substance, if not
formally, a free agreement among a number of independent organs of the
state, none of which can legally coerce the other'.[222] Weber qualifies these
observations by adding that 'in the legal sense, the public official's legally
fixed obligations are not regarded as flowing from a contract of appointment,
as would happen in the case of a freely made contract of private law, but from
his act of submission to the authority of the state as a public servant',[223] and
by noting that even though it may look like a contract, the agreement that
precedes the adoption of a budget in a constitutional regime is really not a
contract from a technical legal point of view. Despite these qualifications,

however, Weber insists that the idea of contractual obligation plays a larger role in modern public law than it has in the past. 'This conception', he asserts, 'has historically not always been the prevailing one and it would not accurately describe political organizations in the past. Formerly the position of a public official was less based upon a free contract than it is today . . . [but] rested rather upon his entire submission to the personal, quasi-familial, authority of a lord.'* Here, too, Weber contrasts contractual obligation established by voluntary agreement with a type of obligation based either upon the natural relations of the household or certain quasi-natural relationships patterned after them. The importance of the idea of contractual obligation in modern public law thus also marks the decreasing significance of family relationships – relationships 'socially and economically regarded as a special and intrinsic quality and . . . attributed to [the individual] by the law independently of his own acts of consocation' – as a basis for determining his legal entitlements. The remarks that Weber makes in an effort to explain his characterization of the 'contemporary type of society' as a peculiarly contractual one all point to a single, fundamental distinction – the distinction between the artificial relationship that is deliberately created by a contract and the natural or quasi-natural relationships that exist between the members of the same household or kinship group. This same distinction is reflected in the differences between what he calls 'status' and 'purposive' contracts. These represent two entirely different forms of contractual association, and the passage in which Weber describes their contrasting characteristics is one of the most important in the *Rechtssoziologie* as a whole.

Status and purposive contracts

According to Weber, ' "contract" in the sense of a voluntary agreement constituting the legal foundation of claims and obligations, has . . . been widely diffused even in the earliest periods of legal history', and can often 'be found in spheres of law in which the significance of voluntary agreement has either disappeared altogether or has greatly diminished, i.e. in public law, procedural law, family law, and the law of decedents' estates.'[224] The 'contracts propagated by [our contemporary] market society', however, are completely different from those 'which in the spheres of public and family law once played a greater role than they do today.'[225] Indeed, modern contract law reflects a 'fundamental transformation of the general character of the voluntary agreement' as a source of legal rights.[226] Weber uses the term 'status contract' to describe 'the more primitive type' of contractual association and contrasts this type with the so-called 'purposive contract'

ES, 670; *LES*, 103. One important exception to this is the 'feudal bond' which according to Weber was 'in its innermost essence based upon contract.' For a discussion of the contractual character of fedual obligation, see M. Bloch, *Feudal Society* (trans. L.A. Manyon, Chicago, 1964) Chapters 32 and 33.

which he considered 'peculiar to the exchange or market economy'. The distinction between these two types

is based on the fact that all those primitive contracts by which political or other personal associations, permanent or temporary, or family relations are created involve a change in what may be called the total legal situation (the universal position) and the social status of the persons involved. To have this effect these contracts were originally either straightforward magical acts or at least acts having a magical significance. For a long time their symbolism retained traces of that character, and the majority of these contracts are 'fraternization contracts'. By means of such a contract a person was to become somebody's child, father, wife, brother, master, slave, kin, comrade-in-arms, protector, client, follower, vassal, subject, friend, or quite generally, comrade. To 'fraternize' with another person did not, however, mean that a certain performance of the contract, contributing to the attainment of some specific object, was reciprocally guaranteed or expected. Nor did it mean merely that the making of a promise to another would, as we might put it, have ushered in a new orientation in the relationship between the parties. The contract rather meant that the person would 'become' something different in quality (or status) from the quality that he possessed before. For unless a person voluntarily assumed that new quality, his future conduct in his new role could hardly be believed to be possible at all. Each party must thus make a new 'soul' enter his body. At a rather late stage the symbolism required the mixing and imbibing of blood or spittle or the creation of a new soul by some animistic process or by some other magical rite. . . .

The agreements of fraternization as well as other forms of status contract were oriented toward the total social status of the individual and his integration into an association comprehending his total personality. This form of contract with its all-inclusive rights and duties and the special attitudinal qualities based thereon thus appears in contrast to the money contract, which, as a specific, quantitatively delimited, qualityless, abstract, and usually economically conditioned agreement, represents the archetype of the purposive contract. As a non-ethical purposive contract the money contract was the appropriate means for the elimination of the magical and sacramental elements from legal transactions and for the secularization of the law.[227]

In this passage, Weber draws three related distinctions between status and purposive contracts. First, a status contract effects a total change in the personalities of the individuals involved, an 'all-inclusive' change in the 'universal position' of the parties, as a result of which each acquires a new soul and becomes another person. By contrast, a purposive contract merely establishes 'a new orientation' in the parties' relationship; it does not involve a change in their 'total legal situation'. Unlike status contracts, which have as their object the creation of an 'all-inclusive fraternal relationship', purposive contracts are 'delimited' in the sense that they 'neither [affect] the status of the parties nor [give] rise to new qualities of comradeship but [aim] solely . . . at some specific (especially economic) performance or result.'

Second, status contracts are contracts of fraternization: they seek to establish a relationship of brotherhood or comradeship between the individuals involved. As the term fraternization implies, relationships of this sort are quasi-familial; they are patterned after and take as their model some natural relationship existing between the members of a household. Status contracts may therefore be said to have their foundation in the household community. A purposive contract, on the other hand, does not require the establishment of a fraternal bond between the parties (who are, and remain, strangers). 'In sharp contrast to all other groups which always presuppose some measure of personal fraternization or even blood kinship, the market is fundamentally alien to any type of fraternal relationship.'[228] Thus, 'where the market is allowed to follow its own autonomous tendencies', individuals engaged in market relationships 'do not look toward the persons of each other but only toward the commodity; there are no obligations of brotherliness or reverence, and none of those spontaneous human relations that are sustained by personal unions. They all would just obstruct the free development of the bare market relationship, and its specific interests serve, in their turn, to weaken the sentiments on which these obstructions rest.'[229] The 'bare' or 'abstract' market-oriented exchange contract is not modelled, even fictively, on the blood relationships that exist between members of a household community; it thus stands in the sharpest possible contrast to all status contracts whose fundamental aim is to establish a real or imaginary bond of the latter sort.

Third, it is characteristic of status contracts that they are effected by magical or supernatural means. According to Weber, 'one whose thinking is embedded in magic cannot imagine any other than a magical guaranty for the parties to conform, in their total behaviour, to the intention of the "fraternization" they contracted.'[230] Even after primitive animistic conceptions have died away, it is still thought necessary 'to place each party [to a status contract] under the dominion of a supernatural power, which power constitutes not only their collective protection but also jointly and severally threatens them in case of anti-fraternal conduct.'[231] This explains why the oath, 'which originally appears as a person's conditional self-surrender to evil magical forces [and] subsequently assumes the character of a conditional self-curse, calling for the divine wrath to strike . . . remains even in later times one of the most universal forms of all fraternization pacts.'[232] By contrast, the market-oriented money contract – the 'archetype' of all purposive contracts – has been an important factor in the *elimination* of 'magical and sacramental elements' from the law. Unlike status contracts, which 'were originally either straightforward magical acts or at least acts having a magical significance', purposive contracts are self-consciously anti-magical and wherever they have gained recognition have tended to accelerate the disenchantment of the legal order.

In summary, status contracts effect a total qualitative transformation in the identities of the individuals involved, seek to establish a familial or quasi-familial relationship between them, and use magical means to do so. Purposive contracts, by contrast, do not fundamentally transform the parties' legal personalities, are non-fraternal in character, and do not require magical acts or the use of magical symbols. Weber obviously considered these three pairs of contrasting characteristics to be connected in some way. To understand the connection between them, it will be helpful to examine more closely the first of the three distinctions he draws – the distinction between an all-encompassing change in the 'total legal situation' or 'universal position' of an individual and the mere addition of a 'new dimension' to the pre-existing set of rights and obligations that constitute his legal personality.

According to Weber, an individual who enters into a contract of fraternization acquires, as a result, a new quality or 'status', the status, for example, of brother, master, slave, client, vassal, lord or comrade. It is characteristic of all such contracts that the acquisition of this new quality marks a fundamental alteration in what Weber calls the 'total [legal] personality' of the individual involved: in acquiring this new status, the contracting party quite literally becomes a new person. Now for it to be possible that a status contract alter someone's 'total legal situation' in this way, it is necessary that the parties to the contract equate the possession of the quality created by it with their legal personality – their recognition by others as the bearers of specific rights and obligations. Indeed, the equation must be so complete that they cannot conceive of their having such a personality apart from or independently of the quality in question. If the parties to a fraternization contract thought of themselves as having a legal identity of some sort apart from the status or quality created by the contract itself, the acquisition of the quality could only modify, but not totally alter, their legal situation. A total alteration requires that no distinction be drawn between the person who enters a status contract and the special quality he acquires by doing so. Put differently, the parties to a contract of fraternization must assume that the bond created by the contract exhaustively determines who they are and what sorts of legally recognized relationships they may and ought to have with others. What is missing, necessarily, in every status contract is the idea of an individual – or more precisely, a legal person – who exists independently of the status created by the contract, for whom the relationship is merely an attribute (with specific legal consequences, to be sure) that can be added or subtracted without fundamentally altering his juridical identity.

It is precisely this latter idea which underlies the 'specific, quantitatively delimited, qualityless, abstract, and usually economically conditioned agreement [that] represents the archetype of the purposive contract.' By entering such a contract, an individual acquires a new set of rights and obligations or, as Weber puts it, a 'new orientation' in his relationship with the other party. He does not, however, acquire a new 'soul' or become an entirely different person as a result. This implies that the individual who enters a purposive contract has an unchanging 'core' identity of some sort, an identity that is independent of the contract itself, that antedates it and survives its destruction.

What does this unchanging core identity consist in? Although he does not answer this question directly, Weber's discussion of the difference between purposive and status contracts suggests the following view. An individual enters a purposive contract for a particular reason or purpose, for example, in order to obtain the money or material goods he requires to satisfy certain needs. Each individual has many different ends or aims, however, not all of which are served by any particular contract. To pursue them all, he must make a number of arrangements with different individuals. As a result, he finds himself at the centre of a web of contractual associations. Who precisely is it that stands at the centre of this web? Since he is not identified, from a legal point of view, with any one of these contracts, but has a legal personality that includes them all (in the sense that each contributes to the sum of his rights and obligations), it is tempting to equate the identity of the individual who happens to be a party to all of these contracts with the series of relationships created by the contracts themselves. But this equation is misleading; since the individual in question can always enter an additional contract without acquiring a wholly new identity, his legal personality at any given moment in time cannot simply be the sum of the contractual relationships he has created for himself but must transcend – be irreducible to – any possible series of such relationships no matter how extensive.

As I have already indicated, each of these relationships is the expression of a particular aim or purpose. To conceive of an individual as a legal person whose identity transcends the sum of his *expressed* purposes we must think of him as having – or, more accurately, as being – a *capacity* for purposive action which his concrete aim-regarding interactions (and, in particular, his contractual relations) with other individuals actualize but never exhaust. The person who stands behind every purposive contract and whose basic identity is unchanged by the contractual relationships he enters must therefore be thought of as a bare power or capacity, the capacity for purposeful action itself. It is this capacity, viewed abstractly, which constitutes the core of his legal personality.

This same point can be expressed in a different way. Weber believed that an action acquires meaning only by being brought into relation with a purpose or intention, and thought that human beings alone have the power to frame purposes and thus to act in a meaningful way. This power or ability – the ability to represent, in advance, the idea of an activity's end and to regulate one's conduct on the basis of such an idea – is identified, in Weber's methodological writings, with the will, the creative power of choice that is exercised in every value judgment and normative commitment an individual makes. A purposive contract may therefore be described as a voluntary association between two or more individual wills. Viewed in the abstract as bare wills, the parties to such an agreement possess an identity that is unaffected by the contract itself; although the agreement creates additional rights and duties for the individuals involved, it does not alter in any way their basic status (using that term in a broader sense than Weber does) as right-bearing persons or wills. By contrast, a contract of fraternization wholly transforms the identities of the parties and makes them into different kinds of persons. As I have noted, for this to be possible, the parties to such a contract must view their own identities as something indistinguishable from the qualities of comradeship created by the agreement. This assumes that they do not regard themselves as bare or abstract wills, for if they did, the mere acquisition of a new quality or status could never transform their total legal situation. The conception of a person as a locus of aims and intentions endowed with a capacity for purposeful action – a will – that underlies but is never exhausted by the concrete choices he actually makes is a conception alien to all contracts of fraternization. Contracts of this sort presuppose a different conception of what it means to be a person, a conception that may be called naturalistic insofar as it treats an individual's possession of some natural or quasi-natural characteristic as the only conceivable basis for ascribing to him an identifiable legal personality.

This helps to explain the second difference between status and purposive contracts emphasized by Weber – that one aims to create a relationship mimicking or reproducing the bond between brothers, while the other rejects all norms of brotherliness and is 'fundamentally alien to any type of fraternal relationship'. Obviously, mere agreement cannot create a biological relationship where none existed before. To this extent, every contract of fraternization that purports to establish an artificial brotherhood between individuals who are not related by blood necessarily rests upon a fiction. The fiction is an important one, however, since it reveals the normative premise underlying all agreements of this sort. If the parties to a fraternization contract deliberately conform their own relationship to the one that exists between brothers, it must be because they believe the latter relationship to be endowed with special normative significance and think that by assimilating themselves to it they can give their own association a similar meaning and importance. The most striking thing about a contract of fraternization is not that it creates an artificial relationship – both status and purposive contracts do this – but that it seeks to legitimate the community or association it establishes by patterning it after a natural relationship of some sort.

Contracts of fraternization thus rest upon a principle of legitimation identical to the one that underlies the authority claims of a patriarchal master. The patriarch's right to command is legitimated by the position he occupies in his household community, a position defined by certain unalterable natural characteristics (age and sex). The relationship between a patriarch and the subordinate members of his household, to the extent it constitutes an authoritarian relationship in Weber's sense, is premised upon the belief, shared by both ruler and ruled, that the natural characteristics which define the positions of each have an inherent normative significance of their own – a belief that implicitly identifies *is* and *ought*. The fact that all status contracts seek to create a normatively binding relationship between two or more individuals by assimilating their association (even if only symbolically) to the truly natural bond between biological kinsmen indicates that a similar identification of the normatively significant with the naturally given prevails here as well.

As a result, all contracts of fraternization are marked by a characteristic tension. Although contracts of this sort create artificial relationships, their artificiality must be ignored or disguised since it is the likeness of these relationships to a natural bond of some sort which gives them normative significance in the eyes of the participants and makes them a source of rights and obligations. Put differently, every status contract establishes a relationship whose normative force is ascribed to the fact it mimics one that cannot be established by mere agreement. The legitimating principle on which status contracts rests thus requires that their own artificiality be suppressed. In an important sense, a contract of fraternization is an agreement that the parties themselves are not permitted to recognize as such. For this reason, all such agreements necessarily exhibit the same lack of self-consciousness displayed by traditional forms of domination and by that primitive type of legal thinking which attributes inherent juristic significance to what Weber calls sense-data characteristics.

In a parallel fashion, purposive contracts and legal-rational authority also share a common normative foundation. A purposive contract binds the parties because they have agreed to its terms and have expressed their consensual arrangement in whatever form the law requires. Like the rules administered by the officers of a legal-rational organization, their private arrangement derives its binding force from the mere fact that it has been intentionally established through a specified process or procedure. In both cases, it is the idea of voluntary enactment that ultimately justifies the exercise of power by one person over another – whether it be a bureaucratic officer issuing an order to someone subject to his jurisdiction or a private individual seeking to enforce the terms of an agreement against the person with whom he has contracted. The legitimacy of the bureaucrat's rule derives from the fact that the norms he applies have been deliberately established, and his claim to authority can therefore be justified only by appealing to the same positivistic principle of legitimation that must ultimately be invoked to explain why the parties to a purposive contract are obligated to respect its terms.

The third feature of status contracts that Weber emphasizes is their magical quality. As an example of the magical processes employed to create a fraternal bond between the parties to such a contract, Weber mentions the ritual 'mixing of blood and spittle', a technique still used at a relatively late stage of legal development to enable each of the individuals involved to acquire a new soul and thus 'become something different in quality (or status)' from what he was before. What gives such techniques their 'magical' character? In the preceding chapter, we saw that Weber contrasts two basic types of legal thinking: one attributes inherent significance to what he calls 'sense-data characteristics' and the other ascribes a juristic meaning to these same characteristics only insofar as they manifest the purposive attitudes of one or more human actors. At several points, Weber describes the first type of legal thinking as 'magical', meaning that it is based upon a belief that certain factual states of affairs have an intrinsic normative significance of their own. Contracts of fraternization are magical in exactly this sense. For such a contract to alter the 'total legal situation' of those involved, their legal personality must be completely absorbed in the new quality created by the contract. The idea of a person who stands apart from the quality and has a legally cognizable personality independent of it is, as I have said, alien to all contracts of fraternization. Consequently, the legal meaning of the quality – its significance as a source of rights and duties – cannot be explained on the ground that it evidences the intentions of the parties, for this would require us to imagine them having an identity that antedates the contract and is unaffected by it. From the point of view of the parties to the contract, the quality must be regarded as having an inherent significance of its own, so that its mere possession determines an individual's legal position even when he has acquired it through artificial means. To call such contracts magical is only another way of describing the basic conflation of facts and values on which this form of contractual association is based.

In sharp contrast, Weber describes the purposive exchange contract as 'the appropriate means for the elimination of the magical and sacramental elements from legal transactions and for the secularization of the law', and he characterizes this type of contractual association as a rationalizing force contributing to the dissolution of those 'sacred, status, and merely traditional bonds'[233] that historically have restricted the development of a universal and impersonal market for the exchange of goods. From a legal point of view, the purposive exchange contract is the product of a peculiarly rational type of juristic analysis. By entering such a contract, the parties seek to create a set of special norms to regulate their dealings with one another – norms that may be viewed as supplementing whatever residual legal obligations they would have in the absence of their contractual relationship. The only justification for enforcing such a contract is that the parties' agreement expresses their intention to do something which the law permits them to do if they wish. In this sense, the 'new orientation' created by the contract has no intrinsic legal meaning of its own; its juristic significance derives entirely from the intentions and purposes of the parties. Thus, unlike contracts of fraternization, purposive contracts are based upon a method of juristic analysis that has its point of departure in the logical interpretation of meaning; they are rational in the same sense, exhibit a similar self-consciousness (in contrast to all primitive or magical forms of legal thinking), and contribute, for the same reasons, to an increase in the overall calculability of the legal order.

In summary, contracts of fraternization rest upon the same principle of legitimation as the authority of the patriarchal master and reflect a type of legal thinking that is rooted in the belief that 'the legally relevant characteristics [of an event] are of a tangible nature . . . [and] are perceptible as sense-data.' By contrast, the binding force of a purposive contract can be explained only by invoking the principle of legitimation on which all legal-rational authority is based and by employing a type of juristic analysis that seeks to establish the legal significance of 'the external characteristics of the facts' through the logical analysis of their meaning, that is, by relating them to the purposive attitudes that constitute the ' "inner" kernel' of individual behaviour. The distinctions Weber draws between traditional and legal-rational authority, magical and rational types of legal thinking, and status and purposive contracts all express the same fundamental distinction between facts and values, a distinction ultimately rooted in his commitment to the principle of positivity.

Special law

The distinction between status and purposive contracts illuminates another problem that Weber discusses, the problem of 'special law communities'. In the past, an individual often had the right to be treated as the member of a special legal order or law community and to demand that the norms of that group – which typically represented only a subpart of some larger political community – be applied in his dealings with other members and sometimes even with outsiders. Thus, for example, 'in those groups which were polit-ically integrated by a common supreme authority, like the Persian empire, the Roman empire, the kingdom of the Franks, or the Islamic states, the body of laws to be applied by the judicial officers differed in accordance with the ethnic, religious, or political characteristics of the component groups, for instance, legally or politically autonomous cities or clans.'[234]

These special law communities often had a consensual foundation in the very general sense that they were based upon the free agreement of their members. Weber emphasizes, however, that an individual's right to be judged by the norms of a particular group 'was initially a strictly personal quality', and hence, if acquired voluntarily, had to be acquired by the kind of agreement he calls a contract of fraternization. 'Prior to the emergence and triumph of the purposive contract and of freedom of contract in the modern sense, and prior to the emergence of the modern state, every consensual group or rational [!] association which represented a special legal order and which therefore might properly be named a "law community" was either constituted in its membership by such objective characteristics as birth, political, ethnic, or religious denomination, mode of life or occupation, or arose through the process of explicit fraternization.'[235]

With the rise of the modern state, these older law communities were sup-pressed or subordinated and their autonomous legal powers denied. 'The state [has] insisted almost everywhere, and usually with success, that the validity of these special laws, as well as the extent of their application, should be subject to its consent.'[236] Even within the modern state system, however, one observes 'a great mass of legal particularisms'[237] – norms that pertain exclusively to certain individuals by virtue of their membership in a partic-ular economic or professional group. Today, for example, 'special legal regulation may . . . be occasioned by the existence of certain purely technical or economic conditions such as ownership of a factory or a farm, or the exercise of the profession of attorney, pharmacist, craftsman of a certain kind, etc.'[238] In a very general sense, then, special law is as widespread a phenomenon today as it was in pre-modern legal systems.

Weber is nevertheless careful to point out that although modern law 'has created anew a great mass of legal particularisms . . . it has done so upon a basis which differs in many important respects from that of the privileges of the older corporate status groups.'[239] The special legal norms associated with groups of the later sort were 'founded not on economic or technical qualities but on status, i.e. qualities derived from birth, mode of life, or group membership ("nobleman", "knight", or "guild fellow") or certain social relationships with respect to material objects such as a copyhold or a manor. It has therefore always been the case [in the past] that the applicability of a special law was conditional upon a particular quality of the person or upon his relationship to some material object.'[240] Modern special law communities, by contrast, rest upon an entirely different conception of how such norms are created and why they are binding.

> The ever-increasing integration of all individuals and all fact-situations into one compulsory institution which today, at least, rests in principle on formal 'legal equality' has been achieved by two great rationalizing forces, i.e. first, by the extension of the market economy and, second, by the bureaucratization of the activities of the organs of the consensual groups. They replaced that particularist mode of creating law which was based upon the private power or the granted privileges of monopolistically closed organizations; that means, they reduced the autonomy of what were essentially status groups in two ways: The first is the formal, universally accessible, but closely regulated autonomy of voluntary associations which may be created by anyone wishing to do so; the other consists in the grant to everyone of the power to create law of his own by means of engaging in private legal transactions of certain kinds.[241]

Today, the special legal norms that apply to individuals by virtue of their membership in a particular group are based not upon their possession of a personal quality or status of some sort, but upon their own voluntary consent and are considered 'valid and binding because one [has] created them for oneself by directly participating in a purposive contract.'[242] Pre-modern special law communities were based upon contracts of fraternization; their modern counterparts rest upon purposive contracts and thus have a basis which differs from 'the privileges of the older corporate status groups'.

The most interesting aspect of Weber's discussion of this problem is his account of the historical process leading from one type of special law community to the other. All special law communities were originally corporate status groups whose members had certain rights and obligations in virtue of some 'objective characteristic' or personal quality which they had acquired through a process of fraternization. An individual's right to insist on 'subjection to the special law [of his group] was initially a strictly personal quality, a "privilege" acquired by usurpation or grant and thus a monopoly of its possessors who, by virtue of this fact, became "comrades in law".'[243] To the extent that an individual's 'total legal status' was determined by his possession of the quality in question, he could have no cognizable legal identity apart from his membership in the law community to which he belonged. This meant that relations with strangers – those outside the community – were, to begin with at least, beyond the law. Since strangers, by definition, do not belong to the same status group, wherever membership in such a group is considered the all-inclusive basis of an individual's rights and duties, a legal relationship between strangers is inconceivable.

Despite this, however, contacts between strangers cannot be avoided – especially 'with the increasing differentiation and economic scarcity of those goods which were munificently [sic] appropriated by the several [status] groups.'[244] These contacts are of essentially two sorts: first, a member of one group may kill or injure the member of another; second, individuals belonging to different groups may find it in their mutual interest to exchange goods or engage in some other economic transaction. In each case, as contacts increase, the need for an agreed-upon set of rules to govern interactions between strangers becomes greater. Historically, the need for such rules resulted in 'freely concluded agreements between autonomous groups'[245] regarding the procedure to be followed in determining liability for wrongs against strangers. According to Weber, 'the arbitration agreement which developed out of the agreement for composition between kinship groups, i.e. the voluntary submission to a verdict or an ordeal, is not only the source of all procedural law but also the point of departure to which even the oldest contracts of private law can, very broadly speaking, be traced.'[246] Increasing economic contacts between strangers also stimulated the development of an independent 'body of norms autonomously agreed upon by the participants or imposed by any one of a great variety of different groups, especially political or religious organizations.'[247] These norms were not those of any particular status group; they were, from the beginning, conceived as the norms of the 'market', a form of association that 'transcends the boundaries of neighbourhood, kinship group, or tribe'.[248]

As these last remarks suggest, a separate institution of some sort, distinct from the various status groups to which different individuals belonged, was required to oversee and enforce the rules established by agreement for the purpose of regulating interactions between strangers. Whether it was primarily political or religious in nature, the institution in question had to be defined in broader and more abstract terms than these status groups themselves; only in this way could it establish a common ground between their members. For obvious reasons, an individual's membership in *this* community, unlike his membership in the corporate status group to which he belonged, could not be based upon the possession of a particular personal quality not shared by those belonging to other status groups. Just as the political association established to administer the norms of the market 'transcends' the various special law groups between which it seeks to mediate, an individual's membership in this association must be based, in theory at least, upon some property or characteristic which transcends the personal qualities that define his rights and duties toward those belonging to his own status group. Implicit in the idea of membership in a political community that seeks to impose 'common legal principles' on a number of otherwise autonomous special law communities is the concept of what Weber calls 'formal legal equality', a concept based upon the same abstract and qualityless notion of legal personality that underlies all market-oriented purposive contracts.*

To begin with, however, this wider political community was regarded as only one particular legal order alongside others – indeed, as a tenuous and relatively insignificant appendage to the corporate status groups that continued, for the most part, to define their members' legal situation. So long as this remained true, a characteristic dualism of legal norms existed. 'At the very origin of all legal history, there . . . prevailed, if viewed from the standpoint of the political power and its continuously growing strength, an important dualism, i.e. a dualism of the autonomously created law between groups, and the norms determinative of disputes among group members.'[249] Wherever such a dualism existed, status groups strove 'for the application of the principle of *personal* law on behalf of the law created by them',[250] that is, for the application of their own legal norms in disputes between members of the same special law community. How successful they were in this regard depended, in each case, on the strength of the opposing forces that favoured expansion of the political community and an increase in its powers of control.[251]

In the modern West, at least, this competition has been decisively resolved in favour of the political community, which today 'appears as [an] all-embracing coercive institution' whose 'legal supremacy' is based upon the fact that it 'either tolerates or directly guarantees the creation of law by organs other than its own.'[252] Thus, while the political association was once viewed as a relatively unimportant adjunct to special law communities based upon status and personal privilege, the present situation is exactly the reverse. Today, the validity of norms established by an autonomous legal order depends entirely on their recognition by the state. To this extent, the 'modern type of special law' rests on 'the official monopoly of law creation by, and the compulsion of membership in, the modern political organization.'[253]

So long as law remained 'largely the autonomously arrogated creation' of numerous, independent special law communities, the legal identity of those belonging to these communities had necessarily to be conceived in the way that every contract of fraternization requires us to conceive it, as a status wholly inseparable from the individuals' objective characteristics or personal qualities. However, with the rise of the state a new and different conception of legal personality was bound to emerge and eventually replace the older one associated with a regime of autonomous special law communities based upon familial or quasi-familial relationships. This new conception had, of necessity, to be more abstract than the one it replaced, since

---

*Hegel's account of the movement from what he calls 'ethical substance' to 'legal personality' is based upon a similar argument. See *Phenomenology of Spirit*, §§ 477–83.

membership in the political community could not be based on any of the special qualities that were the exclusive possession of one or another of the status groups existing within its jurisdiction.

According to Weber, the historical origins of the state are to be found in those various 'inter-group arrangements' that arose in order to make possible binding legal relationships between individuals who had previously been strangers in law with no reciprocal rights or obligations. These new arrangements typically were established by the free agreement of the different groups involved, and it was therefore natural to attribute their legitimacy to the mere fact of their deliberate enactment; in this sense, composition agreements and formalized rules for economic exchange 'constituted step[s] on the way to the purposive contract.'[254] As we have seen, the parties to such a contract must be conceived as having a legal identity distinct from the particular rights and duties it establishes, an identity founded upon their capacity for purposeful action (their will). Since the inter-group arrangements which represented the historical nucleus of the state were themselves based upon purposive contracts rather than contracts of fraternization of the sort associated with the older, status-based type of special law community, it is not surprising that an individual's membership in the political community – his citizenship – came eventually to be conceived in the same abstract terms as the legal personality of the parties to a modern, market-oriented exchange contract. This helps us to understand how a contractarian conception of political authority – a conception that in broad terms is presupposed by all legal-rational forms of public administration – could emerge in the first place, against the background of a world dominated by more traditional and naturalistic views, and underscores, once again, the similarity between the notions of obligation that today underlie the public duties of a citizen and his private responsibilities as a contractual partner.

Limitations on freedom of contract

Modern law does not unambiguously allow the individual greater freedom of contract than he enjoyed in the past, in the sense of permitting him to arrange his relationships with others, regardless of their nature or purpose, in whatever way he wishes. In certain areas of life, according to Weber, there has unquestionably been a dramatic increase in freedom of contract. This is especially true so far as purely economic relationships are concerned. There are, however, other areas of social life in which freedom of contract is today sharply limited – more limited, in some cases, than it was in the past. It is therefore appropriate to speak of an overall increase in freedom of contract only to the extent that one type of contractual association – the market-oriented purposive contract – has gained in importance as a source of legal rights and obligations. Even in this domain, however, the individual's freedom of contract – the extent to which he has 'autonomy to regulate his relations with others by his own transactions'[255] – is limited in two very different respects.

The first set of limitations that Weber describes restrict the scope of an individual's contractual freedom by prohibiting him from making consensual arrangements of one sort or another or by denying legal validity to the arrangements in question. As examples, Weber offers the following: restrictions on freedom of sexual contract, on freedom of testation, on an individual's right to sell himself into slavery, and on his power to create, through contract, permanent encumbrances on land. In each case, according to Weber, the restrictions that exist today were more relaxed and often nonexistent in the past. Thus, although freedom of sexual contract is not to be found among those primitive tribes which are most backward in a social and economic sense, in more developed traditional societies 'freedom of the sexual contract unfolded in many different forms and degrees',[256] with the result that a variety of sexual relationships distinct from legitimate marriage – including 'service marriage, trial marriage, and temporary companionate marriage'[257] as well as prostitution and concubinage – were accorded a legal validity that only legitimate marriage enjoys today. Similarly, 'freedom of testation, i.e. freedom of economic and normally intra-familial disposition, has also met in modern times with restrictive tendencies.'[258] Although Weber notes that 'evidence of complete or almost complete substantive freedom of testation can be found only twice in history'[259] – in republican Rome and England before the nineteenth century – the general tendency of modern democratic legislatures has, in his view, been to restrict or eliminate freedom of testation through a number of different devices (statutory provision for indefeasible shares in the decedent's estate, abolition of primogeniture, the compulsory partition of estates, etc.). An individual's right to enslave himself by voluntarily submitting to 'formally slavelike relations'[260] was also recognized in many earlier legal systems; today, of course, contracts of this sort are prohibited. And as regards the power of individuals to put 'permanent encumbrances on land for the benefit of private parties',[261] this, too, was more extensive in the past than it is today (a notable example being the use of the entailed fee in England to preserve the holdings of the great aristocratic families).

What do these various, pecularily modern restrictions on freedom of contract have in common? Weber never answers this question directly; instead, he offers a variety of different reasons (political, ideological and economic) to explain the origin and contemporary significance of each. A reader may therefore conclude that they have only an accidental, historical connection. At several points, however, Weber hints at a deeper connection by emphasizing that each of these limitations was introduced or exploited by the bourgeoisie in its struggle against the aristocratic privileges of the *ancien régime*. Thus, for example, it is 'bourgeois public opinion' which resists an increase in freedom of divorce and sexual contracts generally out of a concern for 'the real or imagined danger to the children's educational chances'.[262] And while 'in English law freedom of testation aimed at the stabilization of the fortunes of the great families', in France and elsewhere limitations on an individual's freedom of testation helped to destroy 'the old aristocracy' and were employed as legal weapons by the rising middle class in its struggle for political and economic power.[263] The same can be said of modern restrictions on an individual's right to encumber land permanently by voluntary agreement: here, too, 'bourgeois class interests' were 'the cause of such limitations'.[264] Finally, so far as the right of self-enslavement is concerned, it was the emergence of the modern, market-oriented capitalist system of production based on free wage labour – a form of economic organization that Weber specifically identifies with the modern bourgeoisie – which was primarily responsible for the elimination of voluntary slavery (although he also notes that 'for the final and complete elimination of personal servitude, strong ideological conceptions of natural law were ultimately decisive everywhere').[265]

Since Weber identifies the bourgeoisie with the rise of a market economy and hence with the expansion of freedom of contract in the economic sphere, his identification of the same social class with various substantive limitations on freedom of contract suggests that the simultaneous growth and restriction of contractual freedom in different branches of modern private law may be related phenomena which are more consistent than they appear. But Weber does not do more than hint at the internal connection between these developments. The reader is left wondering whether, for example, there is a distinctively bourgeois conception of the family that is meaningfully related to the other aspects of contemporary social and economic life that Weber specifically associates with the bourgeoisie (for example, the impersonal market ethic of modern capitalism).[266] These hints are never explicitly developed, however, and as a result this aspect of his analysis of modern contract law remains inconclusive.

Weber's discussion of the second kind of limitation on contractual freedom is also inconclusive, but in a different way. As we saw in Chapter 4, Weber is careful to emphasize the extent to which freedom of contract may protect and even aggravate inequalities in the distribution of property and economic power.

> The increasing significance of freedom of contract and, particularly, of enabling laws which leave everything to 'free' agreement, implies a relative reduction of that kind of coercion which results from the threat of mandatory and prohibitory norms. Formally it represents, of course, a decrease of coercion. But it is also obvious how advantageous this state of affairs is to those who are economically in the position to make use of the empowerments. The exact extent to which the total amount of 'freedom' within a given legal community is actually increased depends entirely upon the concrete economic order and especially upon the property distribution.[267]

This passage suggests a distinction between what may be called 'formal' and 'effective' freedom of contract.* An individual has formal freedom of contract to the extent the law permits him to arrange his relationships with others in whatever way he wishes. He has effective freedom of contract, however, only if he actually possesses the resources needed to make the arrangements the law allows: even though I am formally free to purchase an expensive automobile, if I lack the financial resources required to do so, my freedom is, in this respect, empty or ineffective. The wage contract is a more important illustration of the same phenomenon: even though a wage labourer may be legally free to make his living in whatever way he wishes, if the only thing he has to sell is his time or labour-power and if he does not have sufficient resources to establish a business of his own, he will be forced to work for someone else and will, as a result, have to subject himself to the commands of another person (at least within limits and during the working day). As Weber observes, a formally free labour contract which the worker may enter or not as he chooses but which his propertylessness forces him to accept often increases the overall constraint to which he is subject.

> The private enterprise system transforms into objects of 'labour market transactions' even those personal and authoritarian-hierarchical relations which actually exist in the capitalistic enterprise. While the authoritarian relationships are thus drained of all normal sentimental content, authoritarian constraint not only continues but, at least under certain circumstances, even increases. The more comprehensive the realm of structures whose existence depends in a specific way on 'discipline' . . . the more relentlessly can authoritarian constraint be exercised within them, and the smaller will be the circle of those in whose hands the power to use this type of constraint is concentrated and who also hold the power to have such authority guaranteed to them by the legal order. A legal order which contains ever so few mandatory and prohibitory norms and ever so many 'freedoms' and 'empowerments' can nonetheless in its practical effects facilitate a quantitative and qualitative increase not only of coercion in general but quite specifically of authoritarian coercion.[268]

A person's economic resources, when they are limited, narrow his set of contractual choices. In this sense, propertylessness and a lack of economic power represent significant limitations on freedom of contract, although they are limitations of a very different sort from the various substantive prohibitions described earlier.

Despite his realistic appraisal of the economic factors limiting an individual's contractual freedom, Weber doubted whether these restrictions could be abolished without introducing others of a potentially more severe sort. In general, according to Weber, it is possible to distinguish three different ways in which an individual may be subject to coercion. First, he may be subject to 'direct coercion exercised on the basis of purely personal claims to authority.'[269] This type of authority and the specific form of coercion associated with it is repudiated by both bourgeois capitalist and

---

*This distinction is akin to the one Rawls draws between 'liberty' and the 'worth of liberty', *A Theory of Justice*, p. 204.

socialist communities. Second, an individual may be subject to coercion 'by the private owners of the means of production and acquisition, to whom the law guarantees their property and whose power can thus manifest itself in the competitive struggle of the market.'[270] This type of coercion is, of course, the one that Weber associates with a capitalist economy based upon private appropriation of the means of production and a formally free market in commodities and labour. Finally, an individual's behaviour may be coerced by being subjected to the 'direct mandatory and prohibitory decrees of a central economic control authority'.[271] Weber identifies this third type of coercion – which is neither personal in character nor based on inequalities in the underlying distribution of property rights – with socialist forms of economic organization.

As between capitalism and socialism '[w]hich system would possess more real coercion and which one more real personal freedom cannot be decided . . . by the mere analysis of the actually existing or conceivable formal legal system. . . . Sociology can only perceive the qualitative differences among the various types of coercion and their incidence among the participants in the legal community'.[272] Thus, despite the impliedly critical language that he uses to describe the increase in authoritarian control which results from the formally free labour contracts that workers in a capitalist economy are forced to make in an effort to adapt to 'the purely economic "laws" of the market',[273] Weber did not believe that the triumph of democratic socialism would necessarily mean more overall freedom for the individual. He does not appear, however, to have been similarly skeptical about the relative coerciveness of pre-modern forms of social and economic organization based on direct claims to personal authority: the different types of coercion associated with capitalism and socialism respectively are both to be preferred, in his view, to the domination of a personal master.

Here, as elsewhere, we see the ambivalence in Weber's conception of modern society. On the one hand, the expansion of contractual freedom and the abolition of all direct forms of personal servitude represent an increase in 'real personal freedom'. At the same time, however, these liberating developments have themselves produced, in Weber's words, 'a special kind of coercive situation which, as a general principle, applies without any discrimination to workers, enterprisers, producers and consumers, viz., in the impersonal form of the inevitability of adaption to the purely economic "laws" of the market', laws whose violation is sanctioned by 'the loss or decrease of economic power and under certain conditions, in the very loss of one's economic existence.'[274] And there is little reason to hope that the introduction of socialism will improve things: whatever freedom is gained by suspending the economic laws of the market and correcting inequalities in the underlying distribution of property rights is likely to be offset by increased restrictions on the kind of arrangements that individuals are permitted to make for themselves on terms of their own choosing. In short, modern society, especially its economic institutions, is characterized at once by an unparalleled expansion of individual freedom and by its restriction in new and important ways, ways that cannot be altered without imposing other, perhaps more coercive restrictions. In chapter 8 I shall examine the philosophical roots of this ambivalent and pessimistic view.

6

Law and capitalism

To what extent has the law influenced material life, either by encouraging certain types of economic activity or by obstructing their development? And to what degree have economic factors shaped legal thinking and been responsible for the invention or modification of specific legal institutions? These questions, which Weber raises at the very beginning of the *Rechtssoziologie*, provide a kind of connective tissue linking many of the historical and conceptual problems that he discusses.

Weber's interest in the relationship between law and economic action is more focused than these general questions suggest, however. Although he discusses the relationship between legal and economic conditions of the most various kinds, Weber is primarily interested in the connection between one particular set of legal institutions – those he associates with the concept of formal legal rationality – and one specific form of economic organization – the modern system of capitalist production, which he elsewhere characterizes as 'the most fateful force in our modern life'.[275] It is only in the modern Western world that one finds 'rational capitalistic enterprises with fixed capital, free labour, the rational specialization and combination of functions, and the allocation of productive functions on the basis of capitalistic enterprises, bound together in a market economy.'[276] One of the main objectives of *Economy and Society* as a whole is to elucidate the 'qualitative uniqueness' of this particular form of capitalism and to identify the different factors that have contributed to its historical development. The *Rechtssoziologie* (which is, after all, only a part of this larger work) is specifically concerned with the contribution that legal ideas and institutions have made to the growth of capitalist enterprise and thus reflects Weber's dominating interest in the nature and origins of 'this sober bourgeois capitalism with its rational organization of free labour'.[277]

For the most part, Weber appears to have conceived this problem in causal terms: to what extent have the demands of capitalist enterprise been responsible for the formal rationalization of the law, and to what degree have juristic factors in turn influenced the historical development of modern capitalism? The answer he gives to this causal question is inconclusive. According to Weber, legal and economic conditions have in all periods exerted a reciprocal influence on one another, the strength and direction of the influence varying from one historical situation to the next. To some extent, the legal and economic orders have also each developed along independent lines, propelled by internal forces of their own. Weber carefully avoids attributing greater causal importance to either legal or economic factors, and he offers no general theory to explain why economic conditions have had an impact on the law in some cases but not others. In short, his analysis of the causal relationship between law and economic action – and, more particularly, between the rational systematization of the law and modern capitalism – does not support a specific causal hypothesis; to the contrary, it seeks to demonstrate that any historical explanation which assigns causal primacy to either legal or economic factors is bound to be overly general or incomplete.

This essentially negative position may fairly be described as one of 'causal agnosticism'. The first section of this chapter examines Weber's views regarding the causal relationship between legal rationalization and the growth of modern capitalism (focusing on the problematic case of England), attempts to show that he was indeed a causal agnostic, and considers some possible responses to the charge that Weber's agnosticism renders his account of the causal relationship between law and economic action empty and unilluminating.

Weber's discussion of the relationship between formal legal rationality and capitalist enterprise is also concerned, however, with the meaningful – as distinct from causal – connection between these two characteristically modern phenomena. What do formal legal rationality and market-oriented capitalism – the 'formally most rational' mode of economic organization – have in common? To what extent can the formal rationality of both be explained by their rootedness in the same beliefs and attitudes? This is a question of exegesis, not of causation, and can only be answered by establishing a relationship of meaning or significance between the institutions involved; to do this, one must show that they rest upon similar normative and epistemological premises.

The demonstration of a meaningful relationship of this sort can be illuminating even where the causal connection between the institutions in question remains obscure or indeterminate. In the second and third sections of the chapter, I attempt to show that formal legal rationality and formally rational economic action, as Weber understands these concepts, do indeed rest upon similar assumptions and reflect a common normative ideal. Weber's account of the relationship between them helps us to understand the sense in which they are related aspects of a meaningfully integrated world. I shall argue that it is Weber's positivistic theory of value and his will-centred conception of personhood which provide the elements of common meaning linking the legal and economic dimensions of modern society. The concept of free labour, which occupies a central position in Weber's discussion of modern capitalism, is especially important in this regard and the third section of the chapter is devoted to its analysis.

The problem of causation

The case of England

In Chapter 2 of *Economy and Society* ('The Sociological Foundations of Economic Action'), Weber lists 'formally rational administration and law'[278] as one of the conditions for achieving the greatest possible degree of calculability in any economic activity, especially those devoted to profit-making. Several of the other conditions that he enumerates could also be considered legal in a broad sense, but this particular requirement points to an especially significant connection between law and economic action and raises important questions regarding the influence of legal rationalization on material life and the development of modern capitalism in particular.

As we have seen, Weber believed that formal legal rationality can be maximized only through the systematization of the legal order. Since he included formally rational administration and law among the conditions for achieving the greatest possible degree of calculability in economic action, it would seem to follow that systematization ought itself to be viewed as a condition for maximizing the calculability of economic behaviour. There are several passages in *Economy and Society* which suggest that Weber did, in fact, hold this view.[279] His well-known account of the role played by legal institutions in the development of capitalist production in early modern England appears, however, to support the opposite conclusion, for it suggests that legal systematization is not a prerequisite for attaining the greatest possible, or even a meaningful, degree of formal rationality in economic action. What, exactly, does Weber's discussion of English capitalism establish?[280]

The English common law was not constructed in accordance with the requirements of a systematic legal logic of the sort to be found, for example, in the work of the Pandectists. It grew, instead, in a conceptually haphazard fashion through the analogical extension of established ideas and procedural techniques – a process that typically involved the use of legal fictions and that emphasized the juridical significance of what Weber calls 'extrinsic facts'. Nevertheless, despite the thoroughly unsystematic character of the common law, market capitalism made greater advances in England in the early modern period than it did anywhere else in Europe. Weber considered this a puzzling fact and in the *Rechtssoziologie* he attempts to identify those features of the English legal order which, despite its lack of formal rationality, helped to facilitate the development of entrepreneurial capitalism.

According to Weber, several factors were of special importance in this regard. First, although it lacked a systematic structure, the common law was nevertheless highly formalistic in certain respects – the stereotyped writ system that provided the basis for common law pleading being an important example. And even though its formalism was largely irrational (a fact that leads Weber to compare the common law with other, more primitive types of legal thought) this aspect of common law adjudication tended to exert a stabilizing influence which increased the overall predictability of the legal order, thereby enhancing the security of market transactions – one of the conditions for the rationalization of economic action.

Second, the peculiar organization of the English legal profession also contributed to the development of capitalist enterprise. In England, lawyers traditionally acted as advisers in business matters; this not only sensitized the English Bar to the requirements of commercial life, but gave them an incentive to shape the law in ways that promoted the interests of their business clients – a tendency that was strengthened by the centralization of the Bar in London, in close proximity to the city's business and financial communities. The monopoly which the Inns of Court enjoyed with respect to the practice of law further contributed to this same result by ensuring that control over legal training, admission to practice and promotion to the Bench remained in the hands of lawyers – a group that in England was 'active in the service of propertied and particularly capitalistic private interests and which had to gain its livelihood from them.'[281]

To these two factors, Weber adds a third – the absence, in England, of a university-based, rigorously formal system of legal education and the dominance, instead, of what he calls 'empirical training in the law as a craft', a process of acquiring legal knowledge in which 'apprentices learn from practitioners more or less in the course of actual legal practice'.[282]

> Not only was systematic and comprehensive treatment of the law prevented by the craftlike specialization of [lawyers in England], but legal practice did not aim at a rational system but rather at a practically useful scheme of contracts and actions, oriented towards the interests of clients in typically recurrent situations. . . . From such practices and attitudes no rational system of law could emerge, nor even a rationalization of the law as such, because the concepts thus formed are constructed in relation to concrete events of everyday life, are distinguished from each other by external criteria, and extended in their scope, as new needs arise [by means of procedural fictions].[283]

Although the intensely practical orientation of English lawyers, and the method of empirical craft training associated with it, prevented the rational systematization of the common law, it also assured that lawyers never lost touch with the actual needs of their clients – in particular, their commercial clients. Education by apprenticeship discourages abstract reflection for its own sake, and focuses the lawyer's attention on what is practically useful, which always means what is useful in serving a client. 'The legal concepts produced by academic law-teaching', on the other hand, often result in 'a far-reaching emancipation of legal thinking from the everyday needs of the public', thereby reducing 'the role played by considerations of practical needs in the formation of the law.'[284] Abstract legal thinking of this sort, often motivated by what Weber calls 'a blind desire for logical consistency',[285] never took root in England and the fact that it did not helps to explain why English businessmen found the law so adaptable to their practical needs.

What is implied by Weber's account of the contribution made by these various legal factors to the development of capitalism in England, and what light does his treatment of this particular problem throw on his understanding of the relationship between law and economy in general? To begin with, Weber's discussion does *not* imply that rational economic action is possible in the absence of a predictable legal order – it does not, in other words, contradict or refute the general claim that some measure of legal predictability is one of the conditions for a system of rational profit-making. What Weber's discussion of English capitalism *does* suggest is that the requisite degree of legal predictability may be realized not only through the systematization of the law but in other ways as well. Even an unsystematized legal order, such as the English common law, may provide a sufficiently predictable framework for entrepreneurial activity if businessmen can count on legal rules being framed and interpreted in a fashion that is consistent with their own extra-legal norms and which protects their common interests – despite the fact that the rules in question are based upon analogies and procedural fictions which are illogical from a purely juristic point of view.

Unlike the legal scholar, the businessman has no interest in the logical clarity of the law (*juris elegantia*) for its own sake. His only concern is that the legal order be as free as possible of surprises that might alter the risks associated with his transactions in ways he cannot anticipate in advance. One way of eliminating, or at least reducing, such surprises is to systematize the legal order: if the law is comprehensive and its organizing principles clear, it will be possible to predict with a high degree of certainty how established rules are likely to be applied in novel situations. However, even if the legal order lacks comprehensiveness and organizational clarity, a sufficiently high degree of predictability may nevertheless be attainable if those responsible for administering its rules understand and respect the contractual agreements and customary understandings that define the terms of most commercial transactions. Judicial familiarity with the needs and attitudes of businessmen coupled with a desire to promote commercial stability by enforcing the norms of the business community may be sufficient to produce the degree of legal predictability required by a system of entrepreneurial capitalism even where the law remains relatively undeveloped in a logical sense: this is the first lesson to be drawn from Weber's discussion of the relationship between law and capitalism in England.

But while we may justifiably infer from Weber's discussion of English capitalism that he did not consider legal systematization an indispensible prerequisite for rational entrepreneurial activity, there are passages which suggest that the formal rationalization of the common law might have increased its overall predictability and thereby facilitated the development of capitalist production to an even greater extent. At one point, for example, he remarks that the absence of a system of title registration prevented the development of 'a rationally organized system of real estate credit' in England – a situation he attributes to 'the lawyers' economic interest with regard to the fees for that title examination which must in every transaction be made because of the uncertainty of all land titles'.[286] Presumably, the rationalization of title registration would have promoted economic activity by reducing the legal risks associated with the transfer of real property. It is reasonable to think that in this and other ways, the irrationality of the common law slowed the development of capitalism in England, even though other factors, such as the close connection between the organized Bar and the business community, may have promoted its development for quite different reasons.

If this is true, Weber's description of the legal forces contributing to the growth of English capitalism can be interpreted in a way that makes it entirely consistent with his assertion that a *maximum* of economic calculability is attainable only where the law has been systematized in a formally rational manner. Undoubtedly, some degree of predictability can be achieved without the formal rationalization of the legal order. Weber's discussion of English law also suggests, however, that an increase in the predictability of the legal order beyond what is minimally necessary for regular entrepreneurial activity may be both possible and desirable (from the standpoint of the business community), and provides at least some support for the view that an increase of this sort can only be achieved through the rationalization of the legal order. On this interpretation, the apparent tension between Weber's claim that 'formally rational administration and law' is a precondition for attaining the greatest possible calculability in economic action and his assertion that capitalist enterprise developed in England despite the irrationality of the common law simply vanishes: a contradiction exists only in case we equate the maximum degree of legal predictability that can be attained through formal rationalization with the minimum degree required to establish an effective system of capitalist production in the first place.

There is, however, one aspect of Weber's analysis of English capitalism that conflicts with this interpretation. At several points , he suggests that capitalism flourished in England precisely *because* the common law was never systematically rationalized, and not merely *despite* its lack of systematization.[287] Legal rationalization often requires that considerations of logic and consistency be given greater weight than 'practical' or 'everyday' needs. As a result, the systematization of the legal order may diminish the usefulness of legal rules from a practical, and especially economic, point of view. Indeed, at one point, Weber suggests that the importance which every effort at systematization attaches to considerations of legal logic may actually reduce the overall calculability of the legal order for economic purposes.[288] It is difficult to see how this view can be reconciled with his claim that 'formally rational administration and law' is a precondition for maximizing the calculability of economic action – unless we construe the term 'formally rational', as it is used here, to mean formalistic but not necessarily systematic. At a minimum, this would create a terminological difficulty since Weber frequently treats formal rationality and systematization as equivalent concepts. Beyond this, however, his account of English capitalism suggests some genuine uncertainty on Weber's part as to whether formal legal rationality is a prerequisite or even a stimulus – rather than an obstacle – to the development of capitalist production.

Weber's causal agnosticism

According to Weber, legal and economic conditions have often influenced one another in a reciprocal fashion. The strength and frequency of the influence, however, have not been significantly greater in one direction than the other. Sometimes, economic factors have been of decisive importance in the development of the law – either negatively, by retarding its growth in a particular direction, or positively, by stimulating the creation of new doctrines and institutions. By the same token, legal factors have often exercised considerable influence on material life, preventing or discouraging the development of certain forms of economic organization while facilitating others. In addition, legal and economic institutions have sometimes developed in entirely independent ways, each driven by internal forces of its own. This is especially true of the legal order, whose development has often been influenced, in a decisive manner, by what Weber calls 'intrajuristic'[289] factors and, in particular, by the 'intrinsic intellectual needs' of lawyers and legal scholars for a clear and comprehensive system of legal concepts.

> Practical needs, like those of the bourgeoisie, for a 'calculable' law, which were decisive in the tendency towards a formal law as such, did not play any considerable role in this particular process. As experience shows, this need may be gratified quite as well, and often better, by a formal empirical case law [as was true in England]. The consequences of the purely logical construction often bear very irrational or even unforeseen relations to the expectations of the commercial interests. It is this very fact which has given rise to the frequently made charge that the purely logical law is 'remote from life'. *This logical systematization of the law has been the consequence of the intrinsic intellectual needs of the legal theorists and their disciples, the doctors, i.e. of a typical aristocracy of legal literati.*[290]

The importance of these intellectual needs helps to explain the relative *lack* of influence that economic conditions have often had on the development of legal thought, even within the modern capitalist world order – a point Weber makes in a passage that seems oddly inconsistent with his assertion that formal legal rationality is one of the indispensible conditions of capitalist production.

> The essential similarity of the capitalistic development on the Continent and in England has not been able to eliminate the sharp contrasts between the two types of legal systems. Nor is there any visible tendency towards a transformation of the English legal system in the direction of the Continental under the impetus of the capitalist economy. On the contrary, wherever the two kinds of administration of justice and of legal training have had the opportunity to compete with one another, as for instance in Canada, the Common Law has come out on top and has overcome the Continental alternative rather quickly. *We may thus conclude that capitalism has not been a decisive factor in the promotion of that form of*

rationalization of the law which has been peculiar to the continental West ever since the rise of Romanist studies in the medieval universities.[291]

Taken together, Weber's various remarks concerning the relationship between law and economic action reflect what I have called his causal agnosticism, his assiduous refusal to assign causal primacy – or even sustained causal efficacy – to either legal or material conditions. In the *Rechtssoziologie*, Weber makes many different claims about the influence of law on economic life, and *vice versa*; indeed, he makes almost every claim that one could conceivably make, leaving the reader with the impression that his principal aim is a negative one – to demonstrate the inadequacy of every theory that asserts more than that legal and economic conditions have sometimes had a reciprocal but unspecificable influence on one other, and sometimes none at all.

The depth and pervasiveness of Weber's agnosticism become clear when his scattered comments concerning the causal relationship between law and economic action are gathered and compared. To begin with, Weber identifies three different ways in which the law can influence material life. The first and most general way in which it can do so is by providing a relatively stable set of rules for the protection of individual entitlements, especially those arising from contractual agreements.[292] By guaranteeing that contracts will be enforced in accordance with fixed rules known in advance by the contracting parties, the legal order significantly increases the probability that promises, once made, will be kept and thereby encourages promise-making and the forms of economic activity that depend upon it (most importantly, market exchange). Weber describes this as the 'most general' (positive) effect of law on economic life. Up to a point, at least, the law can have an effect of this sort whether or not it has been rationalized in a systematic fashion, as his discussion of English capitalism makes clear.

Second, the legal order may promote economic activity in a more particularized way, by providing specific concepts and techniques that are useful, even indispensable, for the development of certain forms of economic organization. As examples, Weber cites the law of agency and of negotiable instruments, both of which played a tremendously important role in the rationalization of modern finance. According to Weber, 'every rational business organization needs the possibility of acquiring contractual rights and of assuming obligations through temporary or permanent agents', and requires 'a method by which transfers can be made legally secure [while eliminating] the need of constantly testing the title of the transferor.'[293] These legal institutions – agency and free negotiability – are 'indispensible for a modern capitalist society'.[294] Similarly, in a 'growing exchange economy', it is necessary that there be 'an unambiguous determination of the significance of every action of every member and every official of an organization,' and some way of fixing 'the position of the organization and . . . the legitimation of its organs in both contractual transactions and in procedure . . .'[295] The 'technical legal solution of this [last] problem was found in the concept of the juristic person',[296] a concept that Weber terms '[t]he most rational actualization of the idea of the legal personality of organizations'.[297] In short, the modern legal order has facilitated the development of rational capitalist enterprise not only by establishing a stable framework for the enforcement of contractual entitlements generally, but also, and more particularly, by providing those engaged in economic activity with a number of specific concepts and techniques – agency, negotiability, incorporation – that have proved especially useful in the rationalization of business practice.

Where these techniques have been missing or under-developed – as they were, for example, in classical Roman Law – the rationalization of economic life has been significantly retarded. To the extent that rational profit-making developed at all under such conditions, '[i]t could and had to get along without technical devices which today seem to us to be indispensible.'[298] In certain cases, substitute legal techniques were invented to achieve some of the purposes that today can be accomplished in a simple and direct fashion. Thus, for example, in Roman antiquity '[s]laves were used as business instruments through whose contracts the master could acquire unrestricted rights but only limited liabilities', the 'treatment of the [slave's] *peculium* in the fashion of a separate fund making it possible to obtain at least part of the results which today are brought about by the various forms of limited liability.'[299] Nevertheless, in the absence of a law of agency or corporations or legal recognition of the principle of free negotiability, commerce can be rationalized only to a limited degree. According to Weber, without these particular legal devices, a stable and continuous system of capitalist production is inconceivable.

A third way in which the law may influence economic activity is through the intentional creation of rules designed to encourage particular forms of enterprise or economic organization. Weber mentions this type of deliberate economic legislation but says little about it other than that it 'presupposes . . . a specific stage of legal development.'[300] As an example of the sort of legislation he has in mind, one might cite the advantageous depreciation rates applied to certain forms of industrial capital under the United States Internal Revenue Code.[301] The aim of such legislation is to encourage particular investments by reducing their relative cost. In some cases, deliberate legislation of this sort seeks to stimulate economic activity in a general way (the favourable tax treatment given capital gains income might be an example); often, however, the purpose of such legislation is to encourage a particular line of economic activity or to protect the interests of a specific group. Protective legislation of the latter sort is by no means an exclusively modern phenomenon, nor does it necessarily enhance the formal rationality of economic action: it may be motivated almost entirely by considerations of substantive justice (as Weber uses that term), and often exerts a retarding influence on the development of formally rational economic activity. Consequently, all one can say about laws that are 'expressly created' to induce 'the emergence of certain economic relations'[302] – the third way in which the legal order may affect economic behaviour – is that they have an indeterminate impact on economic conduct, sometimes promoting its rationalization, in whole or in part, and sometimes obstructing it.

While the law has influenced economic activity in a variety of different ways, economic interests and forms of organization have had a reciprocal, and equally diverse, influence on the development of the legal order. One way in which economic needs have shaped the development of legal doctrine and even the basic orientation of juristic thought has been through the work of private legal counsellors. Wherever private counsellors with an expertise in legal matters have put themselves in the service of commercial interests – as was the case, for example, in England and to a lesser degree in Rome – the result has been the creation of new law and, in particular, 'the invention of new contractual forms'.[303] Indeed, the 'growing demand for experience and specialized knowledge and the consequent stimulus for increasing rationalization of the law have almost always come from the increasing significance of commerce and those participating in it.'[304] Weber qualifies this rather strong claim, however, by emphasizing the independently influential role that legal factors have played in this same process: even if 'changes in the meaning of the prevailing law are initiated by the parties or their professional counsellors, they are consciously and rationally adapted to the expected reaction of the judiciary' and presuppose 'the calculability of the functioning of the coercive [legal] machinery' – a 'technical prerequisite as well as one of the incentives for the inventive genius of the cautelary jurists whom we find as an autonomous element in legal innovation resulting from private initiative everywhere.'[305]

Although economic factors have sometimes stimulated the development of legal doctrine, they have, at other times, had the opposite effect. Thus, according to Weber,

> certain empowerments may be lacking simply because the legal recognition of the particular commercial institutions was not felt at the time as a real need. This would probably explain the absence of negotiable instruments in ancient law, or, more exactly, in the official law of the Roman Empire . . . . The same explanation may hold true of the absence of modern capitalistic forms of association, for which Antiquity had no parallels other than the various forms of state capitalist associations, as ancient capitalism was essentially living off the state.[306]

Weber even goes so far as to describe the non-existence of a developed concept of the corporation in Roman law as 'one of the legal symptoms of that absence of stable capitalistic enterprises with continuous credit needs which [was] characteristic of the Roman economic system',[307] a remark with decidedly materialist overtones. Elsewhere, however, he explicitly rejects the view that certain distinctive features of ancient law can be explained as the mere 'reflex' of existing economic conditions. Even though their recognition 'was not felt at the time as a real [i.e. economic] need',

> the absence of an economic need is by no means the only explanation of the lack of certain legal institutions in the past. Like the technological methods of industry,

the rational patterns of legal technique to which the law is to give its guaranty must first be 'invented' before they can serve an existing economic interest. Hence, the specific types of techniques used in a legal system or, in other words, its modes of thought are of far greater significance for the likelihood that a certain legal institution will be invented in the context than is ordinarily believed. Economic situations do not automatically give birth to new legal forms; they merely provide the opportunity for the actual spread of a legal technique if it is invented.[308]

This passage reflects, more clearly than any other, the idealist side of the *Rechtssoziologie*.[309] While acknowledging that the law has often been influenced in its development by social and economic conditions, Weber at several points describes this influence as an indirect one, at least so far as those 'juristic qualities which are characteristic of [the legal order] today' are concerned.[310] By contrast, 'the direction in which these formal qualities develop is conditioned *directly* by "intrajuristic" conditions' including, in particular, the character of the individuals 'who are in a position to influence, by virtue of their profession, the ways in which the law is shaped' and 'the prevailing type of legal education, i.e. the mode of training of the practitioners of the law.'[311]

Two different types of legal training have had a significant influence on the development of doctrine and the general character of legal thought. The first, which Weber calls 'empirical training in the law as a craft' is illustrated 'by the guildlike English method of having law taught by lawyers.'[312] Under the second type of legal training, 'law is taught in special schools, where the emphasis is placed on legal theory and "science", that is, where legal phenomena are given rational and systematic treatment.'[313] In the latter case, according to Weber, purely intellectual needs for coherence, comprehensiveness and symmetry have often been of overriding importance in the development of the law; wherever an 'aristocracy of legal literati' has had control of legal doctrine and been responsible for its development, their 'intrinsic intellectual needs' have played a more important role than considerations of a practical or economic sort.[314]

As I noted earlier, the 'mere desire for intellectual organization' that is characteristic of academic or scientific legal training has had ambiguous consequences for economic life – on the one hand, promoting the systematic rationalization of the law and thus, at least up to a point, increasing the predictability of economic transactions generally, while on the other hand encouraging the elaboration of doctrinal schemes remote from the realities of commercial life and insensitive to the needs of businessmen. But whatever effect the prevailing mode of legal training has had on economic behaviour, its own development has frequently been determined by intrajuristic factors, conditions internal to the legal order itself, and not by economic forces. Although there are many passages in the *Rechtssoziologie* which suggest that material factors have played an important role in the development of legal institutions, there is an equal if not larger number that emphasize the extent to which legal ideas and techniques 'have followed their own paths' and been determined by the 'internal structure' of juristic thought and the type of training or education associated with it.[315]

To a degree, the same can also be said of the economic order. As Weber's discussion of English capitalism implies, certain forms of economic organization may be driven by internal forces of their own, forces that are largely independent of the legal order and which are powerful enough to promote the development of similar economic relationships against the background of even strikingly different legal regimes. Like the legal order, the economic sphere has to some degree a life of its own; only on this assumption can one explain 'the essential similarity of the capitalistic development on the Continent and in England', a phenomenon that Weber regards as evidence of the independence of the legal order but which also reflects the autonomy of material life.[316]

Throughout the *Rechtssoziologie*, Weber seems determined to avoid a one-sided view of the causal relationship between law and economic action. Every strong claim that he makes regarding the influence of one on the other is qualified, somewhere in the text, by an assertion that the influence has only been partial or indirect and has in any case been exerted in the opposite direction as well. To some extent, this agnostic conclusion is unilluminating. If we are interested in understanding the way in which legal and economic conditions have influenced one another and the role they have played in the development of society generally, it is not much help to be told that each has influenced the other to a degree and, to a degree, followed an independent path of its own. One might legitimately object that it is possible to make progress in our understanding of social institutions only through the construction of theories that attempt to explain the organization of society by assigning causal primacy to a particular element or factor (law, economy, religion, etc.). On this view, the distortion created by assigning causal primacy to a specific dimension of social life and treating the others as its reflex or causal product is the price that must be paid for any theoretical understanding whatsoever. Accordingly, to the extent it is concerned with the causal relationship between law and economic action, one might judge the *Rechtssoziologie* a failure since it presents no claims that are sufficiently strong to be falsifiable (another way of saying that a theory must be one-sided if it is to be interesting or illuminating).

There are two different grounds on which Weber's causal agnosticism can be defended against this criticism. First, even assuming that a theory of society must be artificially one-sided to have explanatory power, it does not follow that progress in the social sciences can be made only through the construction of such theories; their destruction is also illuminating if it successfully demonstrates the need for a new theory more adequate than any that yet exist. Progress in the social sciences has a cyclical character: theories are proposed, elaborated, defended and then destroyed, only to be replaced by new theories that purport to capture the strengths of their predecessors while avoiding their weaknesses. An individual theorist may make a contribution to this process in any one of a number of different ways – by refining an existing theory, by criticizing it or by constructing a new one – and there is no reason why each theorist must carry out all of these tasks himself. Viewed in this light, one can argue that Weber's *Rechtssoziologie* significantly advances our understanding of the causal relationship between law and economic action by discrediting various inadequate accounts of this relationship, even though he offers no positive theory of his own, leaving that task for those who follow.

A second defence of Weber's causal agnosticism emphasizes the importance of specifying the level of historical abstraction at which his views are meant to apply. Weber denies there is an invariant causal relationship between legal and economic conditions that obtains in every historical situation. It does not follow, however, that causal primacy cannot be assigned to legal or economic factors on an individualized, case-by-case basis: legal factors may predominate in certain situations and material factors in others, even though neither predominates in all. If this is true, one can, so to speak, be a causal agnostic at the highest level without denying that primacy may be assigned to one or another factor in particular historical contexts. Interpreted in this way, Weber's causal agnosticism is merely a warning against the dangers of overgeneralization and a reminder that any meaningful analysis of the causal relationship between law and economic action must be confined to particular cases, which provide the necessary context for making strong claims about the influence of either on the other.

Finally, even if one finds these defences of Weber's causal agnosticism unconvincing, it does not follow that his account of the relationship between law and capitalism must be judged a failure. Weber's analysis of this relationship is only partly concerned with the causal connection between law and capitalist production. He was, in addition, interested in the meaningful relationship between these two aspects of modern social life, in the elements of common meaning that link the legal and economic dimensions of modern society and justify our treating them as aspects of a single social world. The contribution that he makes to our understanding of the meaningful relationship between modern law and capitalist production is an important achievement in its own right, and since it is concerned with connections of a different sort, this aspect of Weber's analysis is unaffected by the agnosticism that arguably undermines his causal analysis of the same relationship.

The formal rationality of economic action

According to Weber, both modern capitalism and 'present-day legal science' are distinguished by their high degree of formal rationality. It is natural to wonder whether the concept of formal rationality has the same meaning in both cases. When he describes modern capitalism as the 'formally most rational' type of economic organization, is the characteristic he has in mind identical with – is it even related to – the feature (or features) of modern legal thought that he describes in the same terms? I have discussed Weber's concept of formal legal rationality at some length. We must now examine his concept of formally rational economic action to see what connection, if any, there is between these two ideas.

The basic types of economic action

'Economic action is a peaceful use of the actor's control over resources, which is rationally oriented, by deliberate planning, to economic ends', and an action has an economic end – as opposed to, say, a religious or political one – 'so far as, according to its subjective meaning, it is concerned with the satisfaction of a desire for "utilities" '.[317] This general definition, which is meant to include economic behaviour of every imaginable sort, defines economic action in terms of its 'subjective meaning' for the individual(s) involved. 'All "economic" processes and objects are characterized as such entirely by the *meaning* they have for human action in such roles as ends, means, obstacles and by-products';[318] hence, it is the actors' purposeful orientation to a particular end – the satisfaction of a desire for utilities – which 'alone defines the unity of the corresponding [economic] processes and . . . alone makes them accessible to subjective interpretation'.[319] Weber's subjectivist definition of economic behaviour clearly reflects his own methodological belief that events or states of affairs have meaning only in the context of our purposive endeavours.

Within the field of economic behaviour, Weber distinguishes two fundamentally different types. One he calls 'profit-making activity' and the other 'budgetary management'. Each is defined in terms of the goal that gives the process or activity its meaning for those involved. Indeed, this would appear to be the only possible way of distinguishing these two types of economic action. Since '[t]he administration of budgetary "wealth" and profit-making enterprises may be outwardly so similar as to appear identical', it is necessary to distinguish them 'in terms of the difference in [their] meaningful orientation'.[320]

Weber defines budgetary management as 'the continual utilization and procurement of goods, whether through production or exchange, by an economic unit for purposes of its own consumption.'[321] Budgetary management is essentially concerned with the satisfaction of wants or needs and it is the attainment of this goal that gives the activity its meaning for those involved. The 'basis for an individual or group oriented in this way is the "budget" ', a form of accounting 'which states systematically in what way the needs expected for an accounting period – needs for utilities or for means of procurement to obtain them – can be covered by the anticipated income.'[322] According to Weber, all budgetary calculations of this sort ultimately rest upon the 'principle of marginal utility'.[323]

By contrast, profit-making is a type of economic behaviour 'oriented to opportunities for seeking new powers of control over goods on a single occasion, repeatedly or continuously'.[324] The key word in Weber's definition is the word 'new': every profit-making activity aims at the acquisition of additional 'powers of control' which will increase the total economic value (the net worth) of the individual or enterprise engaged in the activity. Unlike all forms of economic action which seek merely to satisfy certain fixed wants or needs, profit-making is essentially oriented toward the production or acquisition of a surplus, a quantitative increase in the value of the goods belonging to the profit-making unit.

This characteristic of profit-making activity is brought out most explicitly in Weber's definition of 'capital accounting', a 'form of monetary accounting which is peculiar to rational economic profit-making.'[325] Capital accounting 'is the valuation and verification of opportunities for profit and of the success of profit-making activity by means of a valuation of the total assets (goods and money) of the enterprise at the beginning of a profit-making venture, and the comparison of this with a similar valuation of the assets still present and newly acquired, at the end of the process; in the case of a profit-making organization operating continuously, the same is done for an accounting period.'[326] A profit-making enterprise is successful, in its own terms, only if the total value of the assets belonging to the enterprise is greater at the end of the relevant accounting period than it was at its beginning. This alone determines the profitability of the enterprise and is the sole basis for deciding whether its goal – the goal that gives it its meaning – has been achieved.

The distinction between budgetary management and profit-making marks a conceptual difference between two ideal types of economic action, and Weber explicitly states that neither should be viewed as a more 'primitive' form of economic activity than the other.[327] He also emphasizes, however, that these two types of economic action have not been equally prevalent at all times. Profit-making in its purest form is a 'specifically modern' phenomenon; by contrast, 'the budgetary unit has been the dominant form in most periods of the past.'[328] The dominance of budgetary management in the economic life of pre-modern societies reflects the greater importance in them of the household, the original *locus* of 'organized want-satisfaction'. In this historical sense, budgetary management does constitute a primitive phenomenon, along with traditional patriarchalism, which Weber also associates with the household as a social institution.

Formal and substantive rationality in economic action

Weber asserts that 'both [budgetary management and profit-making] can take rational forms',[329] and argues that their different goals can each be pursued in a rational manner. Here, as in the *Rechtssoziologie*, he equates rationality with calculability: whatever its subjective meaning, an economic process is rational to the extent its results are calculable and therefore subject to control.

What does Weber mean by the term 'calculable' in this context? At times, he uses it in a rather technical sense to mean 'relatively risk-free'. If an economic actor knows precisely what the consequences of his actions will be, the decisions he makes are risk-free. Economic conduct becomes risky only if there is a range of different outcomes which the conduct in question may produce. Understood in this sense, there is obviously some risk attached to every economic action. The risk of an action can be reduced, however, by narrowing the range of its possible outcomes and by increasing one's ability to make objectively sound predictions concerning the likelihood of each of the outcomes in question. Insurance is the most obvious example of an institution designed to reduce the riskiness of economic actions in this way, but many different social arrangements – including the very existence of a legal system – may be viewed as having, at least in part, a similar function.

Weber sometimes uses the notion of calculability to measure or describe the riskiness of an activity in the sense just defined: on this view, a particular activity becomes more calculable – and hence more rational – as its riskiness is reduced. Frequently, however, he gives the notion of calculability a broader meaning, using it as a measure of the overall costliness of an economic activity. In this broader sense, a particular activity becomes more calculable as its costs go down – as it becomes possible to perform the same activity by expending fewer resources than had previously been required. Of course, risk is itself a cost and hence any reduction of risk makes an activity more calculable in this broader sense as well. There are, however, other ways of reducing the cost of an activity (for example, by finding less expensive substitutes for the factors of production currently in use); the concept of cost-reduction includes that of risk-reduction but is not limited to it.

Even though it is somewhat misleading to equate calculability with the reduction of cost *simpliciter*, this broad and inclusive definition is the one that best expresses the different – sometimes broader, sometimes narrower – ways in which Weber uses the concept. His assertion that both budgetary management and profit-making can take rational forms should therefore be interpreted to mean that each type of economic activity can be structured in such a way that the costs of achieving its goal, whether it be want-satisfaction or the production of a profit, are as low as possible under existing conditions. If the same goal can be achieved while expending fewer resources, there is room for further rationalization of the activity, in a purely formal sense.

The fact that a particular economic activity is formally rational does not mean, however, that it is either good or bad, where these terms are used to describe its ethical or other normative qualities. An economic process – the manufacture of Zyklon B for use in extermination camps – may be evil despite its formal rationality. Whenever an economic activity is evaluated on the basis of 'certain criteria of ultimate ends',[330] it is its *substantive* rationality that one is assessing, the activity being substantively rational if it tends to advance, and irrational if it tends to thwart, the values that are thought important from the point of view one has chosen for evaluation. According to Weber, although '[t]here is an infinite number of possible value scales for this type of rationality', all such points of view have one feature in common – 'they do not restrict themselves to note the purely formal and (relatively) unambiguous fact that action is based on "goal-oriented" rational calculation with the technically most adequate available methods, but apply certain criteria of ultimate ends, whether they be ethical, political, utilitarian, hedonistic, feudal, egalitarian, or whatever, and measure the results of the economic action, however formally "rational" in the sense of correct calculation they may be, against these scales of "value rationality" or "*substantive* goal rationality".[331]

In his analysis of the forms of economic action, as in the *Rechtssoziologie*, Weber identifies formal rationality with calculability, but repeatedly states that the unqualified pursuit of calculability for its own sake may produce results that are objectionable when evaluated on the basis of one or another substantive ethical criterion. This is especially true, he claims, of modern capitalism. Although the modern capitalist system of production both pre-supposes and makes possible a degree of calculability unknown in any other economic system, those aspects of capitalism which are responsible for this unparalleled increase in formal rationality are also those most subject to criticism on ethical grounds. Among what he describes as the 'substantively irrational'[332] consequences of the formal rationality of capitalist production, Weber includes the growth of authoritarian domination in the workplace and the increased inequality in the distribution of wealth that results from a market-oriented system of production in which goods are produced to satisfy 'effective demand' and production decisions are determined 'by the structure of marginal utilities in the income group which has both the inclination and the resources to purchase a given utility'.[333] In order to understand why the effort to maximize economic calculability should have these substantively irrational consequences, it is necessary to describe the 'quite specific substantive conditions'[334] that must be satisfied if the effort is to succeed.

The substantive conditions of formal rationality in economic action
Although he asserts that both budgetary management and profit-making can take rational forms, Weber emphasizes that a maximum of formal economic rationality is attainable only if certain 'substantive conditions' are satisfied. Many of these conditions – indeed, the most important ones – are fully realized only in a capitalist economy of the modern sort. Weber in fact tends to identify capitalist production with formally rational economic action *per se*; his account of the substantive conditions of formal rationality is therefore also a description of the factors that distinguish modern capitalism from those forms of economic organization which have preceded it historically.

The first of these conditions is the possibility of calculating the value of goods – ideally, of all goods – in money terms. Only in case goods have a specific money value, a price, can the relative efficiency of different processes of production or patterns of consumption be determined with exactness. Weber acknowledges that limited comparisons of this sort are possible using either direct estimates of utility or what he calls 'calculations in kind'. However, 'when it becomes a question of comparing different *kinds* of means of production, their different possible modes of use, and qualitatively different final products',[335] only monetary calculation 'is capable of [providing] a determinate solution in principle.'[336] By contrast, 'for accounting in kind . . . there are formidable problems involved . . . which are incapable of objective solution.'[337] These problems are 'not a matter of circumstances which could be overcome by technical improvements in the methods of calculation', but reflect, instead, 'fundamental limitations, which make really exact accounting in terms of calculations in kind impossible in principle.'[338] The same is true for calculations based upon the direct comparison of utilities. To achieve the highest possible degree of exactness in computing costs and benefits, one must be able to assign a determinate money value to each of the goods or utilities being compared.

Monetary calculation of this sort itself has certain conditions, including, most importantly, the existence of a market in goods and services. According to Weber, a genuine price system can only exist in a market economy, where independent economic units satisfy most of their needs by purchasing goods rather than producing them themselves. In an economy dominated by self-sufficient households or managed by a centralized authority, where the voluntary exchange of goods for money is a limited or marginal phenomenon, it is impossible, in Weber's view, to determine with precision the relative economic value of different utilities. Efforts can be made to avoid this problem – for example, through the use of 'shadow' prices of the sort sometimes employed by socialist planners – but from the standpoint of calculability, there is nothing that compares with the price system generated by a decentralized exchange economy. This is one of the reasons why Weber concludes that a planned economy, at least where it has been 'radically carried out', must accept an 'inevitable reduction in formal, calculatory rationality'.[339] For an economic process to be maximally rational, all of its costs and benefits must be calculable in money terms and this is possible only where a price system has been created by the individual, voluntary exchange of goods for money on a regular and widespread basis.

Even this, however, does not fully describe the conditions required to achieve the highest possible degree of formal rationality in economic action. According to Weber, 'formal, calculatory rationality' presupposes a market with a specific legal structure, a market based upon a particular system of entitlements or property rights. Markets may have different legal structures, but there is only one that permits the complete formal rationalization of economic action. This structure constitutes what Weber calls a 'mode of appropriation'[340] and may be viewed as one of the specifically legal preconditions of formally rational economic action.

The system of property rights required to achieve a maximum of economic calculability has several important features. First, it must be universal in scope: all utilities must be either actually or potentially subject to an ownership claim. According to Weber, the rationalization of economic action is inhibited to the extent that certain utilities have not been appropriated (or more importantly, *cannot* be – for example, because their appropriation would violate a religious taboo). In his view, the calculability of economic action directly increases 'with the degree to which [the] sources of utility, particularly the means of transport and production, are appropriated. For, the higher the degree of marketability, the more will economic action be oriented to market situations. . . . All parties to market relations have had an interest in this expansion of property rights because it increased the area within which they could orient their action to the opportunities of profit offered by the market situation.'[341] In short, a universal market presupposes the broadest possible system of property rights, one in which all economic utilities are, or at least in principal can be, owned by some identifiable group or individual. Less extensive property systems make it more difficult to compare the economic value of different utilities and hence harder to calculate with precision the costs and benefits of various productive and consumptive activities.

Universality is the first and most general feature of the system of property rights required to achieve a maximum of formal rationality in economic action. The particular pattern of appropriation established by this system constitutes its second distinguishing characteristic. Many different patterns of appropriation have actually existed at one time or another and many more can be imagined. Not all, however, promote the formal rationalization of economic action to an equal extent; some modes of appropriation, in fact, sharply limit the calculability of productive activities. This is particularly true with respect to the appropriation of labour power. In Weber's view, slavery – the appropriation of one person's labour power by another – is 'less favourable to rationality and efficiency than the employment of free labour'.[342] Despite the fact that slavery guarantees 'what is formally a more complete power of disposal over the worker than is the case with employment for wages',[343] there are many reasons why it tends to retard the rationalization of economic activity, including: the 'specifically irrational' risk 'attendant on slave ownership' as a result of its exposure 'to all manner of non-economic influences, particularly to political influence in a very high degree'; the extreme instability of slave markets 'which has made a balancing of profit and loss on a rational basis exceedingly difficult'; the special problems of 'recruitment' associated with slave labour and the difficulty of breeding slaves for production; the inability 'to use slave labour in the operation of tools and apparatus, the efficiency of which requires a high level of responsibility and of involvement of the operator's self-interest'; and 'the impossibility of selection, of employment only after trying out in the job, and of dismissal in accordance with fluctuations of the business situation or when personal efficiency declines.'[344] For all of these reasons, Weber concludes that exact calculation is 'only possible on a basis of free labour.'[345]

The formal rationalization of economic action also requires that individual workers not have an indefeasible right to – be the owners of – the jobs they perform. According to Weber, maximum economic calculability presupposes the 'complete absence of appropriation of jobs and of opportunities for earning by workers' and hence 'freedom [of the employer] in the selection of workers'.[346] 'Every form of appropriation of jobs in profit-making enterprises by workers, like the converse case of appropriation of the services of workers by owners, involves limitations on the free recruitment of the labour force'; the appropriation of jobs by workers means 'that workers cannot be selected solely on the grounds of their technical efficiency, and to this extent there is a limitation on the *formal* rationalization of economic activity.'[347]

This last condition can be stated in more general terms. In addition to 'formally "free" labour' – the exchange of labour for money by means of 'a contractual relationship which is formally free on both sides'[348] – economic rationality also requires the complete expropriation of workers from the material means of production (the 'full appropriation of capital goods to the owner').[349] Where workers have been expropriated from the means of production, management enjoys greater freedom with regard to 'the selection and the modes of use of workers', has more control over the combination of different factors of production (including both capital and labour), is in a better position to borrow (since the assets over which it has control are not encumbered by the claims of workers), can more easily enforce the shop discipline required by complex industrial processes, and, finally, is able to take advantage of 'sources of power [which] can be rationally exploited only by using them simultaneously for many similar types of work under a unified control.'[350]

To summarize: a maximum degree of formal rationality in economic action can be attained only where all economic utilities are assigned a monetary value and this, in turn, presupposes the existence of a universal market. The market in question must, moreover, be based upon a particular system of property rights, one in which individual workers own their own labour power but do not own either their jobs or the material means of production. Free labour and the expropriation of workers from the means of production are indispensible conditions for maximizing the formal rationality of economic action. Since they define a pattern of ownership rights, these last conditions should be included among the legal prerequisites of formal economic rationalization along with the other, specifically legal, factors that Weber mentions: the existence of a juridical system in which the results of adjudication can be predicted with a relatively high degree of certainty; a law of contracts that imposes few substantive constraints on the voluntary economic arrangements individuals are permitted to make with one another; and the complete separation, from a legal point of view, of the private wealth of the owners of a firm from the assets of the firm itself.

Free labour

Of the substantive legal conditions required for the formal rationalization of economic action, and hence for capital accounting and the type of profit-making activity based upon it, free labour is in Weber's judgment the most important. 'The peculiarities of Western capitalism', he asserts, 'have derived their significance in the last analysis only from their association with the capitalistic organization of labour. . . . Exact calculation – the basis of everything else – is only possible on a basis of free labour.'[351] But despite his emphasis on the importance of free labour, and his claim that it represents the distinguishing characteristic of modern capitalism, Weber has little to say about the concept itself. Free labour, I shall argue, is a juridical idea and rests upon the same conception of personhood as that presupposed by all formally rational legal thought and by the purposive contract as a mode of association; understood in this sense, it provides a meaningful connection between the modern legal and economic orders and reflects their rootedness in a common normative ideal.

Free labour and legal personality
The term free labour has two different meanings. Understood in a negative sense, it denotes a condition in which workers have been 'freed' or expropriated from ownership of their jobs and the material means of production. According to Weber, the historical process by which workers have been separated from ownership of the means of production exactly parallels the process by which administrative officials have been separated from ownership of their offices (the material means of administration); like the modern bureaucrat, the wage labourer works with material and instruments that belong to someone else – the owner of capital – whether the owner be an individual entrepreneur or the shareholders of a large corporation (a group that may, of course, include many workers, but in a different capacity). Understood in its second or positive sense, the term free labour refers to the fact that an individual's labour power (his capacity for work) can be owned or appropriated only by the individual whose capacity it is, although he may, if he chooses, sell its use to someone else for a limited period of time. Labour is unfree, in this second sense, whenever one person is or can become the owner of another's labour power by acquiring an unrestricted legal right to dispose of it in whatever way he wishes.

In the past, labour has rarely been free in either of these two senses.[352] The appropriation of jobs and means of production by workers and the ownership of some human beings by others have both been characteristic features of most pre-modern economies. Only in the modern West has free labour, in both its positive and negative aspects, become the basis of economic life.

To the extent that it rests upon free labour, modern capitalism presupposes the expropriation of workers from the means of production and rejects the idea, so familiar and widely accepted in the past, that one person can be the property of another. In this latter respect, the modern capitalist order differs fundamentally from all forms of economic organization based on slavery or serfdom. As the following passage from chapter 2 of *Economy and Society* suggests, this feature of capitalist production in turn presupposes the acceptance of a specific conception of legal personality.

The organization of economic activity on the basis of a market economy [one of the conditions for maximizing the formal rationality of economic action] presupposes the appropriation of the material sources of utilities on the one hand and market freedom on the other. The effectiveness of market freedom increases with the degree to which these sources of utility, particularly the means of transport and production, are appropriated. For, the higher the degree of marketability, the more will economic action be oriented to market situations. But the effectiveness of market freedom also increases with the degree to which appropriation is limited to *material* [i.e. non-human] sources of utility. Every case of appropriation of human beings through slavery or serfdom, or of economic advantages through market monopolies, restricts the range of human action which can be market-oriented. Fichte, in his *Der geschlossene Handelsstaat* (Tübingen, 1800) was right in treating this limitation of the concept of 'property' to material goods, along with the increased autonomy of control over the objects which do fall under this concept, as characteristic of the modern market-oriented system.[353]

The system of property rights that underlies the modern form of market-oriented capitalism is characterized by its recognition of a categorical distinction between human beings and non-human or material things. Human beings can own things ('the material sources of utility') but they cannot own one another. From a legal point of view, a thing is an entity that can be appropriated and made the object of an ownership claim by a human being. By contrast, human beings cannot be appropriated or owned by anyone else; unlike things, however, human beings *can* assert ownership rights to their own qualities or attributes (for example, their labour power). In short, the modern concept of property rights – of which the idea of free labour in its positive aspect is merely one expression – presupposes a division of the world, from a legal point of view, into things (entities that can be owned but cannot own either themselves or anything else) and persons, who alone are capable of ownership but can only own things and not other persons.[354]

The organization of economic action on the basis of legally unfree labour is conceivable only if we abandon this distinction between persons and things – or more precisely, only if we abandon the distinction in its modern form and draw it in an entirely different way. Slavery and other forms of unfree labour entail the appropriation of some human beings by others. Since it involves the acquisition of a right or entitlement, appropriation of this sort is possible only if the human beings who are enslaved are considered things – entities of a kind that can be owned by someone other than themselves. Wherever the enslavement of one human being by another is recognized as a legally valid form of ownership, some human beings must necessarily be classed as things rather than persons, understanding these terms in the general sense described above.

This does not mean that the distinction between persons and things lacks all meaning in a legal system which recognizes the legitimacy of slavery. Classical Roman law, for example, acknowledged the legal validity of slavery but at the same time drew a principled distinction between persons and things.[355] What sets Roman law apart from the modern system of property rights that Weber describes is not the rejection of this distinction in one case and its acceptance in the other, but the interpretation that each gives to its basic terms (person and thing), that is, the way in which each legal system defines the classes to which these terms refer. In Roman law, it was possible for a human being to be a thing; by contrast, the modern concept of property limits the class of things to non-human or material objects.

The latter limitation rests upon a more democratic interpretation of the meaning of the differences between individual human beings. Wherever slavery has been legally recognized, certain human beings have been classified as things because of some quality or characteristic they possess – a characteristic that distinguishes them from the class of freemen who are not (and are often considered incapable of becoming) slaves themselves. In pre-modern legal systems, for example, an individual often inherited the status of slave from his parents; if his parents were slaves, he would be considered a slave in the eyes of the law, and treated as the actual or potential property of another person.[356] Wherever slavery has been viewed as an inheritable condition, the law has had to recognize a fundamental distinction between different kinds of men, between those who are property and those who are not. By contrast, the system of property rights that underlies the modern economic order rests upon the assumption that no difference between two human beings can ever justify a distinction of this sort, whatever other consequences it may have for their respective legal statuses.

The assumption that there is no characteristic with respect to which men differ that justifies the inclusion of some human beings in the class of things, represents a significant democratization of the concept of legal personality. This extension of the class of persons to include all human beings parallels, in an obvious way, the destruction of the old, status-based special law communities that Weber describes and the emergence, in their place, of a universal association based upon a more abstract notion of citizenship. The legitimacy of the modern state is premised upon the voluntary association (real or imagined) of equal and independent persons rather than the authoritarian command of natural leaders; similarly, the capitalist system of production is based upon the labour contract – a voluntary exchange, between equally free persons, of services for wages – rather than the direct appropriation of some human beings by others. The fact that the modern labour contract, though free in a legal sense, is made compulsory from a practical point of view by the existing distribution of material resources, provides the basis for a substantive critique of modern capitalism but in no way weakens the fundamental conceptual difference between free labour and slavery.

I have attempted to explain the difference between free and unfree labour in an essentially negative fashion by pointing out that slavery can only exist if certain concrete characteristics of an individual – his family membership, for example – are given a legal significance which they cannot have in a modern system of property rights. I now want to describe, in more positive terms, the conception of legal personality on which the modern view of the class of persons as including all human beings is implicitly based.

Every legal system that recognizes a distinction between persons and things must have some rule or principle for determining who is to count as a person, as an actual or potential owner of things. Since all legal systems that recognize the validity of slavery treat some human beings as things, an individual must be more than a mere human being to be a person in such a system – he must be a human being of a particular sort, for example, a human being born of free parents. Where slavery is legally recognized, the bare humanity of an individual can at most be a necessary condition for his inclusion in the class of persons; it can never be a sufficient condition, since slaves are also members of the human species. By contrast, in a legal system which denies the legitimacy of slavery, the fact that someone is a human being by itself makes it impermissible to treat him as a thing – or, put the other way around, makes it mandatory to treat him as a person. What general characteristic of human beings justifies broadening the class of legal persons in this way?

The concept of ownership itself suggests an answer.[357] In general terms, the class of persons includes all those who are believed to have the capacity to appropriate things and assert ownership rights to them. Now it is one thing to possess an object, and something quite different to own it. Possession requires physical control but nothing more; ownership, by contrast, involves the assertion of a legitimate right to take or retain possession of the object, and acknowledgement of the rightfulness of this claim by others. It is only by justifying the legitimacy of his possession through an appeal to a normative principle which the possessor claims is binding both on himself and those to whom his claim is addressed, that the fact of possession is transformed (assuming the claim is accepted) into rightful possession or ownership. Put differently, possession must be assigned a normative meaning or given a normative interpretation before it can become ownership in a legal sense. Only against the background of such an interpretation does it make sense to talk of ownership at all.

If we view ownership in this way, as a phenomenon which necessarily includes an interpretive element of the sort I have described, it is natural to define the class of persons to include all and only those beings who are able to assert a right to things and to understand the similar assertions of others. This capacity may be described, in Kantian terms, as the capacity to act in accordance with the conception of a rule.[358] When someone asserts a right of ownership, he is demanding that a certain entitlement rule (the rule, for example, that the first possessor of an unowned tract of land acquires title to it) be acknowledged by others and applied, in his favour, in a particular situation. The rule in question is of course only an idea: it does not have physical reality and its application is not itself a physical act like taking possession of an object. To make a claim of ownership, the would-be owner must be able to form such an idea and communicate it to others.

The ability to do so is, at bottom, identical with the capacity for purposeful action. Action is purposeful insofar as it is guided by an idea of the end which the actor is striving to attain and by a conception of the rule to be followed in attempting to reach it. It is not enough that the action in question *have* an end, or even that the actor be *drawn* toward it in an instinctive and unthinking way; an *idea* of the end – its conceptual image, so to speak – must be present in the mind of the actor and must provide the basis, to some degree at least, on which he deliberately organizes his conduct. In this sense, all purposeful action may be said to contain an ideal element; indeed, it is the presence of this element that distinguishes purposeful action from teleological behaviour, as I used that term in Chapter 2. In a precisely analogous fashion, claims of ownership are distinguished from mere possession by their dependence upon the idea of an entitlement rule that functions as a critical standard for the assessment of conduct.[359] Both purposeful action and ownership claims contain an ideal component of this sort and hence presuppose an ability, on the part of the actor or owner, to modify his own behaviour on the basis of an idea – a capacity for action in accordance with the conception of a rule.

Since this capacity is one that all or nearly all human beings possess, we must define the class of persons to include all members of the species and reject any narrower definition that attributes legal personality – the capacity for ownership – to only some human beings (those possessed of an additional characteristic such as free birth). The ability to act in accordance with the conception of a rule is one that is both species-wide and species-specific: with a few marginal exceptions, it is an ability that all human beings, including children, possess and that non-human animals lack. The possession of such a capacity is, moreover, a sufficient (rather than merely necessary) condition for ownership since ownership is itself distinguished from simple possession by the presence of this element alone; it is his claim of right, based upon the invocation of an entitlement rule – and nothing else – which distinguishes the owner, or would-be owner, of an object from someone who merely possesses it.

To summarize: free labour in its positive aspect – the legal prohibition against one human being owning or appropriating another – presupposes that all members of the species are persons rather than things in the sense defined above. This expansive conception of the class of persons in turn rests upon two premises: first, that possession of a capacity for action in accordance with the conception of a rule is a sufficient condition for inclusion in the class of persons (a notion which follows, in a direct way, from the concept of ownership itself); and second, that this capacity is one which all (and only) human beings possess.

By contrast, the legal recognition of unfree labour requires that certain human beings be classified as things rather than persons. This is possible, however, only if some further attribute, in addition to the universal human capacity for action in accordance with the conception of a rule, is made a prerequisite for membership in the class of persons. A rule stating that the children of slaves are themselves to be treated as slaves – a rule making free birth a condition of legal personality – illustrates this more restricted conception of personhood. Aristotle's famous discussion of natural slavery, in which he asserts that the moral imagination of some human beings is so limited as to incapacitate them for anything but a slavish life of service and dependency, illustrates the same view in a different way.[360] According to Aristotle, something more is required to be an owner – a manager of property, as he puts it – than the ability to understand ideas and follow rules, an ability he assumes even the natural slave possesses. In Aristotle's view, this additional attribute (wisdom, virtue, moral imagination) is possessed by only some human beings and so, like the attribute of free birth, demarcates a particular sub-group within the species as a whole; this class alone is endowed with legal personality (the capacity for ownership). Free labour can exist only where all particularizing attributes of this sort are considered irrelevant in determining who is to be included in the class of persons.

The conception of legal personality presupposed by a regime of unfree labour closely resembles the one on which status contracts are based. Every status contract rests on the assumption that an individual's legal personality – the totality of his rights and duties – depends entirely upon his possession of certain natural or quasi-natural qualities that he has acquired by birth or through what Weber calls an act of fraternization. These qualities distinguish the individual who possesses them from other men and make him a member of a special law community. In a world dominated by status-based associations of this sort, an individual can have no legal personality apart from his membership in one or another special law community; apart from the group with whom he shares his defining status qualities, the individual is quite literally nothing, at least in the eyes of the law. In a similar way, the class of persons – those individuals in whom the law recognizes a capacity for ownership – will necessarily constitute a special law community whenever the possession of some particular quality not shared by all human beings, such as free birth or moral wisdom, is made a prerequisite for membership in the class itself. Status contracts and slavery both rest upon the assumption that an individual can have a legal personality, be a bearer of legally protected rights and entitlements, only in case he possesses some determinate quality which distinguishes him, and the others who possess it, from those who lack the quality and the legal standing it confers.

Purposive contracts rest upon a fundamentally different conception of legal personality. A purposive contract binds the parties to it not because it creates a quasi-natural bond that is thought to be a source of obligation in its own right, but because it is the product or expression of the parties' will. As I emphasized in Chapter 5, this conception of obligation is intelligible only if we think of the contracting parties as having a legal identity apart from and antecedently to the various contractual relations they create for themselves, an identity founded upon the possession of a capacity for intentional action rather than any particular attribute created by the establishment of a specific contractual relationship. Viewed simply as wills, as beings endowed with the ability to impose obligations on themselves by entering, voluntarily, into contractual relations with others, the parties to a purposive contract are alike and equal. Unlike the status distinctions to which all contracts of fraternization attach such decisive importance and which, at least originally, entailed a division of the species into numerous independent special law communities, the identification of an individual's legal personality with his will, understood in the abstract sense as a bare capacity for purposeful action, makes it possible to talk meaningfully about the equality of all men and prepares the way for the emergence of a universal community (the state) which transcends all status-based special law communities.

In a similar way, free labour – the denial that any human being can be owned or appropriated by another – presupposes a broadening of the class of persons to include all men. The class of persons can be broadened in this way, however, only if membership in it is not conditioned upon the possession of a quality or characteristic possessed by some men but not others. As I have attempted to show, the concept of ownership itself suggests a broadened membership criterion of this sort: since ownership is distinguished from possession by the would-be owner's appeal to an entitlement rule, it is appropriate to treat an individual's capacity to make and understand such appeals as a sufficient warrant for including him in the class of persons. Different individuals will exercise this capacity in different ways; the capacity, however, is one that all men share.

The capacity for action in accordance with the conception of a rule is, at bottom, identical to the power of self-regulation on which the obligatoriness of all purposive contracts is based; it is, in other words, merely another name for the will. The concept of free labour and the idea of purposive contractual exchange thus both rest upon a similar understanding of what it means to be a legal person, a being with the power to create rights and own property. Each presupposes that an individual's legal personality, his status as a bearer and creator of rights, depends entirely upon his possession of a faculty that may variously be described as the capacity for purposeful action, for voluntary self-regulation or for action in accordance with the conception of a rule.

This link between the concept of free labour and the idea of purposive contractual association is important for two reasons. First, the dominance of purposive contracts as a source of legal rights and the organization of economic life on the basis of free labour are both, according to Weber, distinctively modern phenomena. The dependence of free labour and purposive contractual exchange on the same conception of legal personality thus provides a meaningful connection between what Weber considered the most characteristic features of modern law and capitalist production. Second, the notion of legal personality on which they both rest is the juristic counterpart of the will-centred conception of personhood that underlies Weber's theory of value and his account of the distinctive features of sociological inquiry. The conception of the person as a will – a being endowed with the power to set ends for himself and pursue them in a self-conscious and rule-governed fashion – thus not only links Weber's analysis of the forms of contractual association to his description of the defining characteristics of modern capitalism, but establishes a connection between both of these and his methodological views as well. Here, too, there is a striking convergence between Weber's own epistemological beliefs and the implicit presuppositions of the institutions he considered most characteristic of modern European civilization.

The expropriation of labour from the means of production

Understood in its positive sense, free labour means the non-appropriation of workers by owners. According to Weber, the non-appropriation of workers is one of the essential conditions for achieving a maximum of formal economic rationality and is a distinguishing charateristic of the modern capitalist order. Weber also asserts, however, that economic calculability can be maximized only where workers do not have a right to insist on continued employment or to determine how the material means of production shall be used, where they own neither their jobs nor the material factors employed in the production process itself. It is this that I have characterized as the negative aspect of free labour – labour which is free in the sense that it has been detached or separated from ownership of the means of production. This aspect of free labour also describes a structure of rights or entitlements. It is therefore appropriate to characterize freedom of labour in its negative sense as another of the legal pre-conditions of capitalist production.

In contrast to the non-appropriation of workers by owners, however, the expropriation of workers from the means of production is not tied to a specific conception of legal personality. If owners were allowed to appropriate workers and to treat them as their property, it would be necessary to redefine the class of persons to exclude some individuals that it now includes; to this extent, free labour in its positive aspect is indissolubly linked to a particular conception of what it means to be a legal person. By contrast, appropriation of the means of production by workers, either individually or collectively, is perfectly consistent with a continuing commitment to the idea that every human being is a person, a bearer of rights and entitlements, who cannot himself be appropriated by anyone else. Thus, while it is impossible to deny the freedom of labour in its positive aspect without embracing a narrower conception of legal personality, the appropriation of the means of production by workers need have no such effect on our notion of what it means to be a person, although it would obviously alter the distribution of rights to non-human goods.

According to Weber, appropriation of the means of production by workers would, however, have a significant effect on the formal rationality of economic action. The separation of workers from ownership of the means of production could not be abolished, in his view, without some – perhaps considerable – sacrifice of formal rationality and therefore some increase in production costs. One may, of course, conclude that a sacrifice of this sort is worth the price. It is the negative aspect of free labour – the separation of workers from the means of production – which is responsible for the extraordinary increase in discipline and authoritarian control that Weber associated with the capitalist workplace, something he himself characterized as one of the 'substantively irrational' consequences of the capitalist system of production. Is the decrease in discipline and authoritarian control that might be achieved if workers were given ownership of the means of production, either individually or collectively through state ownership, worth the loss of formal rationality (the increase in production costs) that would result – *necessarily* result, in Weber's view – from altering the capitalist pattern of property rights in this way? Weber considered this question to be the central one posed by modern socialism. But however one answers it – and as we shall see, Weber's own answer was indecisive and ambiguous – it is important to note that this question does not put in issue the soundness of the conception of legal personality presupposed by the freedom of labour in its positive aspect. Like the defenders of the capitalist order, the proponents of socialism are committed to the principle that one human being cannot own another and to the conception of legal personality which this principle presupposes. The freedom of labour in its positive aspect is endorsed by capitalists and socialists alike; their agreement in this respect transcends whatever other differences they may have. It is only with regard to the expropriation of workers from the means of production – the negative aspect of free labour – that the defenders of capitalism and its socialist critics take sharply different positions.

If this is true, however, the defining characteristic of modern capitalism, which Weber states in general terms to be its dependence on free labour, must actually be something more specific, namely, the separation of workers from the means of production – for it is *this* feature of the capitalist order which alone distinguishes it from its most important contemporary competitor. This in turn implies that Weber's concept of modernity is broader than his concept of capitalist production and hence cannot be equated with it. What gives the capitalist system of production its peculiarly modern character and connects it in a meaningful way to the other distinguishing features of modern social and political life is its association with a particular conception of legal personality, one that socialism does not challenge in any deep or fundamental respect (making socialism itself an essentially modern phenomenon, as Weber recognized). Thus, although Weber describes capitalism as the 'most fateful force' in modern life, he viewed modernity as a concept or category embracing both capitalist and socialist forms of economic organization, and believed that the most characteristic features of the modern age would not be eliminated, but rather intensified, by the transition from one to the other – a belief which led him to oppose socialism out of an ambivalent opposition to the rationalizing tendencies of modernity as a whole.

7

The disenchanting religion

Although Weber was fascinated by religion and wrote more extensively on this subject than any other, the *Rechtssoziologie* itself has little to say about the relation between law and religion. It is nevertheless natural to wonder how this branch of Weber's work is related to his study of religious ideas and institutions, given the latter's importance in his sociology as a whole.

The few explicit remarks on religion which the *Rechtssoziologie* does contain are mostly to be found in Weber's discussion of the substantive rationality that typifies priestly or theocratic forms of law-making. 'The distinctive characteristic of a theocratic administration of justice', he asserts, 'consists entirely in the primacy of concrete ethical considerations; its indifference or aversion to formalism is limited only insofar as the rules of the sacred law are explicitly formulated.'[361] However, to the extent such rules *are* formulated, 'the theocratic type of law results in the exact opposite, viz., a law which, in order to be adaptable to changing circumstances, develops an extremely formalistic casuistry.'[362] In short, sacred law tends to produce two contrary results – on the one hand, a high degree of casuistical formality and on the other, an emphasis on the importance of the individual case. These divergent characteristics nevertheless have similar practical consequences since each obstructs the rationalization of economic conduct, one by giving prominence to theological considerations remote from everyday life, the other by reducing the predictability of judicial decisions. For these reasons, Weber concludes that the theocratic administration of law 'must necessarily interfere with the operation of a rational economic system'; only 'the precise extent of this interference . . . varies from place to place'.[363]

There is, however, one important exception to this rule. According to Weber, '[t]he Canon Law of Christendom occupies a relatively special position with reference to all other systems of sacred law. In many of its parts it was much more rational and more highly developed on the formal side than the other cases of sacred law.'[364] A variety of factors help to account for the uniquely high degree of formal rationality displayed by the Canon Law. These include: the influence on it of the Stoic conception of natural law (which Weber characterizes as 'a rational body of ideas'); the incorporation into the Canon Law of 'the rational traditions of the Roman Law' together with 'the most formal components of Germanic Law'; and the 'structure of the occidental medieval university [which] separated the teaching of both theology and secular law from that of Canon Law and thus prevented the

147

growth of such theocratic hybrid structures as developed elsewhere'.[365] Above all else, however, the character of the Canon Law was 'influenced by the fact that the church's functionaries were holders of rationally defined bureaucratic offices.'[366] According to Weber, 'the rigorously rational hierarchical organization of the church' encouraged the view that new law can be created only through deliberate conciliar legislation and was the 'relatively decisive factor' in causing 'the occidental church [to travel] the path of legislation by rational enactment much more pronouncedly than any other religious community.'[367] This tendency, which enabled the Canon Law to serve as 'one of the guides for secular law on the road to rationality', was reinforced by the fact that 'the basic writ of Christianity [contained] such a minimum of formally binding norms of a ritual or legal character that the way was left entirely free for purely rational enactment.'[368]

Although it is brief and merely suggestive, Weber's discussion of Canon Law is noteworthy for the emphasis it places on the idea of 'legislation by rational enactment', an idea that plays a central role both in his theory of authority and in his account of formal legal rationality. There is another sense, as well, in which Weber's treatment of Canon Law reflects themes developed more fully elsewhere in his writings. Weber claims that Canon Law contributed to the extraordinary rationalization of life, particularly economic life, characteristic of the modern West – in contrast to other forms of sacred law-making which tended to retard the process of rationalization rather than promote it. In this respect, Canon Law has had an effect similar to other Judeo-Christian ideas and institutions (such as the medieval monastery and the Calvinist conception of labour in a calling) which have also contributed to the rationalization of modern European civilization. In his writings on religion, Weber attempts to demonstrate the unique effect which this particular religious tradition has had on the development of secular capitalism by examining the ways in which other beliefs and practices have obstructed the growth of a systematic, market-oriented capitalism outside the modern West.

Like the *Rechtssoziologie*, Weber's writings on religion are in large part concerned with a problem of causation: to what extent have religious factors had a causal influence on economic behaviour and to what extent has the reverse been true? Although he makes a convincing case for the view that religious ideas have had a significant impact on material life, Weber also emphasizes the deep and pervasive influence that material conditions have had on the formation of religious beliefs and institutions. (The first point of view is especially prominent in his essay on Protestantism and the second in his discussion of ancient Judaism.) Taken as a whole, Weber's sociology of religion reflects the same causal agnosticism, the same unwillingness to assign causal primacy either to ideas or material conditions, that characterizes his treatment of legal phenomena. At the end of his essay on Protestantism – which demonstrates, perhaps more convincingly than anything written before or since, the influence of religious beliefs on economic behaviour – Weber warns the reader that his aim has not been 'to substitute for a one-sided materialistic an equally one-sided spiritualistic causal interpretation of culture and history.' 'Each is equally possible', he concludes, 'but each, if it does not serve as the preparation, but as the conclusion of an investigation, accomplishes equally little in the interest of historical truth.'[369]

Weber's writings on religion attempt to do more, however, than merely assess the causal influence that religious ideas and practices have had on material life. Here, as in the *Rechtssoziologie*, Weber is also concerned with a problem of meaning: what are the special epistemological and normative premises on which the Judeo-Christian conception of God as a personal, transcendent world-creating deity is based and how do its intellectual presuppositions differ from those that underlie the religions of Asia and the philosophical systems of Occidental antiquity? The Judeo-Christian conception of God rests upon a unique view of the world and man's place in it and one of Weber's objectives is to deepen our understanding of its distinguishing characteristics.

In the first section of this chapter, I shall attempt to show that there is an important convergence between the normative beliefs that underlie the Judeo-Christian conceptions of God and personal salvation and those that implicitly shape the institutions most characteristic of the modern legal order. As we have seen, formal legal rationality and purposive contractual association both rest upon an acceptance of the distinction between facts and values, a distinction that in turn presupposes a particular conception of the person – a conception of the person as a will. The idea of a transcendent, world-creating personal deity entails a similar distinction between what Weber calls the 'logically heterogeneous' spheres of fact and value, and expresses a similar view of what it means to be a person. In his general remarks on the nature of Asian religiosity, Weber acknowleges the connection between these ideas more explicitly than he does anywhere else in his writings. Weber's sociology of religion thus confirms the claim that there is an important philosophical link between the principle of positivity and a will-centred conception of personhood, and makes the effort to organize other aspects of his work around these same ideas more reasonable.

In the second section of the chapter, I examine a more specific connection between the *Rechtssoziologie* and one especially important part of Weber's work on religion – his detailed study of the social and religious foundations of ancient Judaism, whose evolution he describes as 'a turning point of the whole cultural development of the West and the Middle East'[370] that raises problems 'unique in the socio-historical study of religion'.[371] According to Weber, the uniqueness of ancient Judaism is largely attributable to the Israelites' conception of God as a 'contractual partner'.

> In its special relation to God, Israel stood in contrast to all other nations because of this very unique historical event [the 'old covenant with Yahwe'] and the unique conclusion of a covenant. Israel's special relationship to God was not merely guaranteed by God, but had been concluded with God as a party to it. The entire Israelite tradition unanimously traced its origins back to the concrete event

assumed to have set the process in motion. . . . The special permanent obligations of the people to God were justified by the pledges of the people and the promises of God offered in return. This made of Him a God of promise for Israel in a sense unknown of any other God.[372]

The prominence given the notion of contractual obligation in his account of ancient Judaism naturally suggests some connection with the main themes of the *Rechtssoziologie*. One is likely to be struck, in particular, by the connection that Weber himself draws between the conception of God as a contractual partner and the emergence of a form of juristic interpretation employing methods 'at least relatively rational' in character.[373] In the second section of the chapter, I shall try to clarify the relationship between these ideas and to establish their connection with Weber's theory of authority and his own existentialist ethic of ultimate commitment.

The Judeo-Christian conception of God

The relation between man and God

According to Weber, the conception of God as a supra-mundane, personal lord of creation is an exclusively 'Near Eastern concept' which played no significant role in the religions of China and India. Although they differ in many other important respects, Judaism, Christianity and Islam all rest upon the belief that God is a personal deity who stands above the world and brings it into being from nothing. This conception expresses what Weber calls 'the decisive elements of occidental belief in God and creation', and marks a fundamental contrast between the religions of the Near East, on the one hand, and those of Asia, on the other.[374]

The Judeo-Christian conception of God rests upon the following three beliefs: first, that God is a person, rather than an impersonal force or principle; second, that He is not immanent in the world but stands above it; and third, that God is a creator who brings the world into existence out of nothing, not a *demiourgos* who fashions the world from pre-existing material or who generates it through sexual reproduction. The elements of this conception do not fit together in a smooth and consistent way. In particular, there is an obvious tension between the notion that God is a person and the belief that He is a supra-mundane and omnipotent creator. To think of God as a person, we must imagine Him having qualities and powers similar to those possessed by other persons, including human persons, and therefore as being like us in certain respects. This is what is meant by saying that God is a person rather than an impersonal force like order or love. At the same time, however, God is profoundly different from us, for unlike his human creatures, He does not owe His own existence to anyone or anything else. Even in their most creative activities, men are unable to do more than reshape a world (of things and ideas) for whose initial existence they are not responsible; indeed, they are themselves created beings, creatures, who owe their existence to someone else. God, by contrast, brings the world into being *ex nihilo*, without the need for any pre-existing materials, in an act of supreme self-sufficiency. The dependent character of our human existence, and the independence of God's, marks a permanent ontological difference of the most fundamental sort: in every human endeavour we are confronted by our lack of that self-sufficiency that God alone possesses.

These two ideas – that God is a person like us and a lord of creation whose self-sufficiency places Him at an infinite distance from everything human – are not easily reconciled; the more one is stressed, the more problematic the other becomes. This tension is already apparent, for example, in the religion of the ancient Israelite confederacy, whose God is reciprocally bound to His chosen people by a covenant or *berith*, and often wears the human face of a disappointed, but loving, contractual partner. Like any other person, Yahwe is obligated to keep His promises, so long as the conditions of the covenant have been fulfilled. But how can an omnipotent lord of creation bind Himself in this way? It is God's humanity – the fact that He is a person like us – which makes his status as a contractual partner intelligible. Calvinism, with its doctrine of predestination, represents the opposite extreme. One of the consequences (indeed, one of the aims) of this doctrine is to increase the distance between man and God. Although it is assumed that God has reasons for having distributed human fates in the way He has, His reasons are inaccessible to human understanding; the plan of the universe has been framed by an intelligence so utterly unlike our own that we cannot comprehend it from His point of view. The doctrine of predestination emphasizes – indeed, celebrates – the difference between man and God by placing an insuperable barrier between God's perspective on the world and our own. But because it seeks to preserve God's transcendent dignity by insisting on the inscrutability of His thoughts and decisions, Calvinism renders problematic the notion that God is a person and therefore, in certain respects at least, like us; the more one emphasizes the difference between man and God out of respect for God's independence, the less confident one can be that He is a person whose constitution is sufficiently like our own to enable us to adopt His perspective or point of view and grasp His plan for the world through a kind of empathetic understanding.

Either, as in ancient Judaism, God's human qualities are emphasized, in which case the ontological difference between creator and creature is blurred, or, as in Calvinism, God's transcendence is stressed, in which case the claim that He is a person who has certain qualities in common with human beings becomes problematic if not blasphemous. These two beliefs – that God is at once an inhumanly self-sufficient creator *ex nihilo* and a being invested with certain qualities that we also recognize in men and by virtue of which we consider them persons as well – point in different directions and are reconcilable only through an uneasy compromise that requires one or the other to be qualified in some essential respect. Because of this conceptual tension in its basic premises, the Judeo-Christian conception of God as a personal, supra-mundane lord of creation has a characteristic *instability* not to be found, according to Weber, in the religions of Asia.

God's transcendence and the devaluation of the world

The Judeo-Christian conception of God denies His immanence in the world: God stands above the world, and although He is responsible for the orderliness we observe in it, He is not to be thought of as this orderliness itself but rather its architect or creator. Moreover, since God is the creator of the universe, we must think of Him as existing apart from everything that has a worldly existence – from all of the world's 'sense-data characteristics', to borrow a phrase from the *Rechtssoziologie* – and therefore as having an entirely different kind of reality than the things we see about us. By contrast, according to Weber, the religions of Asia identify divinity with the orderliness of the world itself, its eternal Tao or Dharma, and conceive it to be an immanent and impersonal principle rather than a transcendent personal creator. The Judeo-Christian conception of God as the creator of the universe implies an ontological discontinuity between God and the world which is unthinkable in those religions that equate the divine with the inherent and observable structure of the world itself.

The Judeo-Christian conception of God as a transcendent creator has two important implications. First, one cannot accept this view and at the same time ascribe to the world any intrinsic value or significance of its own. By itself, the world has no meaning; it acquires meaning only as the product or expression of God's creative activity, as an artifact of divine will, and therefore only when it is considered from a point of view beyond the world itself. By contrast, the religions of Asia do not require that we establish the meaning of the world from a supra-mundane standpoint; indeed, they do not even allow for the possibility of doing so, since they conceive the world to be a self-sufficient and all-encompassing totality (so that release from the world can only mean the attainment of a state of complete nothingness or non-existence – the Buddhist heaven of *nirvana*).

Second, the Judeo-Christian conception of God as a transcendent creator implies a view of religious authority that is essentially positivistic. The norms which the followers of such a God are required to observe are binding not because they are the expression of an eternal and uncreated natural order but because they are the commandments of God and have been deliberately enacted by Him. It is their origin in an act of divine legislation which gives these norms their obligatory force and hence their normative character. By contrast, the immanent and impersonal principles that in the Asian religions are believed to inform human conduct and determine the fate of individuals derive their ethical significance from the fact that they are considered part of an uncreated and eternally valid natural order.

These two implications of the Judeo-Christian conception of God – the denial that the world has intrinsic value and the acceptance of a positivistic view of religious authority – have obvious parallels in Weber's own theory of value. In his methodological writings, Weber asserts that the domain of facts (the analogue of the world in the Judeo-Christian view) has no inherent meaning of its own, but acquires one only through an act of will that does not itself belong to the sphere of factual occurrences. Like the Judeo-Christian conception, Weber's own rests upon a principled distinction between 'is' and 'ought' and the acceptance of a positivist theory of value. Indeed, one may fairly describe Weber's theory of value as a secular form of Christianity – a Christianity without God. Like the true-believing Christian, Weber denies that the world has an intrinsic meaning of its own; whatever meaning it does have is attributable to a creative act of will that belongs to an entirely different dimension or 'sphere' of reality from the world as it is given to us in experience. According to Weber, however, it is not God who give the world its meaning, but individual human beings, each acting on his own and without divine assistance.

The existentialist ethic that Weber endorses in his own methodological writings results from the combination of three different elements – the notion that men have a 'metaphysical need' to live in a world they can regard as meaningful, the idea that the world has no inherent meaning of its own but must be given one through a kind of deliberate legislation, and the (implicit) assumption that it is man himself who must perform this meaning-giving act. Every religion represents a response to the universal human need for meaningfulness but only the Judeo-Christian conception of God as a transcendent creator entails the radical devaluation of the world and positivistic view of normativity presupposed by Weber's own secular existentialism. Weber's theory of value is, of course, profoundly irreligious in the sense that it places the entire responsibility for guaranteeing the meaningfulness of the world on man himself – it is a theory in which God plays no role whatsoever. Nevertheless, his theory does retain what might be called a *conception* of God's role – the conception of God as a person who gives the world purpose and meaning through the deliberate enactment of norms. Weber remains committed to the idea that some person must perform this legislative function if the world is to have any meaning at all, even though he assigns the task to someone other than God.

Indeed, there is some justification for viewing Weber's own existentialist ethic as the end result of the destruction of the Judeo-Christian conception of God 'at the hands of its own morality' (Nietzsche). This conception, as I have already noted, is an inherently unstable one. In order to preserve God's transcendent dignity, He must be conceived in a way that makes him increasingly inaccessible to human reason and experience (one of the intended consequences, according to Weber, of the Calvinist doctrine of predestination). As the distance between man and God increases, however, the idea of a relationship between them becomes more problematic until one is finally forced to acknowledge that no such relationship can even be thought or imagined without illicitly humanizing God in some fashion. But if a relationship with God is literally unthinkable for this reason, we cannot look to Him for guidance or confirmation but must do the best we can using our own human resources. As a result, it becomes increasingly difficult to view God as a guarantor of the meaningfulness of human experience; if this role is to be filled at all, it must be filled by someone else. But the only candidate for this role is man himself since only man, having been fashioned in

God's image and endowed with a free will, possesses the power to legislate new values into existence and, by imposing them on the world, to give it a meaning it does not have in its own right. Thus, unless one gives up the demand for meaningfulness, or accepts the view that the world has an inherent meaning of its own, the self-destruction of the Judeo-Christian conception of God through the radicalization of its own premises leads in a natural way to the kind of secular existentialism that Weber himself embraces in his methodological writings.

Gnosis and ethical personality
The religions of Asia conceive God or divinity in an impersonal fashion, as a ruling order immanent in the world itself – the world's Tao or the universal Dharma that determines all destinies. This divine order transforms the world into an 'enchanted garden', beyond which there is only the absence of reality or nothingness, and gives it an inherent meaning of its own. As Weber himself observes, the religions of Asia do not acknowledge a distinction between facts and values.

Where divinity is conceived in this way as the world's own order or animating principle, there can be no fundamental gap between man and God of the sort entailed by the Judeo-Christian conception. Along with everything else, man partakes of the divine and participates in it; although he may not understand his situation, man *is* God already and there is thus no insuperable barrier to his becoming more fully (or at least more consciously) Godlike. This immediately helps to explain a fundamental fact that Weber emphasizes in his sociology of religion. According to Weber, it is characteristic of all the Asian religions that individual salvation consists in a process of self-deification, a process that may take different forms but in every case has as its basic aim a union of the individual with God. Unless man and God possessed the same sort of reality and belonged to the same world – unless they stood, so to speak, on the same ontological level – an assimilating union of this sort would be impossible.

Weber uses the *vessel* as a metaphor to describe this process of self-deification: the individual seeking salvation attempts to fill himself up with God as a vessel becomes filled with wine. From a Judeo-Christian perspective, every such effort must be considered blasphemous since it implicitly denies the existence of an ineradicable difference between man and God. If God is a transcendent, personal deity the most one can hope to become is His *tool* – an instrument that serves God and helps Him to realize His plan for the world. A tool cannot direct itself or set its own ends but depends on the guiding hand of the craftsman who employs it. Tools by definition lack self-sufficiency and thus the metaphor of the tool – one of Weber's favourites – reminds us of the lack of self-sufficiency that in the Judeo-Christian conception characterizes the condition of all creatures, placing them at an infinite distance from their creator.

According to Weber, the great religious systems of Asia all imagine personal salvation to consist in the possession of a saving wisdom or *gnosis* which liberates its possessor from the apparent absurdities and meaninglessness of the world. Although efforts to achieve such knowledge may be strenuous and methodical, the end-state that is sought is essentially one of passive intellectual comprehension. By contrast, in the Judeo-Christian conception it is not knowledge or wisdom but the striving for 'ethical personality'[375] that defines the path to salvation. What does Weber mean by *gnosis* and 'ethical personality' and how is the difference between these two conceptions of salvation related to the difference between the vessel (self-deification) and the tool (instrumental activity in the service of God)?

The belief that salvation comes with knowledge and consists in an intellectual state or condition assumes that the world has a definite structure which is intelligible to human beings (can be comprehended by the human mind). This in turn presupposes that the mind itself has a structure that is isomorphic with the structure of the world, so that the latter can be 'taken in' and comprehended by the former. The characteristic Eastern emphasis on *gnosis* as the path to salvation thus reflects a belief in the basic continuity of the human and divine – in contrast, for example, to the Calvinist doctrine of predestination which emphasizes the unintelligibility of God's decisions as a necessary consequence of His distance from man. Indeed, the idea of a saving knowledge or *gnosis* implies a striving for self-deification. This is what is meant by saying that the contemplative mystic is 'taken over' by his vision and reduced to an apathetic ecstasy or by claiming (as Aristotle does in the last book of the *Nicomachean Ethics*) that the philosopher himself becomes godlike through his contemplation of the divine. In either case, the saving *gnosis* that the mystic or philosopher acquires quite literally fills him up with divinity; to think of knowledge as the path to salvation is to think of the human soul as a vessel in which God can be captured or retained. The Judeo-Christian conception of God denies the possibility of a self-deifying *gnosis*, and views any suggestion to the contrary as a blasphemous expression of human pridefulness.

One important consequence of the attempt to achieve salvation through knowledge is the loss of individuality that every effort of this sort necessarily entails. The person who seeks a saving knowledge of the divine order of the world must first prepare his soul to receive such knowledge by ridding himself of all subjective passions and beliefs; only after he has eliminated every interference of this sort can the person seeking *gnosis* see reality with an unclouded eye. This requires, however, that the individual give up everything he had previously thought his own, all of his subjective attachments which now represent obstacles in the way of achieving the union with divinity that he desires. Loss of self-identity is simply the other side of self-deification. In becoming one with God, a person ceases to be the distinct individual he was before: his being is now merged into that of some larger, impersonal reality. Consequently, every philosophical or contemplative technique that is intended to produce a *gnosis* of some sort also entails the systematic eradication of the individual's own distinctive personality and his transformation into an empty and utterly passive receptacle which no longer fears the loss of self-identity that a union with God entails.

Once an individual has achieved the *gnosis* he seeks, he will, according to Weber, automatically do what is right. Right conduct follows immediately from the intellectual state in question, and does not require a further choice on the part of the individual – a choice or decision to do what he knows to be good. This observation is important for two reasons. First, it underscores the essentially passive conception of the self implied by the view that salvation can be achieved through wisdom or knowledge. Once the soul has opened itself up to reality – a process that may require considerable effort and discipline but is intended to culminate in a state of apathy – there is nothing left for it to do. Second, Weber's remark reminds us – indeed, seems intended to remind us – of the Socratic view that knowledge is a sufficient condition for virtue. As we have seen, Socrates' equation of knowledge and virtue presupposes a particular conception of the self, one in which the passive, knowing part of soul – the part that looks at reality and is informed by it – plays the central, defining role. The characteristic intellectualism of the Asian religions rests upon a similar conception of the self, as Weber's own comments on the general nature of Eastern religiosity make clear; indeed, Weber states quite explicitly that the typical Asian belief in *gnosis* as the sole path to salvation implies a conception of the self that is radically different from the conception associated with the occidental belief that salvation can only be secured through the attainment of what he calls 'ethical personality'. The latter view is based upon a conception of the self in which the will – the active, doing, choosing part of the soul – plays the decisive role and gives the self its identity. As Weber observes, this conception locates the self's 'point of gravity'[376] in the will rather than the intellect, and has strikingly different implications for how a person conducts his life.

In contrast to the religions of Asia – which all aim at a 'godlike beholding, possession, property, or obsession of a holiness which is not of this world and yet can, through *gnosis*, be achieved in this world'[377] – the 'occidental ideal of active behaviour – be it in a religious sense concerning the beyond, be it inner-wordly – centrally fixes upon "personality".'[378] It is the concept of ethical personality which lies at the basis of the 'specifically occidental' notion that salvation can be attained only through the 'systematic unification of [one's] life conduct'[379] in accordance with God's commands. In striving to become a personality, an individual is not, like the gnostic sage, seeking to *become* God but only to live in accordance with God's plan or commands, to live a life which is ethical in the sense that it reflects his commitment to God and willingness to obey Him. Even if he achieves an ethical personality in this sense, the individual remains at an infinite distance from God. Ethical personality is a state or condition of the will – the 'purity of heart' (Kierkegaard's phrase) that consists in an unwavering and single-minded commitment to God – and does not itself entail the individual's self-deification. To will god, even without qualification, is not to be God himself. This is the first difference between ethical personality and all forms of self-deifying *gnosis*.

A second and related difference concerns the autonomy of the individual himself. Anyone who seeks a saving wisdom must attempt to eliminate the subjective qualities that stand in the way of understanding, to empty himself of 'worldly relations and worldly cares'[380] and ultimately of 'the real forces of experience',[381] thereby transforming himself into a vessel suitable for receiving God. The Asiatic conception of *gnosis* as 'the single absolute path to the highest holiness'[382] implies a loss of self and requires the individual who seeks salvation from the absurdities of the world to erase his own identity; this loss of self is simply the other side of that union with the divine which the 'apathetic-ecstatic godly possession of *gnosis*'[383] represents. By contrast, the search for ethical personality is a search for what Weber calls 'the individual self in contrast to all others, the attempt to take the self by the forelock and pull it out of the mud, forming it into a "personality".'[384] In the struggle to attain the state of wilful obedience that represents for him the only imaginable form of salvation, someone striving to become a personality necessarily acquires a heightened sense of his own identity as a distinct person, separate from other persons and from the world in general. Consequently, unlike the gnostic philosopher or holy man, he becomes more of an individual, rather than less of one, in his search for salvation. His guiding aim is the creation of an identity, not its obliteration, and he seeks to give his self coherence and value by deliberately imposing an order on his own life. As Weber stresses, this effort is a methodical and comprehensive one that aims at transforming the person's whole life, leaving no part of his conduct or experience untouched. In his search for a personality, an individual seeks to arrange his life so that he can regard it as his own responsibility rather than a piece of good or bad fortune. It is only when he is able to view his life in this way, as the expression of a systematic plan for right conduct, that an individual can feel confident he has attained the condition which alone guarantees his salvation. And this condition, unlike the passive emptiness that is the explicit goal of all gnostic techniques of self-deification, must itself be conceived as an activity, a steady and uninterrupted act of willing in which the soul continuously reaffirms its commitment to God. To be an ethical person is to maintain this state of active willing through the whole of one's life.

As Weber emphasizes, the concept of ethical personality implies a markedly different conception of the self from that presupposed by the gnostic ideal of a 'godlike beholding'. The latter encourages us to think of the self as a being or entity that *knows* and to conceive its knowing as a passive reception of what lies beyond the self, a looking or beholding in which the self is informed by the object of its contemplative gaze. The idea of ethical personality conceives the self as a being that *wills* (chooses, plans, decides) in an effort to actively express its individuality rather than obliterate it.

In this respect, the concept of ethical personality reproduces, at the human level, the Judeo-Christian conception of God as a transcendent lord of creation. Just as God brings the world into being out of nothing and imposes a planful order on the universe by *fiat*, an individual striving to become a personality must, in Weber's words, pull his own self up out of the mud by the forelock. Until he deliberately acquires a personality in this way, a person's life can be nothing but a meaningless jumble of events and experiences. It is of course true that in creating his personality, an individual works on raw material that he finds already in existence – his own talents, needs and dispositions – and in this sense his activity differs from God's, who creates the world *ex nihilo*. The individual is nevertheless responsible for the order he imposes upon these materials and consequently for the meaning (in this context, the religious meaning) of his own life. A person's life has no more inherent meaning than the world does; each acquires significance only when it is viewed as the deliberate expression of a creative plan – as an artifact rather than a fateful datum.

Weber's remarks concerning the religious ideal of ethical personality suggest a direct connection between this ideal and the secular existentialism that he himself embraces. To acquire a personality, an individual must order his existence by living, or attempting to live, in accordance with a plan. Of course, so long as ethical personality remains a *religious* ideal, it is necessary that the plan in question be tied to the divine will and defined in terms of God's own plan for the world, so that the individual seeking a personality must seek it by making himself the willing servant of God or the executor of his decrees. A specifically religious interpretation of the meaning of ethical personality implies that a plan of life is not, by itself, a sufficient condition for salvation; it is necessary, in addition, that the individual's plan have a specific aim or content (obedience to the divine will). If one abandons this last requirement but continues to insist that life has no meaning apart from the plans we invent and willfully impose on it – on ourselves – the result is an existentialist ethic of precisely the sort that Weber defends in his own methodological writings. For Weber, as for the true-believing Christian, salvation consists in the acquisition of a personality through the choice of a plan of life and the intensified sense of responsibility that accompanies it. Unlike his Christian counterpart, however, Weber emphatically denies the existence of any independent, Archimedian point from which the ultimate worth of this choice can be assessed. Indeed, in Weber's view it is precisely the groundlessness of the choice which gives it its meaning and endows the person able to make such a commitment with a kind of heroic nobility. The central role which the concept of personality plays in Weber's own ethical theory, and the irreligious interpretation he gives to this originally religious idea, confirm the view that his existentialism is, in essence, a secularized Christianity without God, an ethic that denies the inherent value of the world but which also denies the existence of God, thereby placing on man's shoulders – by default, as it were – the terrible responsibility for rescuing himself from the pointlessness of what Weber calls the 'world-process'.

God as a contractual partner

The uniquely occidental conception of God as a supra-mundane personal lord of creation has its historical roots, according to Weber, in the Yahwe cult of the ancient Israelite war confederacy. Yahwe was a 'god of social organization', the common war god of Israel. As such, He was the guarantor of the confederacy's unity or cohesiveness, a function he performed in a 'very special manner'.[385]

> Yahwe became war god by virtue of a treaty of confederation. This contract had to be concluded, not only among confederates, but also with Him, for He was no god residing in the midst of the people, a familiar god, but rather a god hitherto strange. He continued to be a 'god from afar'. This was the decisive element in the relationship. Yahwe was an elective god. The confederate people had chosen Him through *berith* with Him, just as, later, it established its king by *berith*.[386]

Because Yahwe was considered a 'contractual partner', an 'ideational party' to the agreement He had made with the Israelite confederacy, violations of the terms of the agreement 'were not merely violations of orders guaranteed by Him as other gods guarantee their orders, but violations of the most solemn contractual obligations toward him personally.'[387] Weber stresses that the 'pre-exilic *b'rithot*' were not fraternization contracts among human partners who placed themselves under the protection of God as a witness and avenger of perjury, but 'covenants with God himself'.[388]

> Hence, in avenging the violation of the covenant He insisted on His own violated treaty rights and not only on the claims of the contract-observing party placed under His protection. This important conception profoundly influenced the development of Israelite religiosity. The God of the prophets based His frightful threats of disaster on the violation of the contractual good faith sworn personally to Him as a contractual partner. He in turn is reminded of the pledges which He has given by oath to the forefathers (thus, first Michah 7:20).[389]

The conception of God as a bearer of rights created by free agreement, rather than the guardian of 'an already existing immutable order of law or a "righteousness" measurable in terms of fixed norms',[390] had important implications for the Israelites' understanding of law in general. 'Since the confederacy was at first a stateless association of tribes, new statutes, whether cultic or legal in nature, could in principle originate only by way of agreement (*berith*) based on oracle like the original covenant. Therewith, all statutes were based on the same ground as the old contract relation which existed between [Yahwe] and the people.'[391] The law of Israel was a *positive* law created through covenant with God; '[i]t had not always been in existence and it was possible that by new revelation and new *berith* with God it could be changed again.'[392]

According to Weber, the conception of God as a contractual partner was a central and unique feature of ancient Judaism. No trace of this idea is to be found in the religions of Asia, and in later Judaism (as well as Christianity) the 'anthropomorphic conception of a bilateral pact' between man and God was eventually replaced by what Weber calls 'the concept of a divine ordainment which is merely guaranteed by a special pledge.'[393] What are the presuppositions of this explicitly legalistic way of understanding the relationship between man and God and how did the conception of God as a contractual partner lead to the development of 'a highly rational religious ethic of social conduct . . . free of magic and all forms of irrational quest for salvation . . . inwardly worlds apart from the paths of salvation offered by Asiatic religions' (the characteristic of ancient Judaism that in Weber's view gives it its world-historical importance)?[394]

The conception of God as a contractual partner clearly presupposes that He is a person rather than an impersonal force or natural process. To view their God as a contractual partner, the Israelites had to think of Him as a person with the power to create new law by imposing binding obligations on Himself through His own promises or agreements. I have described this power of voluntary self-legislation as the capacity for purposive action, for action in accordance with the conception of a rule, or, more simply, as the will – the faculty of choice and deliberate self-rule. To conceive of God as a contractual partner is to view Him as a person with a will – indeed, it is to make God's will the central element in his personality.

The Judaic conception of God as a party to a 'bilateral pact' also implies an equality of sorts between Him and His human partners. The Israelites owe certain contractual duties to Yahwe, the breach of which represents a 'violation of the contractual good faith sworn personally to Him as a contractual partner'. By the same token, however, Yahwe also owes certain duties of support and protection to those with whom He has covenanted – duties which the Israelites, speaking through prophets like Moses and Jeremiah, 'admonish' Him to observe. Each of the parties to the covenant has contractual claims against the other; both are bound by the law they have made for themselves, and in this sense stand on an equal footing.

The conception of God as a contractual partner gives Him a more human appearance and thus in one sense reduces the distance between man and God. However, the idea of a *contract* with God must be sharply distinguished from the entirely different notion that one can actually become God by being united with Him through a process of self-deification. A contractual relationship can exist only if the parties to it retain their separate identities, since it is the essence of such a relationship that each party is bound to someone other than himself. Self-deification, by contrast, entails a loss of identity – a becoming-one with God that is the very opposite of an arms' length transaction in which promises are exchanged and reciprocal claims created. In this respect, the Judaic conception of God as a contractual partner expresses an understanding of the relationship between man and God fundamentally different from the one presupposed by all *gnostic* soteriologies.

Perhaps the most striking feature of the Judaic conception of God as a contractual partner is the positivistic theory of law that it implies. 'The law [created by *berith* with Yahwe] was no eternal Tao or Dharma, but a positive enactment . . . God's ordainments come from his hand and are *as such* changeable. He may bind himself to His enactments by *berith*, but that is the result of His free resolve.'[395] This conception of law, which assumes that all binding legal norms must be traced back to an original act of legislation (an 'original covenant'), had no parallel in the religions of Asia or the philosophical systems of Greek antiquity, both of which attributed the validity of social and religious norms to the timeless and inherently meaningful world-process of which they were thought to form a part – a conception of normativity that also underlies every form of traditional authority. By contrast, the Jewish conception of law rests upon the same principle of legitimation as all legal-rational authority structures: law is binding and has authoritative status only to the extent that it has been deliberately enacted, created through legislative *fiat* and imposed on a world that has no inherent normative meaning of its own. The idea that norms have their origin in the will, rather than the world – the basis of all legal-rational authority and the key to understanding its logical primacy in Weber's typology of the forms of domination – first appeared in connection with the Judaic conception of God as a contractual partner. This helps to explain Weber's assertion that ancient Judaism has had 'world-historical consequences'[396] which make its problems 'unique in the socio-historical study of religion'[397] and illuminates the philosophical connection between his theory of authority and sociology of religion. Each is concerned, at bottom, with the same phenomenon – the intellectual and institutional displacement caused by the disenchanting idea that the world has no meaning in itself and can be given one only through positive enactment.

There is, however, another and even more specific connection between the Israelites' conception of God as a contractual partner and the idea of legal rationality. According to Weber, it was this conception which first stimulated the development of a mode of legal thinking based upon what he calls the 'logical interpretation of meaning'.

[W]hen Yahwe was angry and failed to help the nation or the individual, a violation of the *berith* with Him had to be responsible for this. Hence, it was necessary for the authorities as well as for the individual from the outset to ask, which commandment had been violated? Irrational divination means could not answer this question, only knowledge of the very commandments and soul searching. Thus, the idea of *berith* flourishing in the truly Yahwistic circles pushed all scrutiny of the divine will toward an at least relatively rational mode of raising and answering the question. Hence, the priestly exhortation under the influence of the intellectual strata turned with great sharpness against sooth-sayers, augurs, day-choosers, interpreters of signs, conjurors of the dead, defining their ways of consulting the deities as characteristically pagan.[398]

Given the fundamental importance of their covenant with Yahwe, the historical experience of the Israelites had to be interpreted against the background of the contractual expectations created by the covenant itself. Thus, for example, if the Jews suffered at the hands of their Egyptian or Babylonian neighbours it could only be because they had violated one of the terms of their agreement with Yahwe and earned His wrath as a result.

Behind every historical experience, the Israelites imagined an angry or disappointed contractual partner, acting to protect His rights and punish those
who failed to respect them. Indeed, for the followers of Yahwe, these experiences could have significance only as the expression of God's will, as an
outward sign or manifestation of the 'meaningful, understandable intentions and reactions of the godhead'.[399] Consequently, every effort to understand the meaning of events became a search for the divine intentions that
lay behind them; only when an event had been 'rationalized' as the expression of God's anger at His faithless contractual partners was the goal of
interpretation achieved.

This was, however, always viewed as an attainable goal. '[D]espite His
passionate wrath', the God of the Israelites 'in the last analysis acted rationally and according to plan.'[400] Because they follow a plan, God's actions are
as understandable as the purposive behaviour of any other person; consequently, in order to interpret the meaning of their historical experience, the
Israelites had only to adopt God's point of view as a contractual partner,
much in the way that a sociologist adopts the perspective of those whose
conduct he is attempting to understand.

When Weber uses the term 'rational' to describe the interpretive methods
of 'genuine Yahwism', he is using it in the same way that he does in the
Rechtssoziologie – to describe a type of thinking which 'has its point of departure in the logical analysis of the meaning' of legal propositions and social
actions. Unlike all forms of legal thought which assume that 'the legally
relevant characteristics [of an action or situation] are of a tangible nature'
and hence 'perceptible as sense data', the logical analysis of meaning
attempts to establish the significance of observable events by relating them
to the purposes and intentions of human actors. In a similar way, the
prophets of Israel interpreted the meaning of their own historical experiences by relating them to God's intentions, by treating them as the outward
expression of His deliberate plan. Like all forms of legal thinking based
upon the logical interpretation of meaning, the interpretive method of the
Israelite prophets implicitly assumed that facts ('sense-data characteristics')
acquire meaning – legal, moral or religious – only to the extent they reveal
the aims and intentions of a purposive being.

The Israelite prophets strove for a 'consciously clear and communicable
interpretation of Yahwe's intention',[401] the intention of an invisible being
who stands above the world though His aims are manifest in it. This interpretive attitude, which assumes a profound separation between the tangible
but inherently meaningless order of worldly occurrences, on the one hand,
and the transcendent personal God that invests them with significance on
the other, is reflected, in an interesting way, in 'the superior importance of
. . . auditory experiences to visions' in Israelite prophecy.

> Acoustic experiences of the prophets, as has been discussed in another
> connection, in characteristic fashion much surpassed such visual experience. The
> prophet either heard a voice which spoke to him, commanded him, and charged
> him with a mission to communicate, possibly also to perform, or as . . . in the case

of Jeremiah, a voice spoke out of him, whether he would or not. The superior importance of these auditory experiences to visions, as indicated, was no accident. It was bound with the tradition of the invisible God, which precluded the telling of anything about Him or His appearance. But it also resulted from the one way open to the prophet of realizing inwardly a relationship to this God. Nowhere do we find the prophets mystically emptying their mind of all thought and perception of sense matter and structural objects, a process which initiates apathetic ecstasy in India. Nowhere do we find the tranquil, blissful euphoria of the god-possessed, rarely the expression of a devotional communion with God and nowhere the merciful pitying sentiment of brotherhood with all creatures typical of the mystic . . . [T]he prophet never felt himself deified by his experience, united with the godhead, removed from the torment and meaninglessness of existence, as happened to the redeemed in India, and for him represented the true meaning of his religious experience. The prophet never knew himself emancipated from suffering, be it only from the bondage of sin. There was no room for a *unio mystica*, not to mention the inner oceanic tranquility of the Buddhistic *arhat*. Nothing of the sort existed. Finally, there was no thought of a metaphysical *gnosis* and interpretation of the world. The nature of Yahwe contained nothing supernatural in the sense of something extending beyond understanding. His motives were not concealed from human comprehension.[402]

The God of the Israelites is invisible; He does not have a perceptible form and therefore cannot be seen by human beings. It is also impossible to achieve a union with or take possession of Him. This does not mean, however, that all communication with God is impossible. Like any other person, God speaks and can be spoken to; moreover, God's utterances are comprehensible to human beings because He acts in a purposive way, in accordance with a plan, against the background of which worldly events take on a meaning they would not otherwise possess. These different ideas are all consequences of conceiving God as a supra-mundane person whose defining characteristic is His will, a capacity He exercises both as creator of the world and as a contractual partner. On the one hand, the fact that God is a person endowed with a will makes it possible to interpret concrete historical events as the outward expression of an unseen plan and hence to understand them in the special way that all (and only) purposive actions can be understood. On the other hand, the fact that God stands above the world makes a union with Him unthinkable. By contrast, in the Asian religions which conceive divinity not as a transcendent person but as the inherently meaningful order of the world itself, the idea of self-deification is entirely unproblematic.

These are points I have already emphasized. What I wish to stress now is the parallelism between the method of interpretation employed by the Israelite prophets (a method completely unknown in the religions of Asia) and that type of legal thinking which is oriented toward what Weber calls the logical analysis of meaning. Both presuppose a distinction between facts and values, both assume that concrete events acquire meaning only as the manifestation of a purposive attitude, and both assume that the attitude in question can only be that of a person endowed with a will, the capacity for creative self-legislation. A different, but equally important parallel exists between the religious theodicies of Asia and those primitive forms of legal thought which rest upon a belief that 'the legally relevant characteristics [of events] are of a tangible nature . . . [and are] perceptible as sense data.' In each case, facts (and the world conceived as the totality of facts) are assumed to have an inherent meaning of their own. It is their common denial of the distinction between facts and values and their rejection of the will-centred conception of the person associated with this distinction which leads Weber to characterize both forms of thought as 'magical' and to contrast them with their more 'rational' counterparts.

Finally, we should note the important connection between the Israelite conception of God as a contractual partner and Judaism's 'rational ethical absolutism' (a notion closely related to the idea of 'ethical personality'). According to Weber, 'the special relationship to Yahwe, as personal partner of the *berith* with the confederacy', led Jewish teachers and prophets to place a 'strong accent on "doing justly",' on 'obedience and ethical conduct as over against observance of purely cultic and ritualistic commandments which, given the structure of the confederacy, were necessarily almost completely absent or developed only in a few simple rules in earlier times.'[403] In accordance with His status as a contractual partner, the followers of Yahwe viewed Him primarily as 'a God of just compensation'.[404]

> With this, the commandments of God as well as the expiation of offences were more and more sublimated in the direction of ethical absolutism. What mattered to the heavenly ruler was not external conduct, but unconditional obedience and absolute trust in what, repeatedly, would seem to be problematical promises. The very idea is to be found even in the Yahwistic story of Abraham's call to move to Canaan and the promise of a son. Abraham followed the first blindly and his blind belief in the latter is 'counted to him for righteousness' (Gen. 15:6).[405]

This emphasis on what Weber calls 'unconditional obedience' (in contrast to 'external conduct') 'corresponded to the idea that Yahwe found decisive satisfaction in a contrite attitude *per se*, not sacrificial and expiatory offerings and similar acts of the sinner.'[406] What Yahwe demands of His followers, above all else, is an inner state or disposition, a willingness to do as He says. This conception of religious duty is distinguished by the importance it assigns to the will – righteousness and salvation are states or conditions of the will that cannot be attained merely through the ritual performance of certain prescribed acts. Right actions are important, but what gives them value in an ultimate ethical or religious sense is the 'humility, obedience [and] trusting devotion'[407] with which they are performed: in themselves, the actions are meaningless. This attitude stands in the sharpest possible contrast to all magical techniques of salvation which treat the repetitive performance of certain actions as something meaningful in its own right. The 'rational ethical absolutism' of the Jewish prophets presupposes a distinction between action or conduct, on the one hand, and the inner attitude that gives meaning to conduct, on the other – a distinction which, according to Weber, blocked the development in ancient Judaism of 'magic and all forms of irrational quest for salvation' and set it 'inwardly worlds apart from the paths of salvation offered by the Asiatic religions'.[408]

The ethical absolutism of the prophets, like their interpretative method, rests on the assumption that events have meaning only as the outward expression of the intentions of a person. Whether the person be human or divine, it is his intentions that ultimately explain why his actions have the moral and religious significance they do. This assumption links the religion of the ancient Israelite war confederacy to the formally rational mode of thought characteristic of the modern legal order and explains Weber's insistence on the extent to which ancient Judaism, with its entirely unique conception of God as a contractual partner, 'pushed all scrutiny of the divine will toward an at least relatively rational mode' of interpretation whose basic aim was a knowledge of God's 'meaningful, understandable intentions', a 'consciously clear and communicable interpretation' of Yahwe's will, rather than gnostic self-deification or the development of a therapeutic magic designed to cure souls through the performance of ritually stereotyped acts.

8

Modernity

Beneath its richly detailed surface, Weber's *Rechtssoziologie* exhibits a surprising consistency and unity of purpose. Throughout, Weber is concerned with a single subject – the development of the institutions and forms of thought most characteristic of the modern legal order. 'Our interest', he remarks, 'is centred upon the ways and consequences of the "rationalization" of the law, that is, the development of those juristic qualities which are characteristic of it today.'[409] Whether he is discussing modes of legal analysis, techniques of adjudication, or the forms of contractual association, Weber's fundamental aim is to give an account of those aspects of the present legal order that distinguish 'our contemporary modes of legal thought' from those prevailing in the past.

In this respect, the *Rechtssoziologie* parallels Weber's writings on authority, religion and economic action, all of which also reflect his predominant interest in the structure and meaning of modern social life. Each of his sociological investigations seeks to explain some distinctive component of modern European civilization – legal-rational authority, bureaucratic administration, capitalist production or the uniquely disenchanting Judeo-Christian conception of god as a supra-mundane, personal lord of creation. Indeed, it would not be too far-fetched to describe the entire *corpus* of Weber's substantive writings as a sociology of modernity. The *Rechtssoziologie* is only a part of this larger enterprise. To appreciate its full significance, one must view it in this wider context as a contribution to Weber's general theory of modernity, as one aspect of his lifelong obsession with the meaning of modern social life.

Modernity and rationality

According to Weber, the institutions of modern society are distinguished by their high degree of rationality. What he means by the term 'rationality' is not always clear; nevertheless, despite his own ambiguous use of the concept, Weber's substantive writings all rest on the assumption that modern occidental culture exhibits a 'specific and peculiar rationalism'[410] which distinguishes it from earlier forms of social life. What gives this 'modern occidental form' of rationality its 'special peculiarity'?

The beginnings of an answer can be found in the following passage from Weber's well-known essay, 'Science as a Vocation'.

Scientific progress is a fraction, the most important fraction, of the process of intellectualization which we have been undergoing for thousands of years and which nowadays is usually judged in such an extremely negative way. Let us first clarify what this intellectualist rationalization, created by science and by scientifically oriented technology, means practically.

Does it mean that we, today, for instance, everyone sitting in this hall, have a greater knowledge of the conditions of life under which we exist than has an American Indian or a Hottentot? Hardly. Unless he is a physicist, one who rides on the streetcar has no idea how the car happened to get into motion. And he does not need to know. He is satisfied that he may 'count' on the behaviour of the streetcar, and he orients his conduct according to this expectation; but he knows nothing about what it takes to produce such a car so that it can move. The savage knows incomparably more about his tools. When we spend money today I bet that even if there are colleagues of political economy here in the hall, almost every one of them will hold a different answer in readiness to the question: How does it happen that one can buy something for money – sometimes more and sometimes less? The savage knows what he does in order to get his daily food and which institutions serve him in this pursuit. The increasing intellectualization and rationalization do *not*, therefore, indicate an increased and general knowledge of the conditions under which one lives.

It means something else, namely, the knowledge or belief that if one but wished one could learn it at any time. Hence, it means that principally [in principle] there are no mysterious incalculable forces that come into play, but rather that one can, in principle, master all things by calculation. This means that the world is disenchanted. One need no longer have recourse to magical means in order to master or implore the spirits, as did the savage, for whom such mysterious powers existed. Technical means and calculations perform the service. This above all is what intellectualization means.[411]

If one asks what makes the streetcar's complicated mechanism intelligible – even if it is not actually understood by those who ride it – the answer would seem to be that its operation can be comprehended, at least in principle, because the streetcar itself was made by human beings acting in accordance with a plan and on the basis of known scientific principles. The same is true of the monetary system and the exchange process; these, too, are the products of purposeful human action, of many human beings acting in deliberately coordinated, though not necessarily cooperative, ways.

This idea can be extended to other important aspects of modern social life. Legal-rational bureaucracies, for example, administer laws which are acknowledged to be the deliberate creations of human beings; indeed, it is the artificiality of these laws – the fact that they have been intentionally posited or promulgated – which establishes their validity and grounds the authority of those who administer them. Similarly, the method of juristic analysis that Weber considered most developed from a purely rational point of view treats the legal significance of events as a human artifact, a product of the various meanings that different individuals assign to them rather than an intrinsic characteristic of the events themselves. In an analogous fashion, the Judeo-Christian conception of ethical personality and the contemporary

(Weberian) form of existentialism inspired by it view the human soul itself as something that must be formed in accordance with a plan and that possesses meaning and value only insofar as it displays a deliberately imposed shape of this sort. Finally, even the modern capitalist economy may be viewed as a human artifact to the extent that it rests upon a network of voluntary, purposive contracts rather than prescriptive status relationships thought to be part of a fixed, natural order. Whether one is describing the nature of political authority, the forms of legal interpretation, the meaning of religious ideals or the structure of economic life, the beliefs and institutions that define modern European civilization all rest upon the idea implicit in Weber's streetcar example, the idea that what appears to confront the individual as a given datum (his material circumstances, his political, legal and economic relationships and even his own soul) is in reality a human invention, something that has been deliberately created or arranged by human beings and which therefore belongs to the world of artifacts. It is its artificiality that makes modern social life comprehensible; we can understand its institutions, despite their complexity, because they have been constructed by human beings for reasons or purposes we ourselves can grasp and that need only be recalled for the institutions to become intelligible.[412]

In 'Science as a Vocation', Weber contrasts our world – characterized, he claims, by an 'increasing intellectualization and rationalization' of life in all its departments – with the world of the savage, a world filled with 'mysterious incalculable forces' that must be implored by 'magical means'. If the rationalism of our world is ultimately attributable to the fact that our tools, techniques and institutions are all purposeful human inventions (and known to be such), the mysterious forces that haunt the world of the savage reflect a condition which is just the opposite of this: these forces are mysterious, in some ultimate sense, because they present themselves to the savage as a fateful datum. The powers that confront the savage are not of his own making; they are, in his own eyes, inhuman powers belonging to the world as it is revealed to him in experience, a *locus* of independent forces. Although it is possible for the savage to achieve (or believe he has achieved) some measure of control over these powers by means of various magical techniques, the control they yield is always tenuous and incomplete, and often entirely illusory. In the final analysis, the limited efficacy of the savage's magic is to be explained by the fact that it aims to control a foreign power, a power that can never be completely understood, even in principle, because – unlike a streetcar or the modern system of economic exchange – it is not itself the product of purposeful human action.

This basic characteristic is reflected in each of the institutions and modes of thought (political, legal, religious and economic) that Weber associates, in a general way, with pre-modern society. All forms of traditional authority, for example, rest on the assumption that social norms, far from being human artifacts, belong to a permanently fixed order and form part of an uncreated, pre-existing world in which individuals are assigned a place by the fateful circumstances of their birth. In this view, relations of domination are unalterable facts of life, like the characteristics of age and sexual identity on which they rest. To the extent that pre-modern forms of economic activity are carried on within the framework of a household (whether large or small) and are oriented toward the satisfaction of traditionally stereotyped, status-based needs, the same can be said of them as well: the circumstances and goals of all such activities appear to those engaged in them to be conditions fixed by nature or God or immemorial custom rather than the product of a deliberately established economic scheme of the kind every purposive contract might be said to constitute.

The same is true in the legal sphere. Primitive or magical forms of adjudication are not subject to intellectual control. The judgment of an oracle, unaccompanied by supporting reasons, is a fateful decree which men, with their limited powers of comprehension, must accept but can never understand. Only when human beings assume the role played by divine powers in all oracular forms of law-making and begin giving reasons for their decisions – thereby transforming legal judgments into human artifacts – can the adjudicatory process itself be subjected to intellectual control and in this sense rationalized.

The world of the savage, of the traditional master, of magic and oracular adjudication is above all else a world of *fateful* events and relationships. It is the idea of fate – of what is given to men as a fixed condition of their existence – that best expresses the central, defining quality of this world, a world that provides a home for man and yet confronts him as a fate or destiny rather than the product of his own purposeful activity. In this world, even his most human achievements – the social arrangements under which he lives – belong to a comprehensive, unbroken and unalterable natural order. By contrast, wherever man turns today, he sees only himself, only the arti-facts of his own creative industry; today we live in a world that has been humanized and in this sense disenchanted.

The disenchantment of the world, the result of an historical process that 'has continued to exist in occidental culture for millenia',[413] reflects the revolutionary change in perspective produced by the view that human society is an artifact rather than a fateful datum. Only when social relation-ships and institutions are viewed in this way do they lose their mysterious-ness and become fully comprehensible, at least in principle. The social world in which we live today is transparent to reason because it is our own human creation: as Hobbes observed, a scientific understanding of the organization of society is possible precisely because society is itself a human artifact – something of which we are, in his words, both the matter and the maker.[414] It is this Hobbesian thought – echoed in the writings of many other philosophers including Vico, Kant, Hegel and Marx – that underlies Weber's conception of the 'modern occidental form' of rationality and the age-old 'process of disenchantment' that has defined the historically unique career of Western culture.

Anyone familiar with Weber's writings knows, however, that his view of modernity was more complex and ambiguous than what I have said might suggest. The ambiguity in Weber's conception of modernity is most strikingly revealed by his paradoxical assertion that the very process of rationalization which has produced the belief that 'one can, in principle, master all things by calculation', itself represents a fateful destiny. In 'Science as a Vocation', Weber speaks of the *'fate'* of scientific work, reminds us of the 'fundamental fact' that we are *'destined* to live in a godless and prophetless' age and warns that 'it is weakness not to be able to countenance the stern seriousness of our *fateful* times.'[415] The 'tremendous cosmos of the modern economic order' itself represents an 'iron cage' whose construction has been decreed by 'fate',[416] the same 'inescapable fate' that underlies the 'sober fact of universal bureaucratization'[417] in the political sphere. This idea runs, like an undercurrent, through all of Weber's writings: modernity means enlightenment and greatly enhanced possibilities for human control, but it also means the increasing domination of fateful forces, among which he includes reason itself.[418]

Weber's emphasis on the fatefulness of modernity is indeed paradoxical. Fate means: what is inexplicable and cannot be controlled; but since Weber himself equates reason with control (control in principle), it is difficult to understand how reason can itself be a fate, how the process of rationalization can be regarded as one that, in some sense or other, is beyond our individual and collective powers of control. To the extent the disenchantment of the world has unleashed forces that today dominate us as a fate, it cannot be said to have unambiguously increased the rationality of social life. When Weber says that 'the fate of our times is characterized by rationalization and intellectualization and, above all, by the "disenchantment of the world" ',[419] he implies that the rationalization is less complete or unqualified than it might seem, that the modern world is dominated by peculiar irrationalities of its own – different, to be sure, from those that conditioned the magical experience of the savage or the traditional world of the Abrahamite peasant who 'stood in the organic cycle of life', but equally beyond human comprehension and control. What did Weber believe these peculiarly modern irrationalities to be?

Fate and the loss of autonomy

This question is more difficult than might appear. The reason for the difficulty is that Weber uses the concept of fate to describe two quite different aspects of the rationalization process. Each use in turn suggests a particular critique of modern social life, but these critiques are themselves different and indeed antithetical. Weber's insistence on the fatefulness of reason thus has an ambiguity of meaning which reveals an underlying ambivalence in his attitude toward the most basic features of modern European civilization.

The first of the two meanings that Weber gives to the concept of fate is most clearly revealed in those passages in which he describes the 'substantially irrational' consequences of modern capitalism – in particular, the enervating system of shop discipline imposed by capitalist entrepreneurs in an effort to achieve a 'maximum of formal rationality in capital accounting'.

No special proof is necessary to show that military discipline is the ideal model for the modern capitalist factory, as it was for the ancient plantation. However, organizational discipline in the factory has a completely rational basis. With the help of suitable methods of measurement, the optimum profitability of the individual worker is calculated like that of any material means of production. On this basis, the American system of 'scientific management' triumphantly proceeds with its rational conditioning and training of work performances, thus drawing the ultimate conclusions from the mechanization and discipline of the plant. The psychophysical apparatus of man is completely adjusted to the demands of the outer world, the tools, the machines – in short, it is functionalized, and the individual is shorn of his natural rhythm as determined by his organism; in line with the demands of the work procedure, he is attuned to a new rhythm through the functional specialization of muscles and through the creation of an optimal economy of physical effort. This whole process of rationalization, in the factory as elsewhere, and especially in the bureaucratic state machine, parallels the centralization of the material implements of organization in the hands of the master. Thus, discipline inexorably takes over ever larger areas as the satisfaction of political and economic needs is increasingly rationalized. This universal phenomenon more and more restricts the importance of charisma and of individually differentiated conduct.[420]

This passage has a sharply critical tone – it could have come from Marx's *Paris Manuscripts*[421] – and it seems clear that Weber considers the 'functional specialization' of the human animal in accordance with the work requirements of the modern factory to be one of the most costly consequences of the capitalist system of production. What is not made clear is why the growth of discipline associated with the rationalization of the production process should be viewed as anything more than a cost that must be incurred to obtain the benefits, such as increased material prosperity, that capitalism offers – a price it is arguably rational to pay so long as the benefits of capitalism outweigh its costs. Weber at times seems to imply that the deliberate mechanization of the human worker in the capitalist factory is substantively irrational because it imposes costs on the worker that are not taken into account in calculating the overall profitability of the enterprise. If that were so, however, the irrationality of shop discipline could be eliminated by making its costs explicit, and by deciding whether the harm it does to the 'psychophysical apparatus' of the individual worker is justified by the increase in productivity and consequent rise in material well-being that such discipline makes possible.

There is, however, a second and more troubling sense in which capitalist shop discipline is irrational. The defining characteristic of modern capitalism is its high degree of calculability, and calculability implies control. Although it can never eliminate all risk or contingency, increased calculability reduces the mysteriousness of economic life by permitting its most fundamental processes – the production and exchange of goods – to be deliberately designed and monitored by human beings. One consequence of capitalist discipline, however, is a loss of control on the part of workers. Above all else, factory discipline means a loss of autonomy for the individual worker, a reduction in his ability to control the conditions of his own employment. This follows inevitably from the entrepreneur's effort to maximize the profitability of his enterprise by adjusting the 'apparatus' of his human workers to the demands of the inanimate objects on and by means of which they perform their various functions. In a capitalist factory, workers are required to sacrifice their own psychophysical independence and to subordinate themselves to the inhuman rhythm of the machine (which Weber elsewhere describes as 'mind objectified').[422] For the capitalist worker, the machine is a kind of fate to which he must deliver himself – even though, for the entrepreneur, it represents a powerful instrument of control. To achieve maximum control over his own enterprise, a capitalist factory owner must impose a discipline on his workers that deprives them of the control they would otherwise have over the conditions of their employment and even their own selves. Shop discipline is substantively irrational in the sense that it requires some to give up their self-control so that others may increase theirs. Describing its consequences in this way underscores the extent to which the regimentation of factory life represents a departure from the rationalizing tendencies of capitalism as a whole.

It is possible to view the distributional effects of capitalist production in a similar light. A modern capitalist exchange economy rests upon a complex web of purposive contracts. The utilities that are exchanged in an economy of this sort are transferred through the free agreement of the parties – not in satisfaction of status-based obligations of service and support, as was often the case in the past. Weber emphasizes, in particular, the freedom of the capitalist labour contract: before he can appropriate the labour of his workers, a factory owner must contract for the right to do so by entering an agreement which they are, in theory, entirely free to reject. The contractual freedom that an individual today enjoys in defining his economic relationships with others significantly increases his power of control, his ability to determine, for himself, the interests and even the way of life he shall pursue.

This increase in control may, however, lose much of its meaning if an individual lacks the material resources to make his decisions effective, if his choices are in a practical sense narrowly limited because he can afford to make only a few of them. 'The great variety of permitted contractual schemata and the formal empowerment to set the content of contracts in accordance with one's desires and independently of all official form patterns, in and of itself by no means makes sure that these formal possibilities will in fact be available to all and everyone. Such availability is prevented above all by the differences in the distribution of property as guaranteed by law.'[423]

These differences render pointless, for some, the very freedom on which the capitalist order is predicated. Like the intensified discipline of the capitalist factory, the inequalities in wealth created and sustained by the principle of effective demand – 'the ability of those who are more plentifully supplied with money to outbid the others'[424] – entail a loss of control for the disadvantaged. For those who lack the resources to 'make use of [their legal] empowerments', this loss of control transforms the formal freedom of contractual association on which the capitalist order is based into an 'iron cage' that guarantees the preservation of existing disparities in wealth.

In the concluding paragraph of the *Rechtssoziologie*, Weber describes the analogous loss of control that has resulted from the rationalization of the legal order.

> Whatever form law and legal practice may come to assume under the impact of these various influences [Weber has just concluded a discussion of the 'anti-formal tendencies' in modern law] it will be inevitable that, as a result of technical and economic developments, the legal ignorance of the layman will increase. The use of jurors and similar lay judges will not suffice to stop the continuous growth of the technical elements in the law and hence of its character as a specialists' domain. Inevitably, the notion must expand that the law is a rational technical apparatus, which is continually transformable in the light of expediential considerations and devoid of all sacredness of content. This fate may be obscured by the tendency of acquiesence in the existing law, which is growing in many ways for several reasons, but it cannot really be stayed. All of the modern sociological and philosophical analyses, many of which are of a high scholarly value, can only contribute to strengthen this impression, regardless of the content of their theories concerning the nature of law and the judicial process.[425]

According to Weber, 'the notion must expand that the law is a rational technical apparatus', a tool for achieving certain social, political and economic ends that have been chosen on the basis of 'expediential considerations'. He implicitly contrasts this instrumental conception of law with one that ascribes a sacred meaning of some sort to the legal order: modern law is 'devoid of all sacredness of content', and tends increasingly to be viewed as a tool whose value depends entirely on its success in furthering whatever extra-legal goals we happen to have set for ourselves. In this respect, it resembles the 'fully developed bureaucratic apparatus', a form of administration that enjoys a 'purely *technical* superiority' over every other and 'compares with other organizations exactly as does the machine with the non-mechanical modes of production'.[426]

What this instrumental conception of law expresses, above all else, is the belief that law is a deliberately created artifact, a human invention designed for human ends. Before it can come to be viewed in this way, however, the legal order must be disenchanted and this requires that law be conceived as a product of human legislation. The instrumentalism that predominates today thus presupposes the acceptance of a positivistic conception of law. Acceptance of this idea is also critical to the growth of 'the technical elements in the law and hence of its character as a specialists' domain'. A science of law is possible only if the principles that underlie the legal order – that determine its general structure and define the relationship between its parts – are fully accessible to human understanding. The principles in question can attain this kind of intelligibility, however, only on one condition – that they are themselves conceived, in a positivistic fashion, as rules deliberately formulated by human beings and intentionally employed by them in the construction of the legal order. Modern law resembles Weber's streetcar; we all know that it is fully intelligible in principle and accept the idea of a science of law even though its actual workings are unfamiliar to us. This is because the law is our own human creation. By contrast, primitive law is filled with the same mysterious forces that dominate other aspects of pre-modern life, forces that cannot be mastered except by 'recourse to magical means'. The elaborate techniques of dispute resolution that Weber associates with primitive law are in reality a species of magic which lacks the one distinguishing characteristic of all true science – intellectual control. Primitive law, like primitive life in general, must reckon with 'incalculable forces' that exceed human powers of comprehension; only after these forces have been banished and the responsibility for law-making assumed by human beings, can the legal order be subjected, even in principle, to intellectual control. And only after such control has been achieved can the law be treated as a 'rational technical apparatus' administered by experts in a scientific fashion.[427]

The rationalization of the law has undoubtedly increased the control we have over our own social life. At the same time, however, it has also inevitably increased 'the legal ignorance of the layman', thereby strengthening his dependency on specialists. Legal specialists, in the broadest sense, are a universal phenomenon and have played a role of some sort in every legal system of which we are aware (including even the most primitive ones). Today, however, legal specialists play a larger and more significant role than they have in the past; indeed, Weber describes the increasing importance of legal experts as a 'fate' that 'cannot really be stayed'. For the non-expert, this development entails a loss of control. To an ever greater degree, the layman today requires the assistance of a legal specialist in arranging his personal and commercial affairs, and since he is often not in a position to evaluate, even on purely instrumental grounds, the advice he has been given, he is frequently forced to rely on his legal counsellor for advice of a more substantive nature concerning the ends he ought to set for himself – the things he should care about and strive to attain. In this way, the growing dependence of the layman on legal experts threatens his autonomy in a critical respect by limiting his ability to determine, for himself, the goals that give his conduct direction and meaning.

The transformation of the law into a 'technically rational apparatus' has therefore had the same paradoxical result as the rationalization of other aspects of modern life. We no longer regard the legal order as a medium in which incomprehensible powers declare themselves and determine our destinies, but view it, instead, as a powerful tool for the advancement of human ends, as a device for expanding the deliberate control we exercise over our own social arrangements. At the same time, however, the rationalization of the law has limited individual autonomy by subjecting the layman to an increasing dependence on legal specialists – a consequence that parallels the similar loss of autonomy in the capitalist factory and modern bureaucratic organization (which Weber describes, in a remarkable passage, as a form of 'objectified intelligence' that 'together with the inanimate machine . . . is busy fabricating the shell of bondage which men will perhaps be forced to inhabit some day, as powerless as the fellahs of ancient Egypt').[428] The modern legal order, too, represents a 'shell of bondage', an 'iron cage' in which the individual's power of self-control is increasingly limited by the continuous and irreversible growth of 'the technical elements in the law' – a process that resembles (indeed, is merely one aspect of) the 'irresistible advance of bureaucratization'[429] characteristic of modern political and economic life.

Weber describes the increasing 'legal ignorance of the layman' and his growing dependence on experts in the same way that he describes the progress of bureaucratic organization and market-oriented capitalism – as a 'fate'. In this way, he draws our attention to what he considered their common and most paradoxical feature, the fact that in each case men find the control they are able to exercise over their lives increasingly limited by institutions of their own making. In the past, the control a man had over his life was narrowly bounded by forces that were, or were experienced as being, inhuman in character and origin. Today, by contrast, the forces that constrain the individual and limit his power to determine for himself the kind of life he shall have are, to a degree previously unimaginable, forces that have been deliberately created and set in motion by human beings. It is this fact, more than any other, which distinguishes the special fatefulness of modern society. We live in a world dominated by institutions that we ourselves have made, yet which imprison us in an 'iron cage'. We have, in short, constructed our own 'shell of bondage', a shell whose permanence and indestructability are only enhanced by the fact that it is 'as austerely rational as a machine'.[430] It is the paradox of this self-imposed unfreedom that Weber often appears to have in mind when he speaks of the fatefulness of the process of intellectualization which has liberated mankind from the 'mysterious incalculable forces' that have hitherto dominated his existence – but only by substituting for them a prison of his own construction. A man found the Archimedian point, Kafka says in a parable, but used it against himself; he was permitted to find it only on this condition.

Fate and the decline of leadership

In 1917, near the end of his life, Weber wrote a long and revealing essay with the title, 'Parliament and Government in a Reconstructed Germany'. The essay is in large part devoted to specific political problems facing Germany at the time. It also contains, however, some of Weber's most general observations regarding the nature of modern society and, in particular, the rationalization of political life produced by what he terms 'the irresistible advance of bureaucratization'.[431] At one point in the essay, a question is raised concerning the character of leadership in bureaucratic organizations.

According to Weber the bureaucratization of party politics and of the state's administrative machinery has meant the 'elimination of political talent' and the gradual weakening of those institutions, such as parliamentary government, which in the past have encouraged responsible political leadership and nurtured its development. Similarly, in the economic sphere, the exercise of genuine entrepreneurial leadership has been made increasingly difficult by the rationalization of the firm – a result that Weber believed would only be exacerbated by the nationalization of economic resources under a programme of state socialism. In both realms, 'the directing mind or "moving spirit" '[432] – the politician in one case and entrepreneur in the other – has been replaced by the bureaucratic official with his characteristic 'civil-service' mentality.

> The difference [between the bureaucrat and the leader] is rooted only in part in the kind of performance expected. Independent decision-making and imaginative organizational capabilities in matters of detail are usually also demanded of the bureaucrat, and very often expected even in larger matters. The idea that the bureaucrat is absorbed in subaltern routine and that only the 'director' performs the interesting, intellectually demanding tasks is a preconceived notion of the literati and only possible in a country that has no insight into the matter in which its affairs and the work of its officialdom are conducted. The difference lies, rather, in the kind of *responsibility*, and this does indeed determine the different demands addressed to both kinds of positions. An official who receives a directive which he considers wrong can and is supposed to object to it. If his superior insists on its execution, it is his duty and even his honour to carry it out as if it corresponded to his innermost conviction and to demonstrate in this fashion that his sense of duty stands above his personal preference. It does not matter whether the imperative mandate originates from an 'agency', a 'corporate body' or an 'assembly'. This is the ethos of *office*. A political leader acting in this way would deserve contempt. He will often be compelled to make compromises, that means, to sacrifice the less important to the more important. If he does not succeed in demanding of his master, be he a monarch or the people: 'You either give me now the authorization I want from you, or I will resign,' he is a miserable *Kleber* [one who sticks to his post] – as Bismarck called this type – and not a leader. 'To be above parties' – in truth, to remain outside the realm of the struggle for power – is the official's role, while this struggle for personal power, and the resulting personal responsibility, is the lifeblood of the politician as well as of the entrepreneur.[433]

According to Weber, the increasing rationalization of social life threatens to bring about a uniform 'domination by the "bureaucratic spirit" ' to the disadvantage of real leaders',[434] leaders with 'political ambition and the will to power and responsibility'.[435] Instead of such leaders one finds bureaucratic office-holders, men who possess the expertise required to implement political and economic programmes, but whose 'mentality' or 'spirit' prevents them from exercising genuine leadership. 'If a man in a leading position is an "official" in the spirit of his performance, no matter how qualified – a man, that is, who works dutifully and honourably according to rules and instruction – then he is as useless at the helm of a private enterprise as of a government.'[436] The rule of officials, of professional civil servants who have neither the desire nor the strength to be held personally accountable for their decisions, 'unavoidably increases in correspondence with the rational technology of modern life';[437] in this sense, the increasing dominance of the 'civil-service mentality of the official' is an inevitable consequence of 'the irresistible advance of bureaucratization', a process that itself represents the 'unambiguous yardstick for the modernization of the state'.[438]

This is the second sense in which Weber uses the concept of fate: it is our fate to live in a world in which responsible leadership, of any sort, is increasingly rare. The very conditions that today promote the intellectualization of social life discourage all forms of leadership except those based upon a mass following whose trust and faith have been won through popular demagoguery, a type of leadership that in Weber's view is 'always exposed to direct, purely emotional and irrational influence'[439] and whose basic tendency is to frustrate, rather than promote, the formation of consistent, continuous and – above all else – responsible political programmes. Today, according to Weber, our public life is dominated by the apolitical bureaucrat and the irresponsible caesarist demagogue; this is our fate and we must struggle, as best we can, to preserve a few remnants of responsible leadership while recognizing that in doing so we set ourselves against a centuries-old process of rationalization that only the naïve can hope to reverse. Even socialism is subject to these same rationalizing forces: although 'a progressive elimination of private capitalism is theoretically possible', the abolition of capitalism would not mean 'the destruction of the steel frame of modern industrial work', but only 'that also the *top management* of the nationalized or socialized enterprises would become bureaucratic.'[440]

Why is the spirit of true leadership, as Weber conceives it, necessarily antithetical to the mentality of the bureaucratic official? Weber's fullest answer is to be found in his essay, 'Politics as a Vocation', where he gives a detailed account of the personal qualities required in a political leader. There are, he says, 'three pre-eminent qualities [which] are decisive for the politician: passion, a feeling of responsibility, and a sense of proportion.'[441] A leader must first of all have passion: unlike the bureaucratic official, he must be passionately devoted to a cause, and to 'the god or demon who is its overlord'.[442] The 'proper vocation' of the bureaucrat is 'impartial administration'. He is therefore forbidden to do 'precisely what the politician, the leader as well as his following, must always and necessarily do, namely, *fight*. To take a stand, to be passionate – *ira et studium* – is the politician's element, and above all the element of the political *leader*.'[443]

The passion that distinguishes the true political leader from the bureaucrat is not, however, a 'sterile excitation, a "romanticism of the intellectually interesting", running into emptiness devoid of all feeling of objective responsibility.'[444] No matter how strongly it is felt, mere passion 'does not make a politician, unless passion as devotion to a "cause" also makes responsibility to this cause the guiding star of action.'[445] In this respect, the conduct of the politician

> is subject to quite a different, indeed, exactly the opposite, principle of responsibility from that of the civil servant. The honour of the civil servant is vested in his ability to execute conscientiously the order of the superior authorities, exactly as if the order agreed with his own conviction. This holds even if the order appears wrong to him and if, despite the civil servant's remonstrances, the authority insists on the order. Without this moral discipline and self-denial, in the highest sense, the whole apparatus would fall to pieces. The honour of the political leader, of the leading statesman, however, lies precisely in an exclusive *personal* responsibility for what he does, a responsibility he cannot and must not reject or transfer.[446]

To feel a responsibility of this sort, however, a politician needs the third of the three qualities that Weber identifies – a sense of proportion.

> This is the decisive psychological quality of the politician: his ability to let realities work upon him with inner concentration and calmness. Hence his *distance* to things and men. 'Lack of distance' *per se* is one of the deadly sins of every politician. It is one of those qualities the breeding of which will condemn the progeny of our intellectuals to political incapacity. For the problem is simply how can warm passion and a cool sense of proportion be forged together in one and the same soul? Politics is made with the head, not with other parts of the body or soul. And yet devotion to politics, if it is not to be frivolous intellectual play but rather genuinely human conduct, can be born and nourished from passion alone. However, that firm taming of the soul, which distinguishes the passionate politician and differentiates him from the 'sterilely excited' and mere political dilettante, is possible only through habituation to detachment in every sense of the word . . . Therefore, daily and hourly the politician inwardly has to overcome a quite trivial and all-too-human enemy: a quite vulgar vanity, the deadly enemy of all matter-of-fact devotion to a cause, and of all distance, in this case, of distance towards one's self.[447]

Only if he overcomes his vanity by maintaining a distance towards himself can the politician avoid the constant danger 'of becoming an actor as well as taking lightly the responsibility for the outcome of his actions and of being concerned merely with the "impression" he makes.'[448] Vanity, and the lack of objectivity that it encourages, 'tempts [the politician] to strive for the glamourous semblance of power rather than for actual power', an attitude which represents, in Weber's words, a 'sin against the lofty spirit of his vocation'.[449]

> Although, or rather just because, power is the unavoidable means, and striving for power is one of the driving forces of all politics, there is no more harmful distortion of political force that the parvenu-like braggart with power, and the vain self-reflection in the feeling of power, and in general every worship of power *per se*. The mere 'power politician' may get strong effects, but his work leads nowhere and is senseless.[450]

For the work of the politician to have any meaning at all, it must be continuously informed by a conception of the programme or goal in whose service he places himself; the true politician, according to Weber, will always be prepared to sacrifice his own interests for the sake of his cause, in a spirit of passionate detachment. To do this, however, a man must be 'not only a leader but a hero as well, in a very sober sense of the word . . . Only he has the calling for politics who is sure that he shall not crumble when the world from his point of view is too stupid or too base for what he wants to offer. Only he who in the face of all this can say "In spite of all!" has the calling for politics.'[451]

The intensity of his commitment and the courage he displays in maintaining his 'sense of proportion' – his distance from men and things and even himself – distinguish the experience and conduct of a leader from that of a mere dilettante and set him apart from those who do not have a calling for politics. This fact is of utmost importance: it is not the substance or content of the goal he has chosen for himself that makes someone a leader – a politician, according to Weber, 'may serve national, humanitarian, social, ethical, cultural, worldly or religious ends'[452] – but the spirit in which he makes his choice and attempts to implement it. The politician not only has a goal, he is passionately devoted to it; and he pursues his goal while struggling against the temptations of vanity – which requires the courage and strength of character to keep his own human impulses at a distance.

To make a choice or commit oneself to a cause is not necessarily to do so with passion and courage; these are qualities that any particular commitment, whether shortlived or longlasting, may or may not possess. Since courage and passion are qualities that do not accompany every choice, they must owe their existence to some aspect of a person's character – some part of his soul – other than the will, understood simply as the power of affirming or disaffirming, the power of saying 'yes' to one thing and 'no' to another. Every choice necessarily involves the exercise of this power, but for a choice to possess the special qualities that distinguish a genuine leader's commitment to his cause from the 'sterile excitation' of the political dilettante, something more is required. Courage and passion are qualities that must be brought *to* the choices we make and although it is by no means clear where these qualities come from or how they are to be summoned, there is nothing in the simple act of choice itself that determines their existence or non-existence. The true politician is distinguished by the fact that he is able, for whatever reasons, to draw upon powers in his soul quite different from the general capacity, which he shares in common with other men, for making choices and setting ends. What is decisive, in this respect, is a 'trained relentlessness in viewing the realities of life, and the ability to face such realities and to measure up to them inwardly.'[453] He who possesses this ability is, in Weber's phrase, a *'mature* man'[454] (whether he is young or old in a chronological sense), and it is this quality that we find 'genuinely human and moving' in the actions of such an individual when, with a full sense of responsibility for the consequences of his conduct, he 'reaches the point where he says: "Here I stand; I can do no other." '[455]

The qualities that Weber emphasizes in describing the prerequisites for responsible political leaderhsip – the leader's passionate devotion to his cause, and his courageous self-discipline in maintaining a sense of proportion by resisting the distorting influence of ordinary human vanity – are present either not at all or in a much altered form in the ideal bureaucrat. The perfect bureaucrat, the one who fully lives up to the demands of his vocation, executes his duties with complete impassivity and in a spirit of disinterested neutrality. In contrast to the politician, the bureaucrat strives to eliminate all passion from his work since passion is a personalizing force – passion is the feeling we have for those things that matter to us personally – and it is the bureaucrat's fundamental responsibility to administer the law without regard to his own personal concerns (as distinct from the objective requirements of the legal order, as he conceives them). A genuine politician, on the other hand, identifies in a personal sense with his own programme – it is *his* cause and he takes responsibility for it.

Weber recognizes that the civil servant's tasks, like the politician's, sometimes requires 'moral discipline and self-denial' – as, for example, when he is asked to execute an order that he considers wrong and nevertheless strives to do so 'exactly as if the order agreed with his own conviction'.[456] But the courage required of a politician is different and more demanding, for a politician must be prepared to do something that no bureaucrat need ever do, at least in the performance of his official duties: he must ask others to make sacrifices in order to further a cause for which he alone is personally accountable. Every politician, if he aspires to genuine leadership, must accept the terrible burden this implies, a burden far greater than that associated with even the most extreme acts of *self*-sacrifice. The need for courage cannot be avoided in the struggles of political life; a bureaucrat, by contrast, is not required to be a hero in Weber's sense in order to perform his task (although his work, like that of anyone with a principled vocation, may give him an opportunity to display a heroic devotion to his calling).

There is, however, another and even more fundamental difference between the political leader and the bureaucrat. According to Weber, modern bureaucratic organization 'has usually come into power on the basis of a leveling of social and economic differences', and inevitably accompanies '*mass democracy*'.[457] The leveling tendencies of bureaucratic administration and its close connection with modern mass democracy derive from what Weber calls its 'characteristic principle' – the 'abstract regularity of the exercise of authority, which is a result of the demand for "equality before the law" in the personal and functional sense . . .'[458] When a civil servant issues a command or makes a decision, he does so not in his own name, but in the name of the law; the authority he claims for his official acts is independent of any personal quality he himself happens to possess. Both the bureaucrat issuing an order and the person to whom the order is issued are bound by the system of 'intentionally established' norms that justify the command in question; these norms constitute, in Weber's phrase, an 'impersonal order' to which even the person exercising authority is subject.

Officeholder and private citizen owe obedience to this impersonal legal order only insofar as its rules have been deliberately established by an organization of which each is a member. In their capacity as members of such an organization, the bureaucrat exercising authority and the person subject to his command are 'equals before the law'. Leadership, by contrast, is importantly non-egalitarian. The 'warm passion' and 'cool sense of proportion' that must be 'forged together in one and the same soul' if a man is to be a responsible leader – if he is, in Weber's words, 'to be allowed to put his hand on the wheel of history'[459] – are qualities that are not distributed equally among men. Men differ in the extent to which they possess the 'preeminent qualities' needed for political leadership and hence in their ability to live up to the demands of politics; only he who is able to combine passion and courage in the way Weber suggests can sustain his commitment in the face of the world's stupidity and preserve a sense of responsibility while struggling against both the temptations of vanity and 'the diabolic forces lurking in all violence'.[460] To have a calling for politics, one must have a 'knowledge of [the] tragedy with which all action, but especially political action, is truly interwoven'[461] and be able to act without denying this knowledge or collapsing under its weight. Politics requires an inward strength which only a few men possess and the true leader – the leader who is 'more than a narrow and vain upstart of the moment'[462] – is therefore, in the most literal sense, an *extraordinary* individual, a 'hero . . . in a very sober sense of the word'.

Nothing could be more alien to the leveling democratic spirit of bureaucratic rule with its characteristic principle of equality before the law. A genuine political leader not only reminds us that men are differentially endowed with respect to those personal qualities that are necessary for responsible leadership, he also insists, up to a point, that these same qualities give him the right – a right others do not have – to make demands on himself and his followers. Every true politician, in Weber's sense, feels himself to be an 'innerly "called" leader of men'[463] and finds in this feeling the legitimation for his demand that others, too, make sacrifices on behalf of the cause which is 'the guiding star' of his action. To this extent, all true political leadership has a personal quality that sharply differentiates it from the impersonal authority of the civil servant – indeed, that contradicts the egalitarian premises of bureaucratic rule. 'The devotion of [a leader's] disciples, his followers, his personal party friends is oriented to his person and to its qualities.'[464] This explains why the 'irresistible advance of bureaucratization' poses a threat to the continued exercise of responsible leadership: wherever the bureaucratic spirit prevails, the demands a leader makes on his followers must appear suspect since they are in part legitimated by the possession of extraordinary personal qualities not shared by others. The increasingly bureaucratic world in which we live is a world that has no room for heroes – not for accidental reasons but because bureaucracy itself is predicated upon an egalitarian conception of legitimacy that does not allow us to recognize, as a source of authority, the exceptional personal qualities which all heroism reveals.

The meaning of this last point should perhaps be stated more precisely. To say that our world no longer has room for political heroes does not mean that individual acts of heroism are impossible, but only that we lack confidence in, and to some extent view as illegitimate, the institutions that historically have served as recruiting grounds for political leaders. The very idea of an institution whose fundamental purpose is to foster and reward leadership in Weber's sense must appear suspect from the standpoint of an anti-heroic bureaucratic ethic. According to Weber, the gradual decay of these institutions – in particular, those associated with parliamentary politics – has weakened the conditions necessary for responsible leadership and encouraged a shift in the method of choosing leaders towards what he calls 'the *caesarist* mode of selection',[465] the selection of leaders through mass acclamation achieved by means of demagoguery and tending, at the extreme, to the 'irrational mob rule typical of purely plebiscitary peoples'.[466] To counteract this tendency, which he considered a consequence of 'active mass democratization',[467] Weber argued that faith must be restored in those institutions that in the past have been training grounds for political heroes. This requires, however, that we affirm the value of leadership and hence take a stand against the levelling spirit of bureaucratic rule that increasingly dominates every aspect of our public and private lives. If we do not, we can expect to live in a world divided between the bureaucrat and the plebiscitarian demagogue. This is our fate, a fate that cannot be avoided so long as the responsible heroism which Weber considered the highest form of politics continues to seem an embarrassment from the perspective of the egalitarian ideals that underlie our bureaucratic civilization.

Weber's ambivalent critique of modernity

The peculiar rationality of modern European civilization is to be explained by the fact that its political and economic institutions are deliberately created artifacts which are, in principle at least, intelligible to the human beings who have made them. In Weber's view, however, the rationalization of modern society itself represents a kind of fate or destiny. One encounters this idea in each of Weber's works, including the *Rechtssoziologie* (whose final paragraph characterizes the transformation of the legal order into a 'rational technical apparatus' as an inevitable development that 'cannot really be stayed'). Weber's description of the rationalization process as a fateful destiny seems to be a contradiction in terms: reason means understanding and control, while fate implies a domination by uncontrollable powers. How can reason itself be a fate? This is the fundamental question that any reader of Weber is eventually led to ask.

I have attempted to clarify Weber's concept of fate by describing the two different ways in which he uses it. Weber sometimes uses the concept of fate to describe the loss of individual autonomy that has accompanied the rationalization of political, legal and economic life. Today, we live in a self-imposed shell of bondage 'as austerely rational as a machine', with little control over the forces that determine our material opportunities, work conditions and legal status. It is to the paradox of this self-created unfreedom that Weber is sometimes referring when he speaks of the fatefulness of the intellectualization process. However, Weber often uses the idea of fate to describe a different aspect of modern European civilization – the relentless expansion of the 'bureaucratic spirit', with its profoundly anti-heroic ethic and horror of all personal privilege. This, too, represents an irresistible fate, one that means, above all else, the elimination of real leaders with 'political ambition and the will to power and responsibility'.

Each of these two ways of understanding the fatefulness of the rationalization process – as the paradoxical loss of control that has accompanied the triumphal spread of reason itself or as the disappearance of heroes from a bureaucratically levelled world – provides the foundation for a critique of modern society. Although Weber did not develop either critique in a systematic fashion, there are hints – or more accurately, chronic eruptions – of each in his writings. The first of these two critiques is suggested by certain passages in the *Rechtssoziologie* and by his analysis of the substantive irrationalities of modern capitalism. It can be summarized in the following way: The modern legal order is predicated upon the related ideas of freedom and equality. Today, individuals are free to construct their own legal relationships through voluntary contractual arrangements with others, and consider themselves entitled to equal treatment before the law, regardless of their status or class position. However, despite the very extensive formal freedoms which the modern legal order confers on every individual, material circumstances – in particular, the distribution of wealth and the conditions of work – deprive these formal freedoms of their meaning or value. Freedom and equality cannot be realized in a concretely meaningful sense until property has been redistributed and work routines reorganized so as to eliminate, or at least reduce, the disparities of wealth and the inhuman discipline associated with the capitalist system of production. There must therefore be a fundamental alteration in the material conditions under which individuals exercise their formal freedoms if the egalitarian ideal that justifies these freedoms is actually to be achieved.

This first critique, which Weber states sympathetically without ever actually endorsing, is of course most often associated with the Marxist left, which helps to explain why some Marxist writers have regarded Weber as a cautious fellow-traveller, a materialist who could never quite rid himself of his idealist tendencies.[468] However, it is not the Marxist overtones of this first critique that I want to emphasize, but rather its basic acceptance of equality and autonomy as moral ideas. Someone who accepts this first critique believes that redistribution of wealth and abolition of the factory system are necessary to establish conditions under which individual freedom can flourish to a degree not possible in a society based upon market-oriented capitalism. To this extent, advocates of Weber's first critique embrace the ideal of individual autonomy and disagree with apologists for the existing order only in maintaining that material conditions must be rearranged if a meaningful degree of autonomy is to be secured for everyone. The capacity for autonomous action that will be liberated by a change in material conditions is one that every man possesses and has an equal right to exercise, subject to a similar right in others. Because it celebrates the notion of autonomy as a moral ideal and endorses an egalitarian conception of society, the first critique of modernity implicit in Weber's writings marks an extension or development, rather than a repudiation, of the normative principles that underlie the modern bureaucratic order at its deepest level.

The same cannot be said for Weber's second critique of modern society. This critique challenges rather than supports the ideal of impersonal equality and seeks to rehabilitate the legitimacy of personal leadership in a world dominated by the levelling tendencies of bureaucratic rule. The egalitarian ideal on which the bureaucratic order rests is threatened by the appearance of a leader with courage and passion and a sense of responsibility. A true leader feels entitled, by virtue of his own extraordinary qualities, to call on his followers to make the sacrifices he believes they must; nothing could be further from the attitude of the bureaucratic official who seeks, so far as possible, to eliminate everything strictly personal from his dealings with peers and clients and to perform his duties in a spirit of studied passionlessness. The bureaucrat is devoted, above all else, to the principle that every citizen is equal before the law, regardless of the distinctive personal qualities he happens to possess: from the perspective of the ideal bureaucrat, qualities of this sort can never be a basis for the exercise of authority. A leader, on the other hand, is an extraordinary man who demands to be recognized as such and claims the right to rule others on the ground that only he has both the passion and courageous self-discipline required to lead them, in a responsible way, toward the goal he champions. Every genuine leader draws attention – by his actions and the claims he makes on his followers – to those personal qualities that set him apart as a leader of men and that justify, in the eyes of those devoted to him, the often strenuous demands he makes in the name of his cause. Weber's second critique of modern society insists on the need for responsible leadership in political affairs and hence on the necessity of counteracting the growth of a bureaucratic spirit incapable of tolerating the claims to personal authority which the exercise of genuine leadership always entails. The point of this critique is not to emphasize the extent to which the egalitarian ideals of the legal-rational bureaucratic order remain unfulfilled, but to question these ideals themselves in a fundamental respect. To this extent, it represents a deeper or more radical critique of modern society than the first one.

If the first critique of modern society implicit in Weber's writings is broadly suggestive of the criticisms developed by Marx and his followers, the second parallels, in many respects, the critique of modern society that Nietzsche offers, especially in his later writings.[469] Weber's account of political leadership in 'Politics as a Vocation' reminds one of many similar passages in Nietzsche's own writings and his deliberate use of Nietzschean phrases seems calculated to draw attention to the similarity in their views. In his account of political leadership, Weber stresses the same personal qualities that Nietzsche does – courage, passion, self-discipline, a heightened sense of responsibility, a distance from oneself and the world – and emphasizes (again, as Nietzsche does) the rarity of these qualities and the anti-democratic consequences of treating their possession as a justification for the exercise of authority. Anyone who accepts the democratic principle of equal respect for persons – as the bureaucratic official and Marxist critic of modern society both do – will reject and perhaps even regard as offensive Weber's limited endorsement of Nietzsche's ideas. Similarly, anyone who is sympathetic to Nietzsche's critique of modern society, as Weber obviously was, will dismiss the Marxist programme of reconstructing the material foundations of society in order to achieve a fuller and more meaningful freedom for everyone as a symptom of our disease rather than its cure.

Between these two positions, and the different critiques of modern society they imply, no reconciliation is possible since one embraces egalitarian ideals while the other challenges them. That Weber, at least in a limited and tentative way, adopted both positions reflects an ambivalence in his own attitude toward modern society and the process of rationalization that he took to be its defining characteristic. Weber was by no means a spokesman for the virtues of contemporary European civilization, despite the fact that he made its institutions the point of departure for all his sociological and historical investigations and devoted a lifetime to explaining their development and meaning. But the two criticisms of modernity implicit in his writings – to which his frequent, indeed obsessive, use of the idea of fate provides an important clue – point in different directions and express fundamentally different attitudes toward the egalitarian ideal associated with formal legal rationality and bureaucratic rule. There is, in this regard, something in Weber's writings that can almost be described as an intellectual (or moral) schizophrenia, an oscillation between irreconcilable perspectives that helps to explain why he has found supporters as well as detractors on both the Left and Right.[470]

Whether these two critiques of modernity are justifiable and if so, how one is to choose between them, are questions that lie beyond the limits of this book. In concluding, I shall attempt only to close the circle of my argument by clarifying the connection between the ideas developed in this chapter and the main themes of the book as a whole.

I have called Weber's theory of value positivistic in order to underscore his belief that every value is a posit, the product of a deliberate choice or decision on the part of the individual whose value it happens to be. This theory is to be contrasted with all those that ascribe to the world an inherent meaning or value of its own, a value that antedates the choices and commitments of individual human beings. According to Weber, the very concept of value has no meaning apart from the acts of choice that alone generate norms, norms which the objective 'world-process' can never yield. This positivistic theory of value is the one Weber defends in his methodological writings. It also provides the implicit foundation for his discussion of: the three pure types of authority, the nature of formal legal rationality, the forms of contractual association, modern capitalism, and the Judeo-Christian conception of God.

In addition, Weber's theory of value is associated with a particular conception of personhood. I have defended this claim on independent philosophical grounds, but Weber's own writings – for example, his account of the difference between status and purposive contracts and his description of the Judeo-Christian ideal of ethical personality – suggest that he was himself aware of the connection between these ideas. The conception of personhood associated with Weber's positivism gives prominence to the power of choice exercised in every value-creating act; for this reason, I have called it a will-centred conception of personhood. To be a person, to be qualified to participate in the moral life of the species, one must, on this view, be endowed with the power of deliberate choice – with a capacity for purposeful action or action in accordance with the conception of a rule. Only those beings who possess such a capacity are persons, and Weber's own positivistic theory of value implies that no other quality or characteristic of human beings can have an intrinsic worth of its own – as distinct from the worth it acquires by being affirmed or disaffirmed through an act of choice. Because the capacity for purposeful action is a necessary and sufficient condition for personhood and because it is distributed on a species-wide basis, no human being can be more of a person or have a fundamentally different moral status than any other. The concept of personhood associated with Weber's positivistic theory of value is profoundly egalitarian.

Of the two critiques of modern society implicit in Weber's writings, the first, which emphasizes the loss of individual control resulting from the rationalization of social life, is consistent with the will-centred conception of personhood that I have just described. To be sure, Weber's first critique recognizes – indeed, insists upon – the important influence that material conditions (the distribution of wealth, nature of work, etc.) have on the exercise of human freedom; but it also treats the idea of freedom as the standard against which all social arrangements and programmes of reform are to be evaluated from a moral point of view. It is entirely consistent with this view to assert that human beings have the right to be recognized as persons and enjoy the moral status they do – a status that entitles each individual to a real or effective freedom as great as anyone else's – just because they are autonomous beings with a capacity for purposeful action. Indeed, to the extent that it has been defended on philosophical grounds, the first critique of modern society implicit in Weber's work has typically been justified by an appeal to just such a will-centred conception of the person.[471] In any case, even if the critique in question can be defended on other grounds, it is certainly consistent with Weber's own theory of value and the conception of personhood implied by it.

By contrast, Weber's second critique of modernity challenges this conception. The true leader is set apart from other men by virtue of his special personal qualities – his passion, courage and ability to resist the temptations of vanity by maintaining what Weber calls a 'sense of proportion'. Every political leader chooses a goal of some sort as his 'guiding star', but it is not this choice alone that distinguishes him from other men. Rather, it is the spirit in which the choice is made, the special qualities of character that he displays in making his commitment, which set the leader apart. Even if each of us chooses his own values, some do so with greater passion, courage, steadfastness and modesty than others; these are qualities that are not evenly distributed among men, as the capacity for purposeful action, understood in the most general sense, might be said to be. They are therefore qualities that must be thought of as having their foundation in a part of the soul other than the choosing part, the part that establishes a person's value commitments by affirming some norms and disaffirming others, since there is nothing in the exercise of this capacity alone that can account for the difference between heroes or leaders, on the one hand, and ordinary men on the other. In short, every genuine leader is distinguished by personal qualities not shared by other men, qualities that are rooted in or expressive of some part of the soul other than the will, understood in an abstract sense as the faculty of choice.

From the standpoint of the leader, the possession of these qualities is itself a ground or warrant for the exercise of authority: a genuine leader feels entitled to make special demands on his followers because his courage and self-discipline endow him with a sense of responsibility they do not share. This view is incompatible, however, with a will-centred conception of personhood. For someone who believes that the special qualities of the leader give him a right to exercise authority over others, the possession of a capacity for purposeful action can at most be a necessary but not sufficient condition for determining the moral status of an individual – for deciding what he may rightly demand from others and owes them in return. It is also necessary to ask, on this view, whether the individual in question possesses the special qualities of character that set the true leader apart from ordinary men. A leader is justified in doing things that ordinary men are not and in this sense has a status or identity fundamentally different from theirs. It is uncertain what alternative idea of personhood is implied by the acknowledgement of such differences, but Weber's own will-centred conception must either be abandoned or modified in essential respects if one ascribes inherent value to personal qualities, like passion and courage, in the way his notion of responsible leadership invites and perhaps requires.

That such an incompatibility exists does not mean we must reject Weber's positivistic theory of value; it only means that Weber was himself more uncertain in his commitment to this theory and the conception of personhood associated with it than might appear. Weber's uncertainty is reflected in the ambivalence of his critique of modern society, which as we have seen is really two critiques pointing in different directions, only one of which is consistent with a will-centred conception of the person. Weber never confronted the ambivalence in his criticisms of modern society, and we can only guess how he would have responded if he had. Perhaps he would have said that these are questions for a professional philosopher, a title he emphatically denied for himself.

Despite his disclaimer, Weber's writings are informed by a powerful philosophical intelligence, and I have written this book to clarify the neglected philosophical dimension of his work. Anyone who reflects on Weber's critical account of modern rationalism must eventually confront the questions raised in this chapter. To pursue these questions further, however, would lead us into the domain of moral philosophy. But for those who make the effort, the writings of Max Weber will remain a source of insight and inspiration. No one has thought about these matters on the same scale, or with the same passion as Weber and the fact that his work raises disturbing philosophical questions that it fails to answer is the best proof of his achievement as a philosopher.

A biographical note

Max Weber was born in Erfurt, Germany on 21 April 1864. His father, Max Sr, was a lawyer and politician active in the National Liberal Party. After beginning his career as a civil servant, Weber's father became a parliamentary deputy and represented his party in both the Regional Diet and Imperial Parliament. Weber's mother, Helene, was a woman of intense religious conviction who devoted herself, throughout her life, to humanitarian concerns. According to Marianne Weber (Max's wife), Helene 'always applied absolute standards and in every situation demanded the utmost from herself. Therefore, she was never satisfied with herself and always felt inadequate before God.' Helene's life was marked by 'great inward struggles', to which her husband, absorbed in his political career and unmoved by religious feelings, was largely insensitive.

In 1869, when Weber was five, his family moved to Berlin. The Weber household was a frequent meeting place for the leaders of the National Liberal Party and the scene of many lively political disputes. Weber's father also had a number of academic acquaintances – including Theodor Mommsen, Wilhelm Dilthey and Levin Goldschmidt – and these, too, were regular visitors in his home.

Even as a young boy, Max Weber was a voracious reader. While a *Gymnasium* student, he read widely in history and philosophy (especially Kant in his senior year) and studied the Greek and Latin classics. He also demonstrated a precocious aptitude for scholarship: when he was 14, Weber composed a historical map of medieval Germany and two years later presented his parents, as a Christmas gift, with an essay entitled 'Observations on the Ethnic Character, Development, and History of the Indo-European Nations'.

In the spring of 1882, Weber completed his final examinations at the *Gymnasium* and entered the University of Heidelberg, choosing jurisprudence as his field of primary concentration. In addition to Roman Law, Weber studied medieval history, economic theory, philosophy and theology and participated with enthusiasm (and what Marianne Weber calls 'an outstanding capacity for alcohol') in the social life of the student fraternities. A year after enrolling at Heidelberg, Weber moved to Strasbourg to meet his military service obligations. He spent a rather unhappy year in Strasbourg, complaining, in letters, of the boredom and fatigue of his military existence. In the fall of 1884, Weber resumed his studies, this time at the University of

Berlin where his parents had requested that he enroll for financial reasons. Once again, he turned to law, studying German Civil Law, Administrative Law, International Law, and German legal history (with Otto von Gierke, among others), while also attending the history lectures of Mommsen and Heinrich von Treitschke. In May of 1886, after a semester at the University of Göttingen, Weber took the examination required to qualify as a junior barrister (*Referendar*).

For the next six years, Weber lived in his parents' home in Berlin. During this time, he worked as a *Referendar*, performing various clerical tasks of an essentially mechanical nature while also continuing his legal studies at the University of Berlin. Weber pursued his academic work with a discipline bordering on fanaticism, motivated by a desire to win financial independence from his parents. After completing his doctoral dissertation ('On the History of Trading Companies in the Middle Ages'), he immediately began work on the second dissertation (*Habilitationsschrift*) required of those who wish to be appointed to a faculty position in a German university. Like Weber's first dissertation, this second one, which dealt with Roman agrarian history, combined legal, historical and economic analysis; his *Habilitationsschrift* was completed in 1891 and the following year Weber was certified to teach Roman, German and commercial law. During this same period, he conducted a massive study of the condition of rural workers in East Germany for the *Verein für Sozialpolitik*. The results of this study were published in 1893. In the same year, Weber married Marianne Schnitger, his father's grand-niece, and moved out of his parents' home.

In the fall of 1894, Weber began his teaching career at the University of Freiburg, where he had been appointed to a chair in *Nationalökonomie* (Political Economy) despite the fact that his professional training was as a lawyer and legal historian. The next three years were a period of intense activity for Weber. In addition to his teaching and research, he became increasingly involved in contemporary political debates, writing newspaper articles and giving speeches in an effort to advance his own nationalist and democratic views. Weber expressed some of these same political ideas, as well as his deeply held conviction that ultimate values cannot be derived from scientific research, in the inaugural lecture that he delivered at Freiburg at the beginning of his second semester on the faculty (*Der Nationalstaat und die Volkswirtschaftspolitik*, 'The Nation State and Economic Policy').

In 1896, two years after moving to Freiburg, Weber accepted a position at the University of Heidelberg, where he continued to lecture on political economy as well as more topical matters such as agrarian policy and the labour question. Weber's acquaintances at Heidelberg included many of his former law teachers and also new friends like Ernst Troeltsch the church historian and Heinrich Rickert, the neo-Kantian philosopher, whose writings had an important influence on Weber's own methodological views.

The following year, Weber suffered a nervous collapse that virtually incapacitated him for work of any kind and which eventually forced him to resign his faculty position at Heidelberg. Weber's illness lasted for several years and he did not completely overcome its effects until much later in his life. The precise nature of the illness is uncertain, although its onset was surely related to a disastrous argument that Weber had with his father in the summer of 1897. Relations between his parents had become increasingly strained and Weber assumed the role of advocate in defending his mother's interests – in particular, her right to take separate vacations without her husband. When Max, Sr challenged her right to do so, Weber defended his mother and condemned his father's treatment of her. The argument took place in Weber's Heidelberg home; father and son parted without a reconciliation and several weeks later the elder Weber died suddenly while travelling with a friend. The first symptoms of Weber's illness appeared shortly after the funeral, and increased in severity for the next two years.

During this time, Weber travelled extensively, especially in Italy. It was there, in the winter of 1901–02, that his powers of concentration began slowly to return, to the point where Weber was once again able to read and engage in intellectual conversation (although often with the consequence that he would be physically exhausted by the strain and excitement). In 1902, Weber and his wife returned to their home in Heidelberg and he started work on his first scholarly project in four years – a methodological essay on the foundations of the social sciences entitled *Roscher und Knies und die logischen Probleme der historischen Nationalökonomie* ('Roscher and Knies and the Logical Problems of Historical Political Economy'). The project proved to be an extremely difficult one and taxed Weber's physical and mental capacities to the breaking point; although he frequently despaired of finishing it, the essay on Roscher and Knies was completed in the summer of 1903. At about the same time, Weber accepted an invitation to become an editor of the *Archiv für Sozialwissenschaften und Sozialpolitik,* a scholarly journal that had been acquired by his friend Edgar Jaffé. Weber felt that his editorial responsibilities, while less demanding than a full-time academic appointment, would provide him with a suitable vehicle for the exercise of his reawakened intellectual powers. In 1904, he wrote another methodological essay entitled *Die Objektivität sozialwissenschaftlicher und sozialpolitischer Erkenntnis* ('The Objectivity of Knowledge in Social Science and Social Welfare Policy') which was published in an introduction to the first issue of the new *Archiv* series and shortly after that wrote a piece on agrarian policy which was also published in the same journal.

This burst of renewed productivity was followed, in the late summer of 1904, by a trip to the United States. Weber had been invited to lecture at a scholarly convention in St Louis, and took the opportunity to travel widely throughout the Eastern, Midwestern and Southern parts of the country. Chicago, New York and the boomtowns of Oklahoma all made an impression on Weber and supplied him with a wealth of observations that he subsequently drew upon in his written work.

After returning to Germany, Weber completed the second part of his famous essay, *Die protestantische Ethik und der Geist des Kapitalismus* ('The

Protestant Ethic and the Spirit of Capitalism'), the first part of which had been finished before his trip to America. This was the first of Weber's studies in the sociology of religion, all of which were originally published in the *Archiv*. After a *hiatus* of several years, his essay on Protestantism was followed by similar essays on the religions of China and India, and a massive study of the sociological foundations of ancient Judaism. Although this series of essays, which focused on what Weber called 'the economic ethic of the world religions', was completed in 1913, it did not begin to appear in print until 1915, its publication having been delayed by the First World War and Weber's time-consuming military obligations.

In the intervening years (between 1905 and 1913), Weber undertook a number of other projects in addition to his work on the sociology of religion. During the Russian Revolution of 1905, he learned Russian in order to follow events in the Russian newspapers and published his extensive comments on the Revolution in the *Archiv*. Following this, he wrote some shorter essays on methodology and then a lengthy monograph for the *Handwörterbuch der Staatswissenschaften* entitled *Agrarverhältnisse im Altertum* ('Agrarian Conditions in Antiquity'). Then, in 1908–09, he undertook a research project examining the physical and psychological conse-quences for the factory worker of modern mass-production techniques, a study that had originally been planned by the *Verein für Sozialpolitik* and whose results Weber eventually published in the *Archiv*. Finally, at the request of the publisher Paul Siebeck, he undertook to edit and prepare for publication a wide-ranging series of sociological studies under the general title, *Grundriss der Sozialökonomik* ('Outline of Political Economy'), many sections of which Weber himself agreed to write. His main contribution to the *Grundriss* was not published in its entirety, however, until 1925, five years after his death. This work, entitled *Wirtschaft und Gesellschaft* ('Economy and Society'), is unquestionably Weber's *magnum opus*.

The Weber home in Heidelberg was an intellectual salon. Although he no longer had any formal affiliation with the university and worked entirely as a private scholar, Weber met regularly with other professors and students to discuss political and philosophical issues. His views were eagerly sought on questions of social policy as well as more abstract scholarly matters and he soon acquired an almost mythic stature in the eyes of those who formed the so-called 'Heidelberg Circle'. Karl Jaspers, Werner Sombart, Georg Simmel, Karl Lowenstein and Georg Lukács were among the many regular visitors to the Weber household.

During this same period Weber once again, in his wife's words, 'mounted his charger' and became an active participant in various public debates, publishing several articles in the *Frankfurter Zeitung* on the meaning of academic freedom and making known his own views (mostly in private letters to influential politicians and newspaper editors) on the most important domestic and international issues of the day. In addition, Weber participated in board meetings of the *Verein für Sozialpolitik*, helped to organize a new 'Sociological Society' to facilitate the exchange of ideas among specialists and non-specialists, attended numerous academic conferences and was a party to several rather complicated lawsuits growing out of Marianne's involvement in the women's movement and the (in Weber's eyes defamatory) charge that he had refused to vindicate his wife's honour by accepting a duelling challenge issued by one of her detractors. To the end of his life, Weber remained a controversialist and was highly sensitive to anything that could possibly be interpreted as a slight against his personal integrity.

After the outbreak of the First World War in 1914, Weber served for a period of time as director of the army hospitals in Heidelberg; the job was a demanding one and interrupted Weber's scholarly work, but he took deep satisfaction in the performance of his military duties. Following his discharge, Weber returned to work on the sociology of religion and to his still incomplete systematic exposition of sociological principles (*Wirtschaft und Gesellschaft*). In the tumultuous years of 1916–17, Weber was preoccupied by the many military and political problems facing Germany and expressed his own often quite strong views on these matters in newspaper articles and in a series of treatises on basic constitutional questions. At the conclusion of the war, it seemed likely that Weber might hold a political office in the new government but circumstances and his own principled refusal to be cast in the role of a parliamentary 'seat-hunter' prevented this from happening. In 1918 he did serve, however, as a consultant to the German Armistice Commission in Versailles and as a special adviser to a committee charged with responsibility for drafting the new Weimar Constitution.

During the summer of that same year, Weber taught at the University of Vienna, where his lectures were attended by huge audiences and regarded as public events. In 1919, he accepted a faculty position at the University of Munich – his first full-time professorial appointment since resigning from the Heidelberg faculty, 20 years before – and offered courses in economic history and sociological theory while continuing to work on *Wirtschaft und Gesellschaft*. Following a brief illness, he died of pneumonia on 14 June 1920 at the age of 56. 'During his last night he mentioned the name of Cato and said, with an unfathomable mystery in his voice: *"Das Wahre ist die Wahrheit"* (the true is the truth).'

Suggested further reading

Max Weber's influence on contemporary social theory is ubiquitous and there is an enormous secondary literature which treats virtually every aspect of his work. I offer the following suggestions for further reading in the hope they will provide some guidance for those who wish to pursue further the main themes of this book and to compare my own interpretation of Weber with the interpretations that others have offered. My recommendations are highly selective in two respects. First, with a few exceptions, they are limited to works in English. Second, I have restricted myself to works that deal with problems at the centre of my own concerns; I have tried, however, to indicate the diversity of intellectual traditions influenced by Max Weber's ideas. The selections I have made undoubtedly reveal my own biases; even this, however, may be of some utility.

Two very good books dealing with Weber's methodological views are P. Winch, *The Idea of a Social Science* (London, 1958) and W.G. Runciman, *A Critique of Max Weber's Philosophy of Social Science* (Cambridge, 1972). Winch's book contains an especially good discussion of Weber's concept of meaningful behaviour, and points out some important parallels between Weber's views and Wittgenstein's. In this respect, it establishes an intellectual link (though not an historical one) between Weber and those social and legal philosophers, such as H.L.A. Hart, who have been influenced by the Wittgensteinian notion of rule-governed behaviour (anticipated by Weber's own treatment of the same concept in his *Critique of Stammler*). Runciman discusses Weber's theory of ideal types, the concepts of 'value-freedom' and 'value-relevance', and the nature of interpretative understanding (*Verstehen*); his aim is to 'correct' Weber's methodological arguments by putting them in a more precise and philosophically defensible form. Runciman's own views are strongly influenced by the tradition of analytic philosophy deriving from Frege (although he is familiar with, and draws upon, the work of philosophers in other traditions, such as Husserl and Dilthey).

One of the most interesting essays on Weber's methodology (unfortunately, not yet translated into English) is D. Henrich, *Die Einheit der Wissenschaftslehre Max Webers* (Tübingen, 1952). Henrich develops the neo-Kantian background of Weber's views and stresses the importance of Weber's relationship to the philosopher Heinrich Rickert. Henrich argues that the concept of 'personality' provides the foundation both for Weber's theory of knowledge and his theory of value. The principal limitation of Henrich's book is its failure to consider the significance of Weber's methodological views for his theory of society.

Weber's theory of interpretative understanding is discussed, at length, in A. Schutz, *The Phenomenology of the Social World* (trans. G. Walsh and F. Lehnert, Evanston, Ill., 1967). Schutz attempts to reconcile Weber's views with those of Husserl and to claim Weber for phenomenology. Weber's influence on Schutz and others in the phenomenological movement is described in R. Bubner, *Modern German Philosophy* (trans. E. Matthews, Cambridge, 1981) pp. 41–3.

In the United States, the first really thorough account of Weber's methodological ideas was presented by Talcott Parsons in *The Structure of Social Action* (New York, 1937). Parson's own interpretation of Weber has recently come under attack; see, for example, J. Cohen, L.E. Hazelton and W. Pope, 'De-Parsonizing Weber' (1975) 40 *American Sociological Review* 229. A useful short account of Weber's influence on American sociology may be found in R. Bendix and G. Roth, ' "Value-Neutrality" in Germany and the United States' in *Scholarship and Partisanship* (Berkeley, 1971). As Bendix and Roth point out, the reception of Weber's ideas both in Germany and the United States was importantly influenced by various critical reactions to his controversial distinction between facts and values. The origin and early development of the so-called 'fact-value' debate is described in R. Dahrendorf, 'Values and Social Science' in *Essays in the Theory of Society* (Stanford, 1969). The critics of Weber's distinction between facts and values divide into three camps. In the first are the Marxists and neo-Marxists of the Frankfurt School; for examples, see Lukacs, *History and Class Consciousness* (trans. R. Livingstone, London, 1971) pp. 110–49; H. Marcuse, 'Industrialization and Capitalism in the Work of Max Weber' in *Negations: Essays in Critical Theory* (trans. J. Shapiro, Boston, 1969) pp. 201–26; and J. Habermas, 'Max Weber's Concept of Legitimation' in *Legitimation Crisis*, (trans. T. McCarthy, Boston, 1975). In the second camp are natural rights theorists such as Leo Strauss and Eric Voegelin; see L. Strauss, *Natural Right and History* (Chicago, 1953) pp. 35–80, and E. Voegelin, *The New Science of Politics* (Chicago, 1952) pp. 13–26. Both Strauss and Voegelin criticize the radical positivism of Weber's theory of value from the standpoint of classical rationalism (tempered, in Voegelin's case, by certain Christian ideas). Finally, in the third camp, are the fascist ideologues who have criticized Weber's social theory on the grounds that it represents a degenerate form of bourgeois liberalism; see, for example, C. Steding, *Politik und Wissenschaft bei Max Weber* (Breslau, 1932).

The relationship between Max Weber's methodology and his political theory is discussed in two books by Wolfgang Mommsen, *The Age of Bureaucracy: Perspectives on the Political Sociology of Max Weber* (Cambridge, 1971), and *The Political Thought and Political Theory of Max Weber* (London, 1972).

The general intellectual background that shaped Weber's political ideas is described in Mommsen, *The Age of Bureaucracy*; J.P. Mayer, *Max Weber and German Politics* (London, 1944); D. MacRae, *Max Weber* (New York, 1974); P. Honigsheim, *On Max Weber* (trans. J. Rytina, New York, 1968); L.M. Lachmann, *The Legacy of Max Weber* (London, 1970) Chapter 3; and A. Mitzman, *The Iron Cage* (New York, 1970). Mommsen's and Lachmann's books are the most philosophical; Mitzman takes a psycho-analytic approach to the problem and analyses Weber's attraction to charisma as a reflection of his own repressed eroticism; Honigsheim's book is more historical and anecdotal in character, as is Mayer's; MacRae's (which appears in the 'Modern Masters' series) is brief, readable and contains some interesting remarks on Weber's relationship to Marx and Nietzsche.

A more detailed account of Weber's theory of society is contained in Reinhard Bendix's splendid but rather long book, *Max Weber: An Intellectual Portrait* (New York, 1960). Bendix focuses on Weber's theory of authority and sociology of religion; he makes no effort, however, to relate these aspects of Weber's work to his methodological views (although he does draw attention to the philosophical dimension of Weber's conception of modernity by comparing Weber's ideas with Hegel's). Bendix's book is primarily a descriptive work which accurately and economically summarizes Weber's views for the English-speaking reader.

Equally broad-ranging in their subject-matter, though more critical (and generally more philosophical) in approach are two recent collections of essays, G. Roth and W. Schluchter, *Max Weber's Vision of History: Ethics and Methods* (Berkeley, 1979), and R. Bendix and G. Roth, *Scholarship and Partisanship: Essays on Max Weber*. The latter collection contains essays on a variety of topics, including Weber's relationship to Marx, Durkheim, Burckhardt and Nietzsche, which help to locate Weber's position in the intellectual topography of the twentieth century. Roth and Schluchter's book throws much light on the philosophical links between Weber's methodology, sociology of religion and conception of modernity, and contains some especially acute observations concerning the paradox of rationalization in Weber's theory of society. Roth and Schluchter draw upon the earlier work of Karl Löwith, whose essays on Weber attempt to clarify the philosophical significance of his conceptions of modernity and disenchantment; see K. Löwith, 'Weber's Interpretation of the Bourgeois-Capitalistic World in Terms of the Guiding Principle of "Rationalization" ' in *Max Weber* (ed. D. Wrong, Englewood Cliffs, New Jersey, 1970) – an incomplete translation of Löwith's essay, 'Max Weber und Karl Marx' in *Gesammelte Abhandlungen* (Stuttgart, 1960) – and 'Die Entzauberung der Welt durch Wissenschaft' (1964) 18 *Merkur* 501. Another book, as yet untranslated, which deals with many of the same themes is G. Abramowski, *Das Geschichtsbild Max Webers* (Stuttgart, 1966).

The literature in English on Weber's *Rechtssoziologie* is surprisingly thin. Perhaps the best-known essay on the subject is Rheinstein's introduction to *Max Weber on Law in Economy and Society* (Cambridge, Mass., 1954). Although it contains some useful background material, Rheinstein's introduction has many shortcomings, such as its failure to discuss the relationship between Weber's analysis of legal phenomena and his theory of value. An interesting recent paper which does attempt to clarify the connection between the *Rechtssoziologie* and Weber's methodological views is M. Cain, 'The Limits of Idealism: Max Weber and the Sociology of Law' (1980) 3 *Research in Law and Sociology* 53. Some scattered remarks, along these same lines, can also be found in Roberto Unger's book, *Law in Modern Society* (New York, 1976).

Other recent essays, treating different aspects of the *Rechtssoziologie*, are M. Albrow, 'Legal Positivism and Bourgeois Materialism: Max Weber's View of the Sociology of Law' (1975) 8 *British Journal of Law and Society* 14; S. Andreski, 'Understanding, Action and Law in Max Weber' in *Sociological Approaches to Law* (A. Podgorecki and C. Whelan eds., London, 1981); P. Beirne, 'Ideology and Rationality in Max Weber's Sociology of Law' (1979) 2 *Research in Law and Sociology;* and D. Trubek, 'Max Weber on Law and the Rise of Capitalism' 1972 *Wisconsin Law Review* 3. Trubek's essay contains an especially interesting discussion of the problematic case of English capitalism, and the others touch, at various points, on the relationship between Weber's fundamental methodological beliefs and his analysis of legal phenomena. In one way or another, all are concerned with the long-standing controversy over whether Weber was a materialist or idealist, a dispute I have sought to downplay by emphasizing what I call the 'exegetical' dimension of Weber's sociology.

Reference notes

1. The Biographical Note at the end of the book contains a brief sketch of Weber's life. A much fuller account may be found in Marianne Weber's biography of her husband, *Max Weber: A Biography* (trans. H. Zohn, New York and London, 1975). Some useful insights of a psychoanalytic nature are contained in A. Mitzman, *The Iron Cage* (New York, 1969). See also M. Green, *The von Richthofen Sisters: The Triumphant and the Tragic Modes of Love* (New York, 1974), which throws additional light on certain aspects of Weber's private life neglected in his wife's biography.
2. *Wirtschaft und Gesellschaft* (Tübingen, 1922); *Economy and Society* (trans. Fischoff *et al.*, New York, 1978). The *Rechtssoziologie* has also been separately published in an English translation under the title *Max Weber on Law in Economy and Society* (trans. E. Shils and M. Rheinstein, Cambridge, Mass., 1954).
3. See F. Tenbruck, 'The Problem of Thematic Unity in the Works of Max Weber', (1980) 31 *British Journal of Sociology* 316; S. Kalberg, 'The Search for Thematic Orientations in a Fragmented Oeuvre: The Discussion of Max Weber in Recent German Sociological Literature', (1979) 13 *Sociology* 127.
4. *ES*, 671–73; *LES*, 105–07.
5. See Hegel, *Philosophy of Right* (trans. T.M. Knox, Oxford, 1952) §§ 72–9.
6. See, for example, K. Löwith, 'Weber's Interpretation of the Bourgeois-Capitalistic World in Terms of the Guiding Principle of "Rationalization" ', in *Max Weber* (ed. D. Wrong, Englewood Cliffs, NJ, 1970); H. Marcuse, 'Industrialization and Capitalism in the Work of Max Weber,' in *Negations* (Boston, 1968); and R. Bendix, *Max Weber: An Intellectual Portrait* (New York, 1960) pp. 486–94.
7. *ES*, 775–6; *LES* 96–7.
8. K. Jaspers, *Leonardo, Descrates, Max Weber* (trans. R. Manheim, London, 1965) p. 251.
9. See R. Dworkin, *Taking Rights Seriously* (Cambridge, Mass., 1977) Chapter 4, and 'No Right Answer?' in *Law, Morality and Society: Essays in Honour of H.L.A. Hart* (Oxford, 1977), pp. 58–84.
10. *ES*, 885; *LES*, 307.
11. *ES*, 311; *CS*, 127–34.

12. *MSS*, 7.
13. *ES*, 4311–12; *CS*, 129–34.
14. For a critical discussion of Weber's concept of value-freedom, see Runciman, *A Critique of Max Weber's Philosophy of Social Science*, pp. 49–60; Parsons, 'Value-freedom and Objectivity' in *Max Weber and Sociology Today*, pp. 32–4; A. Dawe, 'The Relevance of Values' in *Max Weber and Modern Sociology* (A. Sahay, ed., London, 1971).
15. See *CS*, 101.
16. See *RK*, p. 125, where Weber makes a similar point regarding the limits of interpretative understanding in general.
17. *CS*, 127–8.
18. See Kronman, 'Legal Scholarship and Moral Education' (1981) 90 *Yale Law Journal* 955.
19. *MSS*, 2–5.
20. *MSS*, 76–9. See also J. Habermas, *Knowledge and Human Interests* (trans. J. Shapiro, Boston, 1971).
21. *FMW*, 140–3.
22. See generally *RK*, pp. 129–74. Weber's conception of empathetic understanding is discussed at great length, from a phenomenological point of view, in A. Schutz, *The Phenomenology of the Social World* (trans. G. Walsh and F. Lehnert, Evanston, Ill., 1967). Weber's influence on the phenomenological movement, and on Schutz in particular, is described in R. Bubner, *Modern German Philosophy* (trans. E. Matthews, Cambridge, 1981) pp. 40–3.
23. *MSS*, 13.
24. See *Charmides*, 174b; *Laches*, 198b–199d; *Protagoras*, 349a–358a.
25. T. Irwin, *Plato's Moral Theory* (Oxford, 1977).
26. *Republic*, 518c–d.
27. See 'Freud's Psychoanalytic Method', 'On Psychotherapy' and 'Analysis Terminable and Interminable', all in Freud, *Therapy and Technique* (Rieff, ed., New York, 1963).
28. See Henrich, *Die Einheit der Wissenschaftslehre Max Webers*. Henrich stresses the central importance of the concept of 'autonomy' in Weber's theory of knowledge.
29. *ES*, 12; *CS*, 138.
30. Something like this seems to have been Holmes's view. See O.W. Holmes, 'The Path of the Law' in *Collected Legal Papers* (Cambridge, 1897). This view is criticized by H.L.A. Hart in *The Concept of Law* (Oxford, 1961) Chapter 3.
31. *RK*, 120–9.
32. *ES*, 7. A very useful discussion of the concept of meaningful behaviour may be found in P. Winch, *The Idea of a Social Science and Its Relation to Philosophy* (London, 1958) Chapter 2.
33. *Physics*, 194b 32.
34. See R. Dawkins, *The Selfish Gene* (Oxford, 1976).
35. For a discussion of the various senses in which this concept may be

understood, see S. Lukes, 'Methodological Individualism Reconsidered' in *Sociological Theory and Philosophical Analysis* (D. Emmet and A. MacIntye, eds., New York, 1970). See also J.W.N. Watkins, 'Holism versus Individualism' (1956) *Proceedings of the Aristotlean Society*.

36. *ES*, 4; 22–4.
37. The example is Weber's. *ES*, 23.
38. See H.L.A. Hart's discussion of 'the internal aspect of rules' in *The Concept of Law* pp. 79–88.
39. *ES*, 34.
40. *ES*, 325.
41. *ES*, 34–5.
42. For an exposition and criticism of this view, usually associated with legal positivism, see Hart, *The Concept of Law* Chapter 6; Dworkin, *Taking Rights Seriously* Chapters 2 and 3; and J. Raz, *The Concept of a Legal System* (Oxford, 1970) Chapter 3. A classical defence of the position can be found in H. Kelsen, *General Theory of Law and State* (A. Wedberg, trans., Cambridge, Mass., 1945) Chapter 10.
43. *ES*, 317.
44. *CS*, 134–6.
45. *Ibid.*
46. *MSS*, 32; 58; 64; 78; 96–7. For a critical discussion of Weber's concept of 'value-relevance', see Runciman, *A Critique of Max Weber's Philosophy of Social Science* pp. 37–48.
47. *ES*, 775–6; *LES*, 96–7.
48. Compare H.L.A. Hart's discussion of the 'rule of recognition', *The Concept of Law* pp. 97–107, with Kelsen's account of the 'basic norm' of a legal order, *General Theory of Law and State* pp. 115–22.
49. For a critical discussion of Weber's theory of legitimation, see R. Bendix, *Max Weber: An Intellectual Portrait* pp. 285–97; J. Habermas, 'Max Weber's Concept of Legitimation' in *Legitimation Crisis* (trans. T. McCarthy, Boston, 1975); M. Spencer, 'Weber on Legitimate Norms and Authority' (1970) 21 *British Journal of Sociology* 133; R. Grafstein, 'The Failure of Weber's Conception of Legitimacy: Its Causes and Implications' (1981) 43 *Journal of Politics* 456.
50. *ES*, 53.
51. This is Weber's own example. See *ES*, 214.
52. Compare Weber's definition of domination at *ES* 212 (where he equates 'domination' and 'authority' – *Herrschaft* and *Authorität*) with his discussion of domination at *ES* 942–3.
53. *ES*, 946. For a critical discussion of this passage, see P. Blau, 'Critical Remarks on Weber's Theory of Authority,' (1963) 17 *The American Political Science Review* 306–16.
54. *ES*, 946.
55. *Ibid.*

56. Compare H.L.A. Hart's discussion of the distinction between 'being obliged' and 'having an obligation', *The Concept of Law* pp. 79–88.
57. *ES* 31; 213.
58. See Aristotle, *Politics*, 1053a 7–18.
59. *ES*, 953; see also *FMW*, 271, 353.
60. *ES*, 953.
61. *FMW*, 271.
62. *ES*, 226.
63. *FMW*, 296.
64. *ES*, 215.
65. *ES*, 376; compare Nietzsche, *On The Genealogy of Morals* p. 125.
66. *ES*, 226.
67. *ES*, 1117.
68. *FMW*, 296.
69. For the classical analysis of the household as a form of social and economic organization, see Aristotle, *Politics* Book I (trans. E. Barker, Oxford, 1958).
70. *ES*, 1111.
71. *Ibid.*
72. *ES*, 377.
73. *Ibid.* See generally *ES*, 370–83.
74. *FMW*, 296.
75. For a fascinating study of the ways in which the sacred and everyday dimensions of life interpenetrated in the routines of the ancient family, see Fustel DeCoulanges, *The Ancient City* (trans. W. Small, New York, 1874).
76. *ES*, 215.
77. *FMW*, 78.
78. *ES*, 217.
79. *ES*, 954.
80. *ES*, 217.
81. *Ibid.*
82. *ES*, 225.
83. *ES*, 218.
84. *ES*, 225. Compare Hegel, *Philosophy of Right*, § 296.
85. *ES*, 983.
86. *Ibid.*
87. *ES*, 957.
88. *ES*, 1006.
89. *ES*, 1111.
90. *FMW*, 149.
91. *ES*, 215.
92. *ES*, 242. See also *ES*, 1113, 1115.
93. *ES*, 1122.
94. *ES*, 1117.
95. *ES*, 1115.

96. *ES*, 1117.
97. *ES*, 244.
98. *Ibid.*
99. *ES*, 1115.
100. *ES*, 244.
101. *ES*, 1112.
102. *ES*, 1113.
103. *ES*, 227.
104. *ES*, 244.
105. *ES*, 1118.
106. *ES*, 245.
107. *ES*, 1121.
108. *Ibid.*
109. *ES*, 246.
110. *ES*, 246–54; 1121–56.
111. *ES*, 1115.
112. *ES*, 217, 954.
113. See *PE*, 13–31.
114. *Ibid.*
115. *ES*, 1399–403.
116. *PE*, 13.
117. *ES*, 1402.
118. *MSS*, 8; 11.
119. *MSS*, 57.
120. *PE*, 181.
121. *ES*, 1006.
122. *ES*, 672; *LES*, 106.
123. For an account of the beginnings of this separation in the great family-owned trading companies of the Italian city states, see Weber's doctoral dissertation, *Zur Geschichte der Handelsgesellschaften im Mittelalter* (Stuttgart, 1889).
124. Aristotle, *Politics* 1252b 10 – 1253a 6. See also Hegel, *Philosophy of Right*, §§ 158–81.
125. Compare Marx, *Capital*, pp. 618–33.
126. See Hannah Arendt's description of the timeless circularity of the labour process in *The Human Condition* (New York, 1959), pp. 84–8.
127. See Aristotle, *Politics* 1256b 26 – 1259a 35; Marx, *Capital* 648–56.
128. See Marx, *Capital*, 185–96; *Grundrisse*, 414–15.
129. *ES*, 981.
130. *ES*, 983; *FMW*, 131.
131. *ES*, 225.
132. For a critical discussion of Weber's concept of charismatic domination, see C. Camic, 'Charisma: Its Varieties, Preconditions and Consequences' (1980) 50 *Sociological Inquiry* 5, and R. Bendix and G. Roth, *Scholarship and Partisanship: Essays on Max Weber* (Berkeley, 1971) Chapter 9.
133. *ES*, 215.

134. *ES*, 241.
135. See *ES*, 1114–18.
136. *ES*, 1112. Hobbes makes many of these points in his account of 'supernatural' or 'formed' religions. See *Leviathan* Chapter 12.
137. See *ES*, 1117–23.
138. For an interesting case study, see M. Rush, *Political Succession in the USSR* (New York and London, 1965). The instability of charismatic movements is also beautifully illustrated by Norman Cohn's discussion of messianism in medieval and early modern Europe. N. Cohn, *The Pursuit of the Millennium* (New York, 1961).
139. *ES*, 656–7; *LES*, 62–4.
140. *ES*, 655–976; *LES*, 61.
141. *ES*, 656–7; *LES*, 63.
142. *ES*, 657, 850, 854–5; *LES*, 64, 271, 276–8.
143. *ES*, 656; *LES*, 62.
144. *ES*, 657, 800; *LES*, 64, 219–22.
145. *ES*, 655; *LES*, 61.
146. *ES*, 655–6; *LES*, 62.
147. *ES*, 655; *LES*, 61.
148. *Ibid.*
149. *ES*, 657; *LES*, 63.
150. *Ibid.*
151. *Ibid.*
152. *ES*, 655; *LES*, 62.
153. *ES*, 657; *LES*, 64.
154. *ES*, 655, 657, 884; *LES*, 62, 63–4, 306.
155. *ES*, 656; *LES*, 63.
156. *ES*, 762; *LES*, 78.
157. *ES*, 812; *LES*, 228.
158. Here I follow in certain general respects the account offered by Rheinstein in his Introduction to *LES*, pp. xlii–lii.
159. *ES*, 761; *LES*, 77.
160. *ES*, 845, 976–8; *LES*, 264.
161. *ES*, 813, 891; *LES*, 229, 317.
162. *ES*, 789–80; *LES*, 205–6.
163. *ES*, 844; *LES*, 264.
164. *ES*, 789; *LES*, 205.
165. *Ibid.*
166. *ES*, 657–8; *LES*, 64.
167. *ES*, 656; *LES*, 62.
168. *ES*, 810; *LES*, 225.
169. *ES*, 758–64; *LES*, 73–82.
170. *ES*, 810–11; *LES*, 225–7.
171. *ES* 810; *LES*, 226.
172. *ES*, 761; *LES*, 78.
173. *ES*, 761; *LES*, 77.

174. *ES*, 812, 830; *LES*, 228, 254.

175. *ES*, 762; *LES*, 78.

176. See Rawls, *A Theory of Justice*, pp. 85–6.

177. See, for example, *ES*, 764; *LES*, 81—2.

178. *ES*, 762; *LES*, 79.

179. Here I follow S.F.C. Milsom's suggestive account of the rise of the common law pleading system as a consequence of the shift in adjudicative responsibility from God to man. Milsom, *Historical Foundations of the Common Law* 2nd edn (Toronto, 1981), pp. 42–3.

180. See, for example, *ES*, 895; *LES*, 321.

181. *ES*, 812; *LES*, 228.

182. *ES*, 655; *LES*, 61.

183. *ES*, 657; *LES*, 63.

184. *ES*, 884; *LES*, 306.

185. *ES*, 656; *LES*, 62.

186. *ES*, 649; *LES*, 53.

187. *ES*, 682–3; *LES*, 123–5.

188. *ES*, 787; *LES*, 201.

189. *ES*, 787; *LES*, 201–2.

190. See generally Raz, *The Concept of a Legal System*.

191. *ES*, 657–8; *LES*, 64.

192. *ES*, 655; *LES*, 61.

193. My explanation of the anti-systematic tendencies of primitive legal thinking draws on E. Cassirer, *The Philosophy of Symbolic Forms* Volume 2 (Myth) (trans. R. Manheim, New Haven, 1955).

194. *ES*, 657; *LES*, 63.

195. *ES*, 884; *LES*, 306.

196. *Ibid.*

197. *ES*, 884–5; *LES*, 306–7. See Llewellyn's discussion of 'situation-sense' in *The Common Law Tradition* (Boston, 1960) pp. 121–57.

198. *ES*, 810; *LES*, 225.

199. *ES*, 812; *LES*, 228.

200. *ES*, 812–13; *LES*, 228–9.

201. For a powerful statement of this view, see F.A. Hayek, *The Constitution of Liberty* (Chicago, 1972) pp. 148–61.

202. *ES*, 811; *LES*, 226.

203. *ES*, 813; *LES*, 230.

204. *ES*, 810; *LES*, 225.

205. *ES*, 811; *LES*, 22–7.

206. *ES*, 812; *LES*, 228.

207. *ES*, 669; *LES*, 101.

208. See E. Durkheim, *The Division of Labor in Society* (trans. G. Simpson, New York, 1933) Chapters 3–5; Marx, *Capital*, pp. 185–96; Maine, *Ancient Law* Chapter 5.

209. *ES*, 668; *LES*, 100.

210. *Ibid.*

211. *ES*, 730; *LES*, 189.
212. *ES*, 668; *LES*, 100.
213. *Ibid.*
214. *Ibid.*
215. *ES*, 671–2; *LES*, 105.
216. *ES*, 669; *LES*, 101.
217. For historical examples of household economies of this sort (drawn from different periods), see M.I. Finley, *The World of Odysseus* (New York, 1965) and G. Duby, *Rural Economy and Country Life in the Medieval West* (trans. C. Postan, Columbia, SC, 1968) Chapter 2.
218. *ES*, 677; *LES*, 113.
219. *ES*, 636–7; *LES*, 192–3.
220. *ES*, 669; *LES*, 101. Compare Hegel, *Philosophy of Right* §§ 179–81; Maine, *Ancient Law* Chapters 6 and 7.
221. *ES*, 670; *LES*, 102.
222. *Ibid.*
223. *Ibid.*
224. *ES*, 671; *LES*, 105.
225. *ES*, 672; *LES*, 105.
226. *Ibid.*
227. *ES*, 672–4; *LES*, 105–9.
228. *ES*, 637; *LES*, 193.
229. *ES*, 636; *LES*, 192. Compare Marx, *Grundrisse* pp. 540–3; *Capital* pp. 81–96 (the 'fetishism of commodities').
230. *ES*, 672; *LES*, 106.
231. *Ibid.*
232. *Ibid.*
233. *ES*, 639; *LES*, 195.
234. *ES*, 696; *LES*, 142.
235. *ES*, 695; *LES*, 141–2.
236. *Ibid.* On this question, see Kelsen, *General Theory of Law and State* Part II.
237. *ES*, 698; *LES*, 145.
238. *ES*, 697; *LES*, 144.
239. *ES*, 698; *LES*, 145.
240. *ES*, 697–8; *LES*, 144.
241. *ES*, 698–9; *LES*, 145–6.
242. *ES*, 700; *LES*, 147.
243. *ES*, 696; *LES*, 142.
244. *ES*, 700; *LES*, 147.
245. *ES*, 671; *LES*, 103.
246. *ES*, 671; *LES*, 104.
247. *ES*, 639; *LES*, 196.
248. *ES*, 637; *LES*, 193.
249. *ES*, 696; *LES*, 142.
250. *ES*, 697; *LES*, 143.

251. For a general historical discussion of this question, from a Marxist perspective, see P. Anderson, *Lineages of the Absolutist State* (London, 1974).
252. *ES*, 698–9; *LES*, 145–6.
253. *ES*, 695; *LES*, 141.
254. *ES*, 678; *LES*, 116.
255. *ES*, 668; *LES*, 100.
256. *ES*, 689; *LES*, 134. For an historical discussion of this subject, and an account of the origins of the bourgeois family, see L. Stone, *The Family, Sex and Marriage in England 1500–1800* (New York, 1977).
257. *Ibid.*
258. *ES*, 691; *LES*, 137.
259. *Ibid.*
260. *ES*, 692; *LES*, 138.
261. *ES*, 694; *LES*, 140.
262. *ES*, 691; *LES*, 136.
263. *ES*, 692; *LES*, 137.
264. *ES*, 694; *LES*, 140.
265. *ES*, 693; *LES*, 138.
266. See Stone, *The Family, Sex and Marriage in England 1500–1800* Chapter 6. A classical philosophical description of the bourgeois family may be found in Hegel, *Philosophy of Right*, §§ 158–81.
267. *ES*, 730; *LES*, 189.
268. *ES*, 731; *LES*, 190–1.
269. *Ibid.*
270. *ES*, 730; *LES*, 189.
271. *ES*, 731; *LES*, 190.
272. *Ibid.*
273. *Ibid.*
274. *Ibid.*
275. *PE*, 17.
276. *ES*, 165.
277. *PE*, 24.
278. *ES*, 162.
279. *ES*, 162; 810–11; 883; *LES*, 225–7; 304–5.
280. For a critical discussion of Weber's account of the development of English capitalism and its relationship to legal rationalization, see D. Trubek, 'Max Weber on Law and the Rise of Capitalism' (1972) *Wisconsin Law Review* 3.
281. *ES*, 892; *LES*, 318.
282. *ES*, 784; *LES*, 198.
283. *ES*, 787; *LES*, 201.
284. *ES*, 789; *LES*, 204–5.
285. *Ibid.*
286. *ES*, 788; *LES*, 203.
287. *ES*, 789, 798–9, 854–5; *LES*, 204–5, 217–19; 276–8.

288. *ES*, 855; *LES*, 277–8.
289. *ES*, 776; *LES*, 97.
290. *ES*, 855; *LES*, 277–8 (emphasis added).
291. *ES*, 892; *LES*, 318 (emphasis added).
292. *ES*, 667; *LES*, 98.
293. *ES*, 681–2; *LES*, 122.
294. *Ibid.*
295. *ES*, 706; *LES*, 156.
296. *Ibid.*
297. *ES*, 707; *LES*, 156.
298. *ES*, 683; *LES*, 125.
299. *ES*, 709; *LES*, 160–1.
300. *ES*, 667; *LES*, 99.
301. See, for example, Internal Revenue Code, § 179 ('Additional first year depreciation allowance for small business').
302. *ES*, 667; *LES*, 99.
303. *ES*, 757; *LES*, 71.
304. *ES*, 775; *LES*, 96.
305. *ES*, 757; *LES*, 72.
306. *ES*, 687; *LES*, 130–1.
307. *ES*, 710; *LES*, 161.
308. *ES*, 687; *LES*, 131.
309. See M. Cain, 'The Limits of Idealism: Max Weber and the Sociology of Law' (1980) 3 *Research in Law and Sociology* 53.
310. *ES*, 776; *LES*, 97.
311. *Ibid.*
312. *ES*, 784–5; *LES*, 198.
313. *Ibid.*
314. *ES*, 855; *LES*, 278.
315. *ES*, 655; 683; *LES*, 61, 124.
316. *ES*, 891–2; *LES*, 318.
317. *ES*, 63.
318. *ES*, 64.
319. *Ibid.*
320. *ES*, 98.
321. *ES*, 87.
322. *Ibid.*
323. *Ibid.*
324. *ES*, 90.
325. *ES*, 91.
326. *Ibid.*
327. *ES*, 89–90.
328. *ES*, 90.
329. *ES*, 89.
330. *ES*, 85.
331. *ES*, 85–6.

332. *ES*, 138.
333. *ES*, 108, 138.
334. *ES*, 107.
335. *ES*, 101.
336. *ES*, 104.
337. *ES*, 102.
338. *Ibid.*
339. *ES*, 111.
340. *ES*, 117, 144.
341. *ES*, 113.
342. *ES*, 162.
343. *Ibid.*
344. *ES*, 162–3. For a further discussion of some of these problems, in particular those concerning the breeding of slaves, see Weber, 'The Social Causes of the Decay of Ancient Civilization,' (1950) 5 *Journal of General Education* 75–88, and M. Bloch, 'Comment et pourquoi finit l'esclavage antique', in *Slavery in Classical Antiquity* (M.I. Finley, ed., Cambridge and New York, 1960). See also Marx, *Capital*, p. 219n.
345. *PE*, 22.
346. *ES*, 162.
347. *ES*, 128.
348. *ES*, 127–8. See Marx, *Capital*, pp. 185–96.
349. *ES*, 138.
350. *ES*, 137.
351. *PE*, 22.
352. See generally M.I. Finley, *Ancient Slavery and Modern Ideology* (New York, 1980), and *Economy and Society in Ancient Greece* Part Two: Slavery and the Economy (New York, 1982).
353. *ES*, 112–13. See also *ES*, 75.
354. Compare Hegel, *Philosophy of Right*, §§ 41–5; 62–3.
355. See W.W. Buckland, *The Roman Law of Slavery* Chapter 1 (Cambridge, 1908).
356. *Op. cit.* pp. 397–401.
357. Here I follow Hegel's treatment of the distinction between ownership and possession in *The Philosophy of Right*, §§ 45–58.
358. Kant, *Fundamental Principles of the Metaphysic of Morals* p. 45.
359. See H.L.A. Hart, *The Concept of Law*, pp. 83–4.
360. Aristotle, *Politics* 1253b 23 – 1255b 15; 1259b 18 – 1260b 7.
361. *ES*, 813; *LES*, 230.
362. *Ibid.*
363. *ES*, 823; *LES*, 244.
364. *ES*, 828; *LES*, 250.
365. *ES*, 828; *LES*, 251.
366. *Ibid.*
367. *ES*, 829; *LES*, 251–2.

368. *Ibid.*
369. *PE*, 183.
370. *AJ*, 5.
371. *AJ*, 3.
372. *AJ*, 118.
373. *AJ*, 205-18.
374. See *RI*, 329-43. An interesting discussion of the ethical implications of Weber's conception of the uniqueness of the Judeo-Christian conception of God's relation to the world may be found in W. Schluchter, 'The Paradox of Rationalization: On the Relation of Ethics and World,' in G. Roth and W. Schluchter, *Max Weber's Vision of History* (Berkeley, 1979) pp. 11-64.
375. *RI*, 336.
376. *RI*, 338.
377. *RI*, 331-2.
378. *RI*, 338-9.
379. *RI*, 336.
380. *RI*, 338.
381. *RI*, 342.
382. *RI*, 330.
383. *RI*, 337.
384. *RI*, 342.
385. *AJ*, 130.
386. *Ibid.*
387. *Ibid.*
388. *AJ*, 78.
389. *Ibid.*
390. *AJ*, 131-2.
391. *AJ*, 131.
392. *AJ*, 132.
393. *AJ*, 78.
394. *AJ*, 4.
395. *AJ*, 132.
396. *AJ*, 5.
397. *AJ*, 3.
398. *AJ*, 167.
399. *AJ*, 223.
400. *Ibid.*
401. *AJ*, 297.
402. *AJ*, 312-14.
403. *AJ*, 220.
404. *AJ*, 216.
405. *AJ*, 216-17.
406. *AJ*, 217.
407. *AJ*, 247.
408. *AJ*, 4.

210 *Reference notes*

ES, 775–6; *LES*, 96–7.
410. *PE*, 26.
411. *FMW*, 138–9.
412. For a similar characterization of the modern world, see H. Arendt, 'The Concept of History', in *Between Past and Future* (New York, 1963).
413. *FMW*, 139.
414. Hobbes, *Leviathan*, p. 5.
415. *FMW*, 137, 149, 153.
416. *PE*, 181.
417. *ES*, 1400–3.
418. This paradox is discussed in G. Roth and W. Schluchter, *Max Weber's Vision of History: Ethics and Methods*, and in H. Marcuse, 'Industrialization and Capitalism in the Work of Max Weber'.
419. *FMW*, 155.
420. *ES*, 1156.
421. See, for example, K. Marx, 'The Meaning of Human Requirements' in *The Economic and Philosophic Manuscripts of 1844* (trans. M. Milligan, New York, 1964).
422. *ES*, 1402.
423. *ES*, 729; *LES*, 188.
424. *ES*, 93.
425. *ES*, 895; *LES*, 321.
426. *ES*, 973.
427. For an account of this attitude toward law-making, see Bruce Ackerman's discussion of 'scientific policy-making' in *Private Property and the Constitution* (New Haven, 1977) pp. 23–40.
428. *ES*, 1402.
429. *ES*, 1403.
430. *ES*, 1402.
431. *ES*, 1403.
432. *Ibid.*
433. *ES*, 1404.
434. *ES*, 1448.
435. *ES*, 1459.
436. *ES*, 1404.
437. *ES*, 1401.
438. *ES*, 1393.
439. *ES*, 1459–60.
440. *ES*, 1401–2. See also Weber's essay, 'Socialism', in *Max Weber: The Interpretation of Social Reality* (trans. J.E.T. Eldridge, London, 1971), pp. 191–219.
441. *FMW*, 115.
442. *Ibid.*
443. *FMW*, 95.
444. *FMW*, 115.

445. *Ibid.*
446. *FMW*, 95.
447. *FMW*, 115–16.
448. *FMW*, 116.
449. *Ibid.*
450. *Ibid.*
451. *FMW*, 128.
452. *FMW*, 117.
453. *FMW*, 126–7.
454. *FMW*, 127.
455. *Ibid.*
456. *FMW*, 95.
457. *ES*, 983.
458. *Ibid.*
459. *FMW*, 115.
460. *FMW*, 125–6.
461. *FMW*, 117.
462. *FMW*, 79.
463. *Ibid.*
464. *Ibid.*
465. *ES*, 1451.
466. *ES*, 1460.
467. *ES*, 1451.
468. Useful accounts of the relationship between Marx and Weber may be found in G. Roth, 'The Historical Relationship to Marxism,' in *Scholarship and Partisanship: Essays on Max Weber*; W. Mommsen, *The Age of Bureaucracy: Perspectives on the Political Sociology of Max Weber* (Oxford, 1974) Chapter 3; W.G. Runciman, *Social Science and Political Theory* (Cambridge, 1969) Chapter 3; K. Löwith, 'Weber's Interpretation of the Bourgeois-Capitalistic World in Terms of the Guiding Principle of "Rationalization" '; and H. Marcuse, 'Industrialization and Capitalism in the Work of Max Weber'.
469. The relationship between Weber and Nietzsche is discussed in W. Schluchter, 'The Paradox of Rationalization: On the Relation of Ethics and World'; W. Mommsen, *The Age of Bureaucracy* Chapter 5; E. Fleischmann, 'De Weber à Nietzsche,' (1964) II *Archives Européennes de Sociologie*, 190–238; R. Bendix and G. Roth, 'Weber's Generational Rebellion and Maturation' in *Scholarship and Partisanship: Essays on Max Weber*; and A. Mitzman, *The Iron Cage* Chapter 6.
470. See G. Roth, 'Political Critiques' in *Scholarship and Partisanship: Essays on Max Weber*.
471. There are passages in Marx's own writings that seem to suggest such a view. See, for example, *Grundrisse*, pp 487–8, and *The Economic and Philosophic Manuscripts of 1844* pp. 47–64 ('The Meaning of Human Requirements').

Index